D1108474

A Gift From

Harvey W. Scott

Memorial Library

Hundreds of thousands of readers are familiar with the special qualities of Ann Bridge's fiction — thrilling narrative skill, local color of sharp immedi... rich... characters... a

(Continued from front flap)

aristocracy, the contrasts of wealth and squalor, the Creole glamor, the hatred of the occupation forces. Equally fascinating are Miss Bridge's accounts of her New England forebears, such characters as her great-great-grandmother, Abigail Hinman, who shot at the traitor, Benedict Arnold, from the window of her home. And particularly memorable is Miss Bridge's portrait of her father, who, as a youth, bought a ton of copper with a hundred borrowed pounds, and then went on to build a fortune in iron and steel; who "took the pledge" in middle age to save the soul of a dangerous alcoholic.

Whether she is describing her own varied life, or the exciting lives and times of her parents and ancestors, Ann Bridge writes, as always, with great spirit and compelling charm. Her book is full of scenes that are vividly realistic, peopled with characters who are in every way refreshingly and memorably alive.

A Family of Two Worlds

A PORTRAIT OF HER MOTHER

A Family of Two Worlds:

A PORTRAIT OF HER MOTHER.

by Ann Bridge

THE MACMILLAN COMPANY

NEW YORK   1955

LC # 55-13550

Published in England under the title
Portrait of My Mother

Marie Louise Day, the author's mother, aged 30

M. L. S.
Benemerenti dilectae

Acknowledgements

I HAVE received so much help in the preparation of this book that to mention here by name all the individuals, and institutions, who have taken the trouble to answer my questions and supply me with information would be impossible. To all I am grateful; and I hope that those whose names are omitted will accept this expression of my gratitude.

My first indebtedness is to the members of my Mother's family in America. To my cousin Dr. E. C. Day, who very generously placed at my disposal the original manuscript papers of Captain Elisha Hinman, never hitherto published, and gave me leave to print extracts from them, as well as from the correspondence of Hannah Hinman, our great-grandmother; Dr. Day and his wife also furnished me with invaluable information about New Orleans and the lives of the Day family there. To my cousin Mrs. Norris of New Orleans and her daughter Edith for many similar details, and for books and information about the Washington Artillery and General "Teaspoon" Butler. To my Mother's first cousin, Mrs. Richard Brinkley Snowden, for permission to reproduce the portraits of Abigail Hinman and Captain James Day, both in her possession, and to her daughter Mrs. Stanley Rowe for a similar permission in respect to the Sully portrait of Hannah Hinman; also to Mr. Robert Borland Day for permission to reproduce the copy (by Daniel Huntington) of the Hudson portrait of my great-great-grandfather Captain William Day—and in each case

vi

for their kindness in having the portraits specially photographed for this book. To Mrs. Leroy Halsey for copies of several early letters from my Mother to hers, much other family correspondence, and for giving me access to the results of her genealogical researches; also to my cousin Mr. Ingersoll Day Townsend for a photograph of my grandfather James Ingersoll Day. Finally, I must express my gratitude to my distant kinsman Mr. Frank Bunnell for the use of his Day family tree, and for endless help in supplying and checking data about my forbears. I am also very grateful to my sisters for their recollections, their advice, and numerous family photographs.

In England, I am indebted to the Librarians of the Admiralty and the War Office for searching their records and supplying me with information, as well as to the Information Department at Chatham House; to Mr. H. P. R. Finberg for permission to quote from his *Devonshire Studies*, and for further information about Tavistock; to Mr. Finnie of the Bedford Office in that town, and to the Town Clerk, for searching the records and valuable corroboration and amplification of my Mother's earlier work. Mr. A. C. Notley, Secretary of the London Metal Exchange, most kindly allowed me to see and quote from the early accounts of that institution. The editors of *The Engineer, Engineering,* and *The Locomotive* went to endless trouble to supply me with such information as is still available about the use of American engines in Russia and on the Chinese Eastern Railway; Professor Prendergast of Galway University deserves, and hereby receives, very special thanks for his kindness in having search made through back numbers of *The Engineer* on my behalf. The Iron and Steel Institute in London also lent themselves with tireless energy to the pursuit of that curiously neglected branch of modern industrial history, the impact of American steel production on railway development in the Old World, and I am grateful for their assistance. Nor must I omit to thank Sir George Campbell of Succoth, Bart., and his chauffeur Donald Urquhart—both my friends for thirty years—for producing background information and stories about Gruinard in the old days.

In America I am indebted to others besides my immediate relations for help. Place of honour goes to Mr. John C. Long, of the Bethlehem Steel Company, for going to the trouble of unearthing the original draft of my Father's agreement with the Pennsylvania Steel Co. and much of his correspondence with them, and sending me photostat copies—a most exceptional kindness. Mr. Lockhead of the Mariners' Museum, Newport News, sought out and sent me delightful extra details about my great-great-uncle John Day's migration from Massachusetts to Ohio in 1816, and the News Printing Company of Oberlin, Ohio, kindly gave me leave to use extracts from their reprint (in 1913) of the *Genealogical Register of the Descendants of Robert Day*. *The Iron Age* in New York and the Canadian Pacific Railway in Montreal were very helpful too. To all these I tender my grateful thanks, as also to Morris L. Ernst of New York and his wife—for advice and help, and in particular for putting me in touch with Mrs. Beth Silverman, who carried out much research for me with resourcefulness and promptitude.

Finally I must thank Mr. Garland C. Routt, lately of the American Embassy in Dublin, for the kind interest which he has taken in this book from the outset and the help, of all sorts, which he has given me; and two quite exceptionally busy English friends who have never failed to find time to answer my many questions: Miss Ursula Nettleship about the composers of songs, Mr. Peter Harris about relatively obscure painters. Memory is a tricky thing; but a book based on memory is based on reality, and ought to be accurate, and I cannot be grateful enough to all those people who have helped me towards the difficult achievement of accuracy.

ANN BRIDGE

Illustrations

SELECTIVE PEDIGREE OF

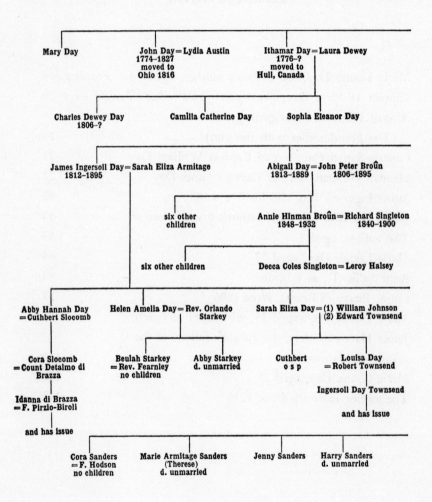

Robert Day = (1) Mary......
1604–1648
emigrated to
America 1634

Mary Day

John Day = Lydia Austin
1774–1827
moved to
Ohio 1816

Ithamar Day = Laura Dewey
1776–?
moved to
Hull, Canada

Charles Dewey Day
1806–?

Camilla Catherine Day

Sophia Eleanor Day

James Ingersoll Day = Sarah Eliza Armitage
1812–1895

Abigail Day = John Peter Broûn
1813–1889   1806–1895

six other
children

Annie Hinman Broûn = Richard Singleton
1848–1932   1840–1900

six other children

Decca Coles Singleton = Leroy Halsey

Abby Hannah Day
= Cuthbert Slocomb

Helen Amelia Day = Rev. Orlando
Starkey

Sarah Eliza Day = (1) William Johnson
(2) Edward Townsend

Cora Slocomb
= Count Detalmo di
Brazza

Beulah Starkey
= Rev. Fearnley
no children

Abby Starkey
d. unmarried

Cuthbert
o s p

Louisa Day
= Robert Townsend

Idanna di Brazza
= F. Pirzio-Biroli

Ingersoll Day Townsend

and has issue

and has issue

Cora Sanders
= F. Hodson
no children

Marie Armitage Sanders
(Therese)
d. unmarried

Jenny Sanders

Harry Sanders
d. unmarried

THE DAY FAMILY—1604 TO 1954

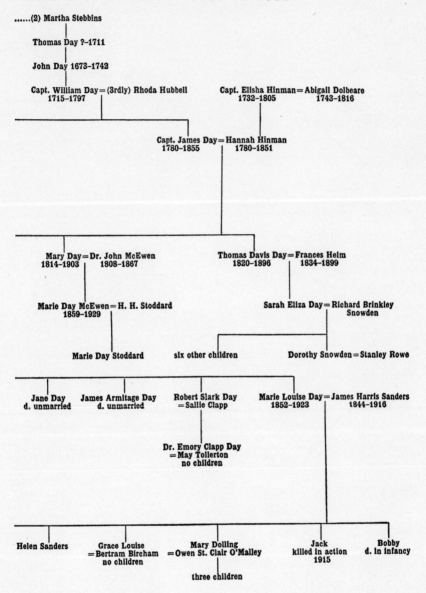

......(2) Martha Stebbins

Thomas Day ?–1711

John Day 1673–1742

Capt. William Day = (3rdly) Rhoda Hubbell
1715–1797

Capt. Elisha Hinman = Abigail Dolbeare
1732–1805   1743–1816

Capt. James Day = Hannah Hinman
1780–1855   1780–1851

Mary Day = Dr. John McEwen
1814–1903   1808–1867

Thomas Davis Day = Frances Helm
1820–1896   1834–1899

Marie Day McEwen = H. H. Stoddard
1859–1929

Sarah Eliza Day = Richard Brinkley
Snowden

Marie Day Stoddard   six other children   Dorothy Snowden = Stanley Rowe

Jane Day   James Armitage Day   Robert Slark Day   Marie Louise Day = James Harris Sanders
d. unmarried   d. unmarried   = Sallie Clapp   1852–1923   1844–1916

Dr. Emory Clapp Day
= May Tollerton
no children

Helen Sanders   Grace Louise   Mary Dolling   Jack   Bobby
                       = Bertram Bircham   = Owen St. Clair O'Malley   killed in action   d. in infancy
                       no children   1915

three children

Chapter 1

A CHILD sees its parents, and especially its mother, at first entirely in the flat, a surface of love and attention directed towards itself; what lies behind that loving and attentive surface it neither asks nor grasps. But presently it can begin to take in incidents from that mother's childhood, if these are vouchsafed, and to compare them with its own childish experiences—this is amusing and interesting. The process continues as the child grows; and between a mother and daughter, if their relationship is a normal one, there gradually arises on the daughter's side a certain curiosity about what her mother's life was like, and what it meant to her as she lived it. As her own experience advances and expands —a bigger child; a growing girl; a young woman with her young men and her proposals and refusals; a bride, at last herself a mother—the daughter probably comes in the end, if she and her mother are fortunate, and the proper happy sympathy between them persists, to a true knowledge of her mother as a person, in the round; and this knowledge is perhaps as close and intimate as is possible between any two different categories of mortals.

But a daughter, slowly and almost unconsciously picking up the various threads that give the clue to her mother's life, usually shares with the mother, in some measure at least, a common background, social and national; and even more important, the visual and physical background of one country, one set of trees and birds and small wild animals, the supreme interests of the country-

1

bred child; shares the same familiar panorama of sky and weather and the recurrent cycle of the seasons, with their scents and flowers; both have known always some similar country speech, and the deeply grounded country pattern of behaviour. All these things, for the rooted country-bred as opposed to the rootless dwellers in cities, constitute the very fabric of life; and the young human being, doing its delightful growing and learning among them, finds there yet more clues to a parent's youth. But for me, when I began to take an interest in my Mother's past, it was not so. Her far-away childhood lay in another continent; three thousand miles of the Atlantic rolled between her remote background and my own vividly present one. For her the Mississippi, for me the Thames; for her long summers the shores of New England, for mine the Dorset coast; my rows of wheat-sheaves along the whitened stubbles at harvest-time had to be translated into her Louisiana cotton-fields, with the singing darkies picking steadily among them, and the dear familiars of my childhood, the cheerful maid-servants indoors, the gardeners and grooms without, into the devoted slaves who brought her up, with their black loving faces, gaudy bandannas, and haunting songs.

The process of translation was not really so difficult as one might suppose. My Mother had a remarkable memory for words, tunes, and scenes, and an unassuming vivid power of description, as well as a passionate love of flowers and birds and all wild natural things; moreover in her the delicious gift of association was strong, so that the first sight, in spring, of the pale-green spears of the wild arum, Lords-and-Ladies, rolled like tiny umbrellas along the banks of our English ditches would bring at once to her mind the rhubarb-bronzy buds of the skunk cabbage, the first sign of spring in New England swamps and coppices, as she had seen them during the years of the Civil War. And being an expansive and expressionist person, all this would come out in joyous exclamation and relation; and my little self, trotting at her side in my button boots and buttoned gaiters, and my fur-trimmed bonnet tied with a bow of thick watered ribbon under my small fat chin, would listen entranced to her account of another world than mine—not remotely guessing, then, the deep nostalgia, the standing sick for home in alien fields that prompted her happy-seeming outbursts. Or did I guess, even then? Did I really always know, in some subterranean fashion, what it all meant for her? I cannot tell. It has somehow so become part of my own life, at one remove, that it is impossible to analyse the stages of comprehension too closely. What I am quite sure of is that it was love, her love of her home scenes that made the translation and the comprehension so easy. Pirandello would agree with this—he knew how love and affection supply the key to riddles which to the intellect alone are locked doors.

Another thing that helped my comprehension of that far-away world immensely was her songs. Simple people—and all children are simple—get from rhymed words fitted to tunes a quite particular impression, half mental, half emotional; they create an impact almost as sharp as the visual impact. When I was suffering from some childish ailment—often influenza, then becoming fashionable, and an uncommonly severe complaint in the nineties —my Mother would sing me songs which her black Mammy had sung to her almost half a century before, and there swam gently into my sleepy or feverish ken scenes from an unknown world, borne in on me with the peculiar compulsion of rhyme and melody.

> *Oh, well do I remember, remember, remember—*
> *Oh, well do I remember, how we picked de cotton,*
> *cotton, side by side.*
> *'Twas in de mild September, September, September—*
> *'Twas in de mild September, dat we picked de cotton,*
> *cotton, side by side.*
> *Oh, list to de mocking bi-rd, Oh, list to de*
> *mocking bi-rd,*
> *De mocking bird a-singin' on de tree.*
> *Oh list to de mocking bi-rd, Oh, list to de*
> *mocking bi-rd,*
> *De mocking bird a-singin' on de tree.*

Well, I knew about "mild Septembers," magical misty days of dimmed blue and gold; but we picked blackberries, not cotton, reaching up into the hedgerows for the dark gleaming beaded fruit to put into our little baskets, bordered with pink and blue straw. Nevertheless I somehow managed to envisage that cotton-picking, and the rows of dark brightly-clad figures, as I lay in my brass-barred bed in that cosy Victorian room, with the firelight shining on the maple furniture, ash picked out with mahogany, while against the fading sunset our English starlings, in the four tall poplars beyond the lawn, were sibilantly chorusing their evening chant. From my Mother's detailed description I even got some idea of the tormenting note of the mocking-bird, though my own children were grown up before I ever heard it with my own ears.

Other evocations were more complicated.

When de autumn leaves were fallin',
When de frost got cold,
'Twas hard to hear old Massa callin'
'Case he was so weak and old.
Now de orange-trees am bloomin'
Along de sandy shore,
Now de mockin'-bird am singin',
Massa nebber calls no more.

I only knew orange-trees in tubs in the conservatory, and along the one sandy shore familiar to me, near Poole Harbour, heath and sea-holly were all that grew. However, I accepted the orange-trees growing in the sand as I accepted the dark figures picking cotton; what was unmistakable was the grieving melancholy of the refrain:

Hark, from de corn-field
Hear dat mournful sound—
All de darkies am a-weepin'
Massa's in de cold, cold ground.

5

Massa, much loved, was dead, and black people mourned for him lovingly; I identified him with my Grandfather, James Ingersoll Day, whom I knew only as a portrait of a stately, intelligent, benevolent old gentleman with thick curly white hair and a wonderful white beard, since he lived in America and died when I was four. But I did get also an immensely definite impression of the relation of slave-owners to slaves, and in particular—since that was what came closest to me—of the relation of the children of slave-owners to those slaves. My Mother—as I now see—spoiled her English servants more than any woman I have ever seen keeping house; however, they adored her, and stayed on an average for twenty years of service—three were with her for thirty-five years. But she dinned into us, as little ones, the essential duty of courtesy to all servants, and of strict obedience to our nurses and nursemaids, set over us in authority; illustrating this uncongenial theme with accounts of how her black Mammy used to slap her for minor crimes, and in what awe she stood of Old Ben, the coachman, and Old Joe, the butler. More, she related how the few punishments she ever remembered as being administered by her parents were inflicted for being either impolite or disobedient to those parents' slaves.

After this no one will be surprised to learn that we were not given *Uncle Tom's Cabin* to read, like most English children of our day. "An *untruthful* book," my Mother would say, her fine level lips closing in a sharp line, "written by a foolish, presumptuous woman, who never knew the South." Untruthfulness, especially about ascertainable facts, was to my Mother the crime of crimes, far worse than the childish lies of fear or silliness of which we were so bitterly ashamed; and to lie in print was unpardonable. She chose our nursery books with extreme care, on this basis, so that we read little Henty and much Mayne Reid, whose natural history was by the standards of his day impeccable: straight fairy-tales, like Grimm and Hans Andersen, she rather reluctantly permitted, but stories about talking humanised animals she abhorred, and when the Peter Rabbit books began to come out, in time for my youngest brother's amusement, her mouth took on much the same close line for Miss Beatrix Potter as it had done for Harriet Beecher Stowe.

She admitted freely that slavery was essentially wrong in itself; what she minded was calumnies about it—"untruthfulness." She recognised that there had been cruel hardships, under bad masters and an implacable system; and these, too, were represented in her songs. I could hardly bear to hear her sing "Nellie Gray"; her deep beautiful voice brought out the pathos of words and air as I have never heard them brought out since. But in fact I often asked for it simply to hear that wonderful matching of voice with pathos.

> *Oh, my darling Nellie Gray,*
> *Dey hab taken her away*
> *And I'll nebber see my darling any more—*
> *Dey hab taken her to Georgia,*
> *   for to wear her life away,*
> *And she's gone from de ole Kentucky shore.*

I must make one thing clear. My Mother's rendering of plantation songs owed nothing to Mr. Stephen Foster; I am not sure that she had ever heard of him. If she had, I am afraid that he too would have qualified for the condemnatory phrase "untruthful," or its lesser but also pejorative relation, "inaccurate." What she sang to us she had learned direct from darky lips. When I myself first came across the Stephen Foster collection, in a house in Ross-shire, my mother had been in her grave for five years, and I must say that I was astounded by his modifications and simplifications, all in the direction of the Boosey Ballad. To give one example: in the song "Dere was an ole man an' his name was Uncle Ned" (which I had known by heart, words and tune, since I was five), in the third line of the chorus, "Dere's no more hard work for poor Uncle Ned," there comes a drop of a full octave between the words "more" and "hard"—most expressive and touching. But Mr. Foster has ironed it out.

It strikes me now as an odd thing that my Mother never sang

7

us any Negro spirituals. As she was by nature a deeply religious woman, who loved the hymns which we sang in the hall to a small organ every Sunday evening, I can only suppose that she knew none. Why was this? I have tried to guess at the reason. The Day family's slaves were extremely devoted to their employers—or owners—as we shall see presently; since my Grandmother was a Quaker and my Grandfather an Episcopalian, possibly those good black creatures deliberately withheld from the children whom they brought up, and gently bullied, their own religious songs. Anyhow, I never heard one. But not all the songs which my Mother sang to us, by any means, were filled with pathos; some were lively and rumbustious to a degree.

> *Way down by de gate dere lived a gal*
> *And her name was Uncle Zebedee's Sal,*
> *And Zebedee was a fisherman bold,*
> *And Sal was a gal nineteen years old.*
> *Hi Jim-a-long, Jim-a-long José*
> *Hi Jim-a-long, Jim-a-long Joe!*

(It is interesting to find embedded in this fragment, like a fly in amber, the name "José," presumably dating from the Spanish dominion in Louisiana.)

There was another song which as children we loved best of all, for its lovely air and the lively hammering chorus. I have tackled every Negro singer I ever encountered in later life to find out if they knew it, but to all it was unfamiliar. I give both words and tune here, in the hope that some reader somewhere may rise up and furnish me with further verses:

> *I used to love a yaller girl*
> *And her name was Susie Brown.*
> *She lived in ole Virginia, an'*
> *Was de fairest in de town.*
> *Her eyes so bright dey shine at night*
> *When de moon am gone away,*
> *I used to call dis darkie up*
> *Jest afore de break ob day*
>   *Wid a who-da? who-da? who-da?*
> *An a who da knockin' at de door?*
> *Is dat you Tom? No 'taint, 'tam Jim—*
> *Well, you better stop dat knockin' at de door.*
> *Stop dat knockin', knock dat stoppin',*
> *Stop dat knockin', knock dat stoppin'—*
> *Oh you better stop dat knockin' at de door!*
>   *LET ME IN.*

I as a child, still seeing my Mother mainly in the flat, the loving attentive surface directed towards myself, could nevertheless take in and enjoy anything I learned of her childhood, and relate it to my own as best I might. I could not hear enough of Old Ben and Old Joe and Mammy, the nurse, later promoted to be my Grandmother's personal maid; above all of Aunt Patsy, the cook, who died when my Mother was quite small at the presumed age

I used to love a yall-er girl And her name was Su-sie Brown. She lived in ole Vir-gin-ia, an' Was de fair-est in de town. Her eyes so bright, dey shine at night When de moon am gone a-way. I used to call dis dar-kie up Jest a-fore de break ob day. Wid a Who da? Who da? Who da? An' a who da knockin' at de door? Is dat you Tom? No, 'taint 'tam Jim! , Well you bet-ter stop dat knock-in' at de door, Stop dat knockin' knock dat stoppin', Stop dat knock-in' knock dat stoppin', Oh, you bet-ter stop dat knock-in' at de door! let me In!

of 110, though no one knew for certain exactly how old she was. But she could not, it was reckoned, have been less than that, and she undoubtedly remembered Africa, and her journey thence in the slave ship—a thing very rare among nineteenth-century Negroes. She was so old, and my Mother so young, that almost nothing survives to me from Aunt Patsy's recollections of her native jungles—only the words, deeply imprinted on the mind of that earlier enquiring child: "It was very dark, an' dey was drums." Perhaps that is sufficient—as much as one may expect to have come down across nearly two centuries—for old Louisa died when my Mother was seven or eight years old, and if my Mother were alive to-day, in 1954, she would be 100. I expect that it *was* dark, and that there were drums; I am glad to have so much, verbatim, if only at second hand.

But it was quite another matter for the possessive child when live human beings, not dead darkies or remote grandparents, impinged upon her little world and began to turn the attentive surface of love and care into a person with other facets, directed elsewhere. This happened when my American aunts came to visit us, as they did fairly often. They swept in, tall, dark-haired, with flashing dark eyes, usually swathed in crape, at least as to their bonnets and the broad bands on their voluminous flowing skirts; Southern women in those days mourned, sartorially, as deeply as Frenchwomen, brought up as they were in a French tradition, and in a family as large as my Mother's somebody had always died within the last eighteen months. I liked the crape, which I felt furtively with small inquisitive fingers; its crinkly stiffness was stimulating to the touch, and moreover I thought it looked very odd and dignified. And I liked hearing my aunts talk, in their rich deep Southern voices—oh, the incommunicable magic of the tones in which they said "My *dear!*" But what was insupportable was the way they called my Mother "Marree" (Marie). Her name was Mummie and nothing else; how dared they call her Marie? And talk and talk about Cousin Walton Glenny and little Marie-Elise Whitney and Morgan Whitney and his photography

11

and his admiration for tall distinguished Cousin Emma Glenny, and a score of other strange names: names, I was to learn forty years later, still remembered in New Orleans. At the time I found it, as I say, intolerable; it took my Mother in some fashion away from us, from *me*, and made of her a person with aspects unrelated to our life; and our demands and wants. In fact, to begin with, my aunts made me bitterly jealous.

I was not really mollified by the material compensations which these richly clad, richly voiced relations admittedly brought. I remember well when Aunt Abby Slocomb, my Mother's eldest sister and nearly twenty years her senior, first came to spend Christmas with us, a formidable lady with curly white hair and the flashing dark eyes characteristic of the family, but without the neat elegant aquiline nose of my Mother and my other aunts; she was already the widow of the much-loved "Uncle Cud," Cuthbert Slocomb—to me, like my Grandfather, merely a picture and a name, with a legend of gallantry from the Civil War attached to him. Aunt Abby brought fantastic presents for my elder sisters—I was the youngest daughter of six, and there was nearly as long a gap in years between me and my oldest sister Cora as between my Mother and Aunt Abby; for us little ones, red-trimmed white calico stockings nearly three feet long, stuffed from end to end with pecan nuts, "peanut brittle," a delicious dark crystalline toffee with the small kernels set into it, guava cheese, winter-green sweets, and above all maple sugar. This delicious product of the splendid trees which, again more than forty years later, I was to see, golden as bunches of daffodils, in all their autumn splendour up in New Hampshire, really enchanted me; and I was still more enchanted by my Mother's descriptions of tapping the trees in the brisk spring sunshine, and boiling the syrup in great iron cauldrons out under the trees themselves, as she had seen it during her four winters in the North. Mrs. Slocomb also brought over the syrup itself in huge tins, and we ate it with our porridge and on waffles, that most delicious of American foods; but not even these good things could mollify me to begin with, greedy as I was, for what she did when she made my Mother less my own.

There were two other aunts whom we liked much better than we did Aunt Abby: Aunt Jane, who remained unmarried and died plain Miss Day, and Aunt Sallie, who when I first knew her was already Mrs. Townsend. She had been married before to a Mr. Johnson, by whom she had two children: Cuthbert, whom most of us never knew, since he died in early manhood, and my Cousin Louisa, who was later to become a great figure in my life. Cousin Louisa married Mr. Townsend's son Robert, thereby making her mother her mother-in-law, an unusual connexion.

Aunt Sallie I can only describe as a "card"—in the grand manner, indeed in the grandest possible manner, but nevertheless a card. Like all her sisters—except Aunt Jane, who was tiny—she was very tall, and held herself superbly; her hair remained till her death of a brown so deep as to be called black, and till the day of her death she could sit on the thick plaits which, spurning the littleness of fashion, she wore piled like a crown round her splendid head, with alluring curls or waves in front. She had the most enchanting eyebrows I have ever seen, arched, but tinily narrow; her enemies—and a woman so gay, so handsome, so *free*, and so reckless with her lively tongue of course had plenty of enemies—vowed that she painted them. How delighted she was when badger-streaks of white at last crept into those miraculous eyebrows!—the only hairs on her ever to change colour; she paraded them triumphantly round New York and Long Island, where she lived next door to the Roosevelts at Oyster Bay. She loved nothing better, at any time, than making a little good honest mischief, and I can remember now the relish with which she related the affair of the black pearl earrings. Both her husbands were fairly rich men, and Aunt Sallie's jewels, though sparingly worn, were both splendid and carefully chosen; owing to her Quaker ancestry the idea of wearing imitation jewellery was normally as abhorrent to her as that unthinkable thing, wearing imitation lace. However, on one occasion when she was in Paris, getting her clothes, as she always did, from Worth, her eye was caught in the Rue de la Paix by a pair of solitaire black pearl earrings—imitation ones, and huge. She looked at them; she went in; she tried them on; they were entrancing on her, and she bought them and wore them, the card in her this time—as indeed I think it often did—triumphing over her Quaker blood. Of course, she made no bones about their being sham to us; my Mother was horrified, and Aunt Abby made some of her usual arbitrary and comminatory remarks.

But Aunt Sallie didn't care a bit, and presently sailed home to the States wearing her huge sham black pearls in her ears. Now it happened that there was one woman in particular in New York who had always envied her, and sought to rival at least her clothes and her jewels—it was hard to rival her spirit and overcoming zest for life. This lady, meeting her one day, exclaimed hopelessly at the earrings, "My dear, where *did* you get those?" "In the Rue de la Paix," says my aunt, wickedly and truthfully. It never occurred to her unfortunate rival that Mrs. Townsend's immense pearls could be other than real, and after trying Tiffany's in vain she betook herself to Paris in search of black pearls. She returned with only one; and in despair sought out Aunt Sallie. "I gave seven thousand dollars for that," she said, "but I can't find the match to it. You *must* be kind and tell me where you got yours." Aunt Sallie was unkind, and told her—and I can hear her deep ringing laughter now as she recounted the episode. My Mother, always pitiful, was rather shocked.

Aunt Sallie's second husband, Mr. Townsend, commonly known as "Pa T.," was a regular Northerner, who took pleasure in deliberately accentuating both the idiom and the accent of his native speech, a Yankee nasal drawl of the most pronounced description. He hated Europe, and came as seldom as he could—much to our regret as children later on, for we had never seen or heard anything in the least like Pa T., and though his sharp drawled comments on us and on our world as we knew it, and his stony pale eyes were intimidating, we listened enthralled to his accent,

14

and to the comments themselves. During one summer—I must have been a good deal older then, about ten—on one of his infrequent visits we dragged him down to our beloved Dorset and took him over to Swanage; in his hideous mustard-coloured overcoat (which his wife invariably referred to, with affectionate contempt, as "the yaller dawg") he walked through the small streets, he walked along the—then rather rudimentary—"front," he sampled, with the rest of us, the lunch at the principal hotel. Finally he uttered his verdict:

"H'mm. Quite a little town. It must be dull down here when it is dull."

He suffered a great deal from Aunt Sallie's impetuous eager ways. Even as children, in a semi-conscious fashion—much like the awareness of dogs, I always think, of adult human reactions—we realised this. Aunt Sallie was always positively effervescing with the desire to do things for other people, and generally did them "spang off," as both she and my Mother termed it; that is, without much prior consideration. Pa T. hated this trait. He had one great motto for all occasions: "Let the shawl drag." This derived from an early experience of his, when as a young and shy man, walking along the beach at Newport, he observed a beautiful lady draped in a wonderful Indian shawl, of which a long corner was trailing behind her in the wet sand. Hat in hand, bowing humbly—so he told us—he approached her and said, "Pardon me, Madam, but your shawl is dragging on the sand." The lady replied, coldly, "I like it to drag."

That taught Pa T. his lesson for life—but nothing could teach it to his wife. Sometimes her hasty helpfulness produced appalling results. On one occasion she and the hapless Mr. Townsend were travelling down from New York to visit Aunt Abby and Uncle Cud in New Orleans; the train, an express, only stopped at intervals of several hours and some hundreds of miles. Sitting near them in the Pullman car was a woman with two small children and a baby, which she proceeded to deposit in the large rack above her head, where it slept peacefully. At some point the train made a halt of ten minutes; the woman got up, shepherding her two children, and went out, leaving the baby still asleep in the rack. As the ten minutes ticked away Aunt Sallie's audibly expressed anxiety increased; and in spite of poor Pa T.'s almost impassioned adjurations to let the shawl drag, when there was barely a minute to go and the mother had still not returned, she threw up the window, put out her head, summoned some station officials in her deep beguiling voice, and explaining volubly and hurriedly that "some lady with two little children had gotten out and left her baby behind in the rack," thrust the sleeping bundle through the window just as the train drew out. Then, satisfied with her good deed, she sat back, relaxed and content. Five minutes later the door at the rear of the car opened, and in walked the mother with her mobile offspring. They had got out to buy food and drink coffee in the station restaurant, and had boarded the train again several coaches farther back, and slowly made their way through to their seats. But while Pa T. recounted the appalling scene that had then ensued, Aunt Sallie gurgled with laughter as deep and impenitent as when she was telling us about the black pearl earrings. She was incorrigible.

And adorable. Even Pa T. grudgingly recognised her power to charm, albeit with a certain resentment. I must have been nearly fifteen, and beginning to guess a little at what the power to charm meant, when I heard him, on his last visit to England, describing a dinner which he had given to his oldest friend on his engagement to Aunt Sallie. He was then a more than middle-aged man and Aunt Sallie a middle-aged woman, each with a grown-up son and daughter apiece; however, Pa T., loyally and characteristically, laid a bet of a thousand dollars with his old friend that when the friend met the fiancée (whose identity he refused to divulge in advance) he would agree that she was "the finest woman in New York." Late, of course, Aunt Sallie appeared, trailing into the restaurant "in a *white* dress, for Gaard's sake—with *her* skin!" said Pa T. indignantly. (My Mother and all her sisters had complexions of a delicate sallowness: beautifully clear, but sallow

from the deep Southern heat and periodic attacks of yellow fever.)
"She was tired, too; great rings under her eyes—she looked like
the wrath of Gaard! I said Goodbye to that thousand dollars."
But no. They went in to dinner, and Aunt Sallie used her eyes,
used her brilliant tongue, bent the bow of her charm and launched
its unerring arrows—and before the guest departed, completely
subjugated, he silently handed over a thousand dollars in notes
to the still resentful but triumphant Mr. Townsend.

I have stepped forward a little down the years in order to give
some sort of picture of "Aunt Sallie T."—so-called to differentiate
her from "Little Aunt Sallie," my Uncle Robert Day's wife—
but it will be evident already that as I grew older my small-child
jealousy and resentment of the American aunts' incursions into
our life gave place gradually to a fascinated admiration, especially
where Aunt Sallie was concerned. Alongside this there were growing all the time a deepening interest and curiosity about my
Mother's childhood and girlhood: the background of it all, and
about herself, as a child and as a girl, set against that background.
These vivid aunts, so unlike my rather humdrum English home
surroundings, in themselves supplied one part of that background;
and their talk of her, always tinged with strong affection, supple-
mented her own recollections, so casually and spontaneously
slipped out, with third-party accounts of her as a child: her
gaiety, her obedience, her passion for the open air and boyish
occupations, her occasional madcap escapades, her persistence and
determination in mastering thoroughly anything she wished to
learn. And even as a child I began to feel the greater power and
flavour of third-party assessments.

There were certain parallels between us. She was the youngest
of five daughters, and the seventh of seven children; I was the
youngest of six daughters, and the seventh child in a family of
nine. It was not till I was quite grown up that I began to realise
for what they were the mysterious attributes which attach to the
seventh child of a seventh child, which I was and my Mother was

not: the veridical dreams, the power to read character from hand-writing, the peculiar bursts of "second sight"—though these last began to show themselves when I was only eleven or twelve. But it was borne in upon me at a very early age what it meant to have five sisters older than oneself!—and it was not difficult to imagine the little Marie Day's position as the youngest of five, especially with *such* older sisters. The fourth of these was a shadowy figure, known to me only by her name, "Aunt Helen"; from my other Aunts, comminatory remarks I learned that she had married a poor man, who was also lazy, and had to feed the pigs; and that after her husband died she went as a missionary to the Indians. That is all I ever knew of her. She had two daughters, one gifted and one not; the ungifted one married an Episcopalian parson, and had no children; the gifted one never married. They are all dead now.

Chapter 2

*L*IKE most lively and attached families the Days revelled in stories about one another, which they told with the utmost zest and a strong dramatic sense; but they were just as enthusiastic about earlier generations, of which their accounts were equally lively and dramatic. This trait, this taste for narrative, taken in conjunction with my Mother's own nostalgic recollections, combined to give me, bit by bit, the picture of her youth that I shall try to draw; but it also gave me a vivid idea of some of my American forbears, about whom she delighted to tell us; and family characteristics tend to reappear down the generations in a most entertaining manner.

Her tales also accounted for something rather peculiar, for English children brought up in the last years of Queen Victoria's reign in the home counties; namely, our youthful preoccupation with such matters as the War of Independence, let alone the Civil War. While our small contemporaries, in their nurseries, were reading or having read to them Mr. Henty's stories about the feats of British arms in various dark continents, we were reading *The Green Mountain Boys*, or *The Deerslayer* and *The Pathfinder* and *The Last of the Mohicans*. True, a good many English children did read the immortal works of Fenimore Cooper, and all at some time played at Red Indians; but I never met any besides ourselves who fought for the temporary privilege of impersonating Ethan Allen in their woods and shrubberies, still less of representing Abigail Hinman shooting at the traitor Benedict Arnold out of the window with her husband's flint-lock at the siege of New London. We did all these things constantly; we each possessed a little saucer or plate fired with a very fine small engraving of Mrs. Hinman, in a low-necked dress and holding a very long gun in her hands, looking malevolently out of a high window at a horseman in a tricorne hat from under arched eyebrows exactly like Aunt Sallie T.'s. (These saucers used to be on sale in New London—perhaps they are still.) We called her "the Grandmother with the Gun," and rightly, since she was in fact my great-great-grandmother. The smallest and least resistant child was forced to get on a pony, wearing one of my Father's deerstalker hats (we had no tricorne) and ride along the terrace path between the standard roses under the night-nursery windows, representing the despised Benedict Arnold; at a bang (made with the voice) he or she had to duck the head and drop the hat, since all Mrs. Hinman's shot achieved was to knock the traitor's hat off his head. But we felt that it was a good gesture, and we loved to re-enact it.

However, "the Grandmother with the Gun" managed to bring off a good deal more than a traitor's hat on that occasion. She and her husband, who was away at sea at the time, had known General Arnold quite well before he turned his coat; most of the inhabitants of New London fled before the approaching enemy, but she remained—ostensibly to watch over her husband's property, but also, I should guess, to see what was going on and to make any mischief she could, after the manner of her great-granddaughter, Aunt Sallie T. When Arnold first rode into the town she was in the front window of the house of one Judge Law, and the wretched traitor, recognising a familiar face in a hostile town, came up and shook hands with her, and asked her to point out to him the Post Office, the printing-house, and Judge Law's dwelling—these being the three he particularly wished to destroy. From Judge Law's own window Mrs. Hinman (with a convincing flourish, I feel sure, very like that of Aunt Sallie T. handing the

Abigail Hinman, great-great-grandmother
(The grandmother with the gun)

Captain William Day, great-great-grandfather

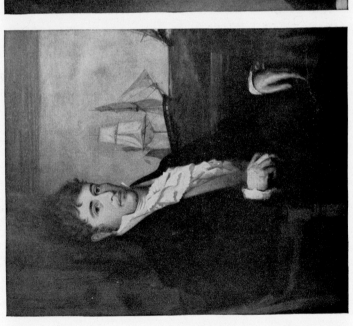

Captain James Day, son of Captain William Day

Hannah Hinman, wife of Captain James Day

baby out of the train window) designated three quite unimportant buildings as the ones in question; then she implored him to spare her own property, indicating the house in which she stood, the Post Office, the printing-house, and her actual home, so when most of New London was burned, these were saved. But that did not in the least prevent her from taking a pot-shot at her unconscious benefactor later in the day.

This spirited and unscrupulous lady, born Abigail Dolbeare, had married a certain Captain Elisha Hinman, another individual in whom as children we took the liveliest interest. He appears, briefly, in the *Dictionary of American Biography;* and he lived in Connecticut, as the Day family then did. Captain Elisha's and the doughty Abigail's daughter Hannah married Captain James Day, my grandfather's father—a sailor too, who deliberately wrecked his ship off Point Judith to prevent her being captured by a British frigate during the war with England in 1812; his portrait by Daniel Huntington, very elegant and severe, is in a cousin's house in Memphis. Elisha Hinman took to the sea at the age of nineteen; to quote an account of him published some fifty years after his death, "he shipped as Captain of a brig . . . and traded at the French and English islands in the West Indies, and remained there for three years at one time. . . . And so popular was he on the islands, that the planters and merchants would not allow him to reside at the hotels, but took him to their own houses, where he formed an extensive and useful acquaintance . . . which not only then but afterwards, was a source of not only profit but pleasure, while in other countries."

Just how profitable this "extensive and useful acquaintance" was to prove in after years in at least one country we shall soon see. Then, as now, many of the West Indian Islands were British possessions, and were known to the Royal Navy as "the America and West Indies Station." The popular young merchant adventurer, staying in the houses of the "merchants and planters" who wouldn't allow him to go to an hotel must inevitably have met in those houses, over and over again, the officers of the Jamaica

21

squadron; and the sequel shows that among them, too, he became popular. At the outbreak of the War of Independence he entered the Revolutionary service as a Lieutenant; in 1776 he appears as No. 20 in the list of Captains, and by 1777 he was in command of the *Alfred*, "a ship of 32 guns," as his monument in New London proudly declares. Alas, the *Alfred* came to grief; with her companion ship the frigate *Raleigh*, under a Captain Thompson, she fell in with a British force—the *Raleigh* fled, the *Alfred*, left alone, was forced to surrender, and Elisha Hinman was taken prisoner. The record before quoted gives this account of his first interview with his captor, a certain Commodore Prindle.

"Who was that damned rascal that ran away?" the Commodore enquired.

"Sir, he is your countryman."

"He is a rascal, come from where he may."

"Had I his ship, I would have taken you, Sir."

"That is loud talking, Captain Hinman."

"Well, Sir"—stating the gun-power, crew, and advantages of the *Raleigh*—"could you not have taken these ships?"

"I think I could."

"I think, Sir, I could do as much as you."

"I believe you can."

And the Commodore, who seemed to find Captain Hinman as agreeable as the West Indian planters had done, promptly presented his prisoner with "two trunks of prize property," containing gold lace and "brocade silks," which he sent home to his Abigail by his purser, Nathaniel Richards.

Hinman had another lively interview with the magistrate before whom, on landing, he was brought for examination—a Scotsman.

Magistrate. "How dare you fight His Majesty's ships, you rebel of His Majesty's Colonies?"

Hinman. "I dare fight His Majesty himself, if I meet him on the high seas."

"Who are you, Sir?"

"Elisha Hinman, Sir."

"What's your occupation?"

"I commanded the *Alfred*, commissioned by the Government of the United States of America" (*sic*).

"Where was you born?"

"In Woodbury, Sir."

"And where" (with great scorn) "is Woodbury?"

"Ten miles from Darby, Sir."

In this last statement Captain Hinman was having a little fun with the Scotsman. In Connecticut there is a Derby, and there is also a Woodbury—which last in Hinman's day was a large straggling district which included his birthplace. However, it seems to have gone down well with the magistrate, who "laughed, and said, 'Give me your hand,' holding out his own: and called for some wine."

The *Raleigh's* performance was considered highly discreditable, and Thompson, her commander, was court-martialled and dismissed from the Navy. On his return to his country my great-great-grandfather was also tried by court-martial, but was acquitted. The faded document notifying him of the verdict, with a covering letter, lies before me as I write. Both are signed "John Brown."

But this is history, and as children we cared little for history as such; what we enjoyed enormously was to hear my Mother relate, as she loved to do, and did very well, the story of "your great-great-grandfather Hinman's escape from prison at Portsmouth." Forton Prison, the books call it; Hinman, who was very free with his spelling, refers to it as "Fortin" in his list of "Expences" in connection with his escape—which list also lies before me, on frail ribbed paper yellow with age, the bold handwriting standing out clearly, though the ink has turned sepia-brown. (Or was it always sepia ink?)

In May, 1778, at "St. Kits" he "payed £2.15.—. for yames, foules and sondres," and the same sum for fresh pork—"in Barbadus currency," as he carefully notes. Then comes the sombre entry:

"Expences at Portsmouth from the 7 July until the 14 for

fresh meet, bread, buter, greens, chese &S Tra, £5.5.0.," and "Sondres at ditto from the 14 July until we were landed for articuls as above." The next item is more cheerful—"Payed for 13 gallons of Rum wilst in prison at Fortin £5.8.0." However, my ancestor did not drink that thirteen gallons of rum all by himself: "the above account," he says, "was wilst in company with my officers viz—Lt. Richard, Lt. Buckley, Capt Welsh & Lt. Hammilton."

What became of these gentlemen when Captain Hinman broke prison I do not know—his accounts in connection with his journey to France relate only to himself, as the following entries show:

Payed sondre exspences for myself in macking my escape from prison, pasing threw France to Brest, viz—

gave a soldier to let me pass	£4. 4. 0.
gave an old woman to conceel me in her house	5. 5. 0.
exspences on the Rode to London for chase hire and sondres	2. 10. 0.
Payed Mr. Jackson for frayting me to London	5. 5. 0.
Payed Mrs. Bayley at London for conceling me and eating	1. 1. 0.
Payed Mr. Hardy for ditto	2. 2. 0.
Payed exspences from London to Deal, shaise hire & S.Tr.	4. 6. 4.
Payed a botte to carry me to Duncarck	5. 5. 0.

And he does the sum: £29.18.4, the price of escape from incarceration to freedom—for France then was freedom to rebelling Americans. Later he records the cost of getting from "Duncarck" to "Parris," and finally from "Parris to Brest," the most expensive single item of the lot, £12.19.0. At Brest, one is glad to learn, he spent another 15 shillings on "one case of gin" before writing, with a satisfaction that still breathes from the bald and laconic statement, "I am now on board the Providence Frigit.

E. Hinman."

However, lists of expenses are of their nature curt and dry; fascinating as it is to hold them in one's hand after little short of two centuries. Here is the story my Mother told us, as it had come down to her. Hinman made his way from Portsmouth towards London easily enough till he reached Hounslow, where he was alarmed by the sight of bills stuck up, describing his person and offering a large sum for information which would lead to his recapture. He seems to have assumed that there would be some sort of *octroi* or customs post at the entrance to the metropolis, and therefore got himself concealed under a load of cabbages going in to Covent Garden Market—presumably the cart belonged to the Mr. Jackson who received the five guineas "for frayting me to London." Emerging from under the cabbages he eventually went to a house in a street off Portman Square, where he stayed for some days; the accounts mention two individuals who were "payed for conceeling me and eating," but my Mother only spoke of the second, Mr. Hardy. This gentleman, by her account an old friend, sheltered Captain Hinman for the greater part of his stay in London, while the escape to France was being organised. It was arranged that Mr. Hardy should cross to the Continent himself, taking the American as his servant, and later return alone. During that period of waiting Hinman only ventured out for air and exercise after dark, often seeing by the faint and infrequent light of street lanterns more of those notices pasted up on walls, describing his appearance, and offering a large reward.

When everything was in train they set out for Deal. Hardy had carefully planned that they should arrive late, and only go on board the "botte" which was to carry them to Dunkirk after dark. But the ports were being watched, and a young British naval officer was on the quay, lantern in hand, examining the papers and persons of all travellers to France. This was a facer. Captain Elisha, in his servant's dress, pulled his hat down over his eyes and his scarf up round his mouth as he stood behind his improvised master, hearing his false name and occupation given.

But the officer was young and zealous, and was taking no chances. As the servant stepped onto the gangway he raised his lantern in one hand, and with the other pulled down the scarf, tilted up the hat, and flashed the light in the Captain's face. It was one he knew well; out in the West Indies, before the Revolution, he had often met this man, on whose head a price was now set.

"Good God! it's Captain Hinman!" he exclaimed under his breath. "Get on board, Sir, as quickly as you can."

There was always an extreme pleasure in my Mother's face and voice as she repeated those words.

After his return to America, and when the wearisome business of the court-martial was over, Hinman, though honourably acquitted, decided to leave the Navy, and took to privateering, commanding amongst other ships the *Deane* and the *Marquis de Lafayette*. "Little is known," the *D.A.B.* remarks, "of his success in these ventures." His family, however, had the best of reasons for knowing a good deal; from the prize-money that he earned, paid largely in silver and subsequently melted down, he was able to fit out all his children with silver for their tables—and numerous as his descendants were, some of his daughter Hannah's spoons have come down to me, with her monogram, two delicate *H*'s intertwined, engraved on them.

Though there is no portrait of Captain Hinman extant, to my great satisfaction I have a description of him, written on the back of his Letters of Marque for the *Marquis de Lafayette*, which are signed by President Huntington. It is headed:

State of Connecticut
By the Governor.
To all whom it may concern.
These certify that the description of Capt Elisha Hinman within named is as follows viz
Aged forty-five years, five foot nine inches high, slender built, pitted with Smal pox, long sandy hair somewhat grey, light grey eyes, light complexion.

Given under my hand and seal at Arms at Hartford—13th June, 1781.

JON TRUMBULL.

This is the earliest version of a passport that I have ever actually had in my hand. I think that the episode on the gangway at Deal was quite enough to make the "long sandy hair" turn somewhat grey before he was forty-five.

As we grew older and came to take a more intelligent interest in such things, the Hinman story and the Hinman spoons took on an added point for us children. This was on account of another naval forbear of ours, English this time—Admiral Brooking, my Father's great-uncle. He saw service in all the skirmishings and forays in and about the Caribbean after the War of Independence proper, being on the West India and America Station, and was eventually presented by the House of Representatives of Jamaica with a dress sword, 100 guineas wherewith to have his portrait painted, and a massive plated salver with a solid oblong of finely engraved lettering in the centre—to reward him, as the inscription states, for his services in "defending the West Indie Islands from the American pirates." Since our great-great-grandfather on one side was almost certainly one of the pirates against whom our great-great-uncle on the other side took action, it amused us, on the occasion of those large Victorian or Edwardian parties when all the silver had to be got out and polished up, lying on acres of green baize on the big pantry table, to arrange the Hinman tea-spoons in the saucers set out on the Brooking salver—a delightful marriage of heirlooms, we felt it to be even then.

We knew less about the Admiral than about Captain Hinman, except as to his appearance. He laid out that hundred guineas to good purpose in having his picture painted by Northcote; and a beautiful portrait it is, the dress sword held lightly in one long shapely hand; it looks down at me daily from above the dining-room mantelpiece, and the sword itself hangs on a rack in the hall; the salver is still in use for cocktail-parties. But we heard no

27

stories of him, save that as a Lieutenant, and later as acting Commander, he was serving on the West Indies Station at the same time that little Prince William, afterwards King William IV, was there as a midshipman on H.M.S. *Barfleur*. The Lieutenant and the little middy Prince made friends, and when they parted company they exchanged the small brooches with which in those days men pinned their stocks, each having a lock of his own hair enclosed for the other. All through my childhood I heard "the Admiral's brooch" spoken of as a revered relic, but we never saw it, for it belonged to an aged Brooking relation of my Father's called "Cousin Gus," a bachelor parson who came to visit us but seldom. However, three days before I was married a little registered parcel arrived, addressed in an unfamiliar wavering hand; when I opened it, there was the Admiral's brooch, which Cousin Gus, bless him, had decided to send me for a wedding present—with the faded royal hair done into a tiny plaited scroll under a minute piece of crystal set in small pearls. I wore it pinned in my dress on my wedding day, as my "something old."

In a book of this sort, inevitably one gets out of step; the Admiral and his brooch have brought me to my wedding, but I must return to my childhood and the figures who came alive for me—shadowy in their far continent, but very much alive—through the talk of my Mother and her sisters. So far, except for "Pa T.," I have spoken mostly of our aunts, but there were also uncles; Uncle Jim, Uncle Cud, Aunt Abby's husband, and Uncle Bob. Of these, Uncle Bob, the youngest brother, was the only one I ever saw in the flesh; I must have been very small indeed when he came over, for he died early, and my impression of him is a childish one—of great height, of a dark moustache, and of dark eyes and a warm, caressing voice. For the child as for the adult, Uncle Bob was all attraction; his heart was as warm as his voice, and wherever he was known he was also loved.

Uncle Jim was the stray-away—I think even his family saw little of him after he wandered off to the great opening tracts of the West. But his death I do remember. During one of my

Father's absences on a business trip, my Mother suddenly had an overwhelming conviction that her brother Jim was in some mortal danger, and she cabled to her parents to ask for news of him. Now my Father was extremely particular about accounts; therefore my Mother, having sent a groom in on horseback to the village postoffice with that very expensive cable, logged up the item, and the date, in her account-book. The answer came next day—"No news of Jim for six weeks was well then." But presently came first a cable, then a letter, telling of Uncle Jim's death. He had died on the very day on which that cable of enquiry had been jotted down in my Mother's accounts.

Usually, in those Victorian days, children were not told much about deaths, or nothing very factual or satisfying; black sashes instead of cherry-coloured ones were tied round our white frocks when we went down to the drawing-room after tea, and we were adjured to "be very good, and not make a noise and bother your Mother," because poor Cousin or Aunt So-and-so was dead. Our reactions were of a vague discomfort, tinged with a rather awed resentment. But for me, at least, Uncle Jim's death was not like that. He died in spring, when the daffodils were out. Now my Mother was an impassioned gardener, and in a small steep cirque in a strip of woodland on the slopes below our house she had planted daffodils in thousands; a flight of steps edged with small boles of timber led down to a pool below. On that spring day, after our nursery dinner, I felt a sudden need for her presence; or at least I felt that it was important that I should be with her. In the grounds we were allowed to run about freely —though never to set foot alone outside the gates; having sought her in vain in the house, I pattered off by myself in pursuit of her. She was not, as so often of an afternoon, talking to Hastings, the head gardener; she was not among her beloved flowering shrubs beyond the vast lawn. Then probably she was in Combe Wood among her daffodils—and thither I sped, down the steep path between the funereal cryptomerias, and through the rosery, into the wood that fringed its lower edge.

She was there. She was sitting on one of those earthen steps, looking out over the daffodils on the curved slope; there was something about her face, and her whole attitude as she sat there —so still—that filled me with an agonisingly intensified love. But there was something about her stillness that I dared not interrupt, and I crept away. Later she told us, herself, that Uncle Jim was dead; that he was her eldest brother, and that she had loved him very much.

Chapter 3

ANOTHER person whom my Mother loved very much was her brother-in-law, my Uncle Cud. I wish I had ever known him, he sounds such a darling; but I was born too late. He was a very important factor in my Mother's life, for my Grandfather, like so many Southerners, found himself pretty well ruined after the Civil War, and when it ended Aunt Abby took over the little youngest sister, young enough to be her own child—indeed, only a few years older than her own one—and to a great extent finished her upbringing and brought her out. The mental and moral climate in which a young person lives during the later teens is of extreme importance, whatever the psychologists may say about the first three years; and I think that the time she spent under Cuthbert Slocomb's roof exercised an immense influence over my Mother, which lasted throughout her life. Gentleness; an invincible courtesy; a profound charity based on Christian humility—these qualities she possessed to a high degree, and I am sure that in part she absorbed them from him.

This curious pair, gentle gracious Uncle Cud and his competent, busy, overbearing and rather charmless wife Abby, bring us on to the American Civil War—still seen by me, though at one remove, as a *family* thing, through what was told to me by, and about, those who lived through it—Uncle Cud and Aunt Abby, who were active participants, and my Mother, who though still a child had sharp experiences of her own while it lasted. But not in the South

31

—for she spent the whole period of the War, from her ninth to her thirteenth year, in the North, for reasons which I must explain; and the explanation involves some account of her parents' forbears and their background, which was also hers.

The Days were not originally a Southern family at all. They were descended from a certain Robert Day, of Cambridge in the eastern counties, who in the year 1634 emigrated with his wife Mary, sailing from Ipswich in the "bark *Elizabeth*," and eventually settled down in Hartford, Connecticut, where he died fourteen years later. Two hundred years after his death, in 1848, there was published a register of his descendants in the male line, who by then numbered over three thousand! The compiler of the register, after noting that during two centuries the Days appeared to double their numbers every twenty-five years, permitted himself to guess that "if the increase should continue at the same rate for the next hundred years, the descendants of Robert Day, in the male line, would amount in the year 1948 to from thirty to fifty thousand souls." I find it fascinating to come of such a philo-progenitive stock, many of whom bore delightful names like Adonijah and Epaphroditus; but in our branch of the family, at least, the rate of increase has not been maintained; from my Grandfather's family of seven sons and daughters there are today only five great-grandchildren, of whom I have personally furnished three. The next generation, with another seven, looks a little better—but it is a sad recession.

There were the Days, then, settled in New England, producing huge families of Jameses and Roberts and Adonijahs and Epaphrodituses. But in the year 1816 my great-grandfather, Captain James Day's elder brother John, with his wife Lydia Austin, his children, and one of his sisters moved west to the then practically virgin territory of Ohio. John had lived in Sheffield, Massachusetts, and gave the name of Sheffield, Ohio, to his new abode; with his friend Jabez Burrell and some other neighbours he had prospected there a year earlier, when he and his associates in the new venture selected their "lots." The journey took nearly three months, and in the best American style was made in "covered wagons," though, surprisingly, the heavy household effects and farming utensils went by water, in a fifteen-ton schooner called the *Fire Fly*, which they had specially built for the purpose, presumably with a pretty shallow draught. The *Fire Fly* was launched at Schenectady, and half rowed, half sailed up the Mohawk River; passed through some rudimentary locks at Little Falls, and via a canal of sorts proceeded into Lake Oneida and thence via the Oswego River to Lake Ontario. Below Niagara Falls a curious *portage* was arranged: the schooner was unloaded, mounted on cart-wheels, drawn across to Lake Erie and relaunched; her cargo, which included a load of that great essential for the coloniser of the wilderness, salt, followed her on carts, and was reloaded for the sail up Lake Erie to French Creek. The Burrells stayed behind to oversee the laborious *portage;* the Days went on ahead in a twenty-ton schooner called *The Black Snake,* reaching their destination a fortnight sooner than the others, on July 26th. There followed the typical colonising work of felling trees and building a log house to shelter twelve souls in the few weeks before winter came: then clearing forest, planting crops, shooting the abounding deer and bears for food, and catching fish in the river. To keep house in such circumstances with a family of ten children sounds an impossible task by modern standards, especially when one realises to what a degree these pioneering families were self-supplied. Eleanor Day, one of the daughters, gives an account of some of the work that went on in her home in the new version of Sheffield, in Ohio:

"The flax was to be spun, woven into cloth, and whitened, for the household use. Later in the season the same process of spinning and weaving the wool was to be gone through with, for their winter clothing; all this cloth had to be made up of course." Made up—stitched by hand, before the days of Mr. Singer and his boon to women, the sewing-machine. Eleanor adds: "Besides, there was the butter and cheese to make, a large family to be fed and cared for; washing, ironing, baking, brewing, cleaning, and the many other things all housekeepers find to do went on continually. Into this home with its stirring activities came every two years or more a fresh consignment of responsibility and a demand for care, and they called it John or Norman or Fanny, and so on as it pleased them, and proceeded to make a place in the Day family for this fresh piece of pink humanity."

It is a staggering picture, this, and makes our contemporary lives look somehow rather thin and small. My Mother was not descended directly from John Day and his Lydia, they were only her great-uncle and aunt; but though she never did any of these things with her own hands she greatly admired that kind of life, and as we grew older fed us with a lavish diet of books about it: not merely *The Wide, Wide World*, but any number of now forgotten works by the Misses Susan and Anna Warner, such as *Queechy, My Desire, What She Could*, and its two sequels, and Mrs. Adeline Whitney's exquisite classic *Hitherto*. So that throughout my girlhood the sort of life led by my great-grandfather's sister-in-law seemed perfectly normal and proper to me.

Hard as the work was, the John Days prospered; two years after they reached Ohio John was already selling to his brother Captain James "corn, sugar, and rackoon skins." Nor was education forgotten; a log-built school-house was promptly erected in the new Sheffield, and two generations later a certain May Day, a grand-daughter of John's, had so mastered the botany of her immediate surroundings, Lorain County, that she was consulted by professors from the neighbouring college of Oberlin, to which she ultimately presented her herbarium. Small wonder that my Mother, with such relations, should have made collections not only of plants but even of seaweeds wherever she went, and that I, her daughter, for the sheer delight of the thing should have filled my novels—probably *ad nauseam* for most of my readers—with descriptions of wild flowers.

Captain James with his naval experience evidently saw possibilities in the Great Lakes, and decided to build boats there; he soon launched a trading vessel, built at Buffalo. Ultimately he seems to have been running several sailing boats, carrying passengers and freight; lists of payments for these services, receipts for nautical supplies, and accounts of seamen's wages paid out still repose in an old tin deedbox—in fact Captain James undoubtedly prospered also, and he spent a good deal of his active life about Lake Erie. But he was not a very satisfactory character, however enterprising; it was only the ceaseless exertions of his wife Hannah which kept his affairs in order. She inherited much of that sense of fair dealing which had made her father, old Elisha Hinman, so popular in the West Indies, and I judge also some of her Dolbeare mother's ruthlessness. There is an interminable correspondence between her and that Jabez Burrell who had gone out to Ohio with the John Days. Captain James had acquired some land in the new Sheffield too, but he didn't look after it; and poor Jabez, who seems to have acted as his man of business, is forever writing to Hannah begging her to get her husband to answer letters, to sign documents sent weeks before, to pay up mortgages, and to acknowledge the receipt of "bills" forwarded to him—the usual way of transmitting money before banks and cheques became the normal means of doing so. The whole correspondence furnishes an extremely lively picture of what was involved in property-holding out in the Middle West in the 1820's and 1830's: the sales of standing crops, the leasing of farms till after the harvest, and so on; but also of the devoted family friend on the spot trying to deal with the tiresome, feckless, absentee owner through his competent sensible wife. Occasionally there is a rather tart letter from my great-grandmother to her James, urging him to sign or pay; there are many from her to Jabez: evidently they understood one another perfectly, and also what they were up against.

Hannah Day was intensely religious, but also shrewd and practical; in 1842 she is already writing to her son-in-law John Peter Broûn in Alabama, advising him to transfer his property from the South to the North, since the abolition of slavery cannot be long delayed. There are two portraits of her. One, by an unknown but forcible artist, shows nothing but her severity—the rigid, squarely planted figure, the austere black dress, the muslin folded plainly round the head and neck, the sombre eyes and level lips; this picture almost explains the family legend that her husband was unfaithful to her. The other was commissioned by her son Thomas Davis Day, who adored her, from Thomas Sully, that curiously hybrid artist. Sully, with his current reputation, was an obvious choice for the wealthy and devoted son who desired to put his darling Mother on record, and this second portrait is a striking variation on the original theme. Now the black dress is bordered with a thread of silver; the figure is slender, and just inclined to the right, losing its stiffness; the muslin folds round the head have become a little cap bordered with lace. But the face, while it has lost none of its force, is youthful and gracious; there is a hint of quizzical amusement round the mouth and in the dark eyes, so like my Cousin Louisa's amused eyes and mouth. That likeness makes me think that the charm of this second picture is not entirely due to Sully's genius, and that it is a truthful portrait as well as a delightful one.

Thomas Day felt so strongly about his Father's behaviour to this charming mother that he would not allow them to rest in the same grave; poor James lies in Springfield, Massachusetts, while Hannah reposes at New London. Such action may strike one as exaggerated, but Great-Uncle Thomas was evidently a man of strong and stubborn feelings, and this probably helps to explain the astonishing persistence of the quarrel which took place between him and my Grandfather in the year 1868. What it was all about I have not been able to ascertain, but after the breach they never spoke or wrote to each other again, though both died only more than a quarter of a century later. Their two sisters took sides, one with each brother—Mary, married to Dr. John McEwen, stuck to my Grandfather, and she and her daughter and grand-daughter were household words to me all my life; but the other sister, Abigail, who married John Peter Broûn, adhered firmly to her brother Thomas. (The Broûns were French Huguenots from Bordeaux; the name was originally Brohun.) The family was "cleft in twain," in the Old Testament phrase, and with an Old Testament thoroughness; at one time the Broûns were living in New York in the next block to Aunt Sallie T., but though they constantly met in the street they never spoke to one another!—and it was only in the year 1953 that I myself so much as learned of the existence of my Great-Uncle Thomas and my Great-Aunt Abigail and their descendants. These are my very good friends now, and this book owes much to their help and collaboration. The actual date of the "grand family split," as my newly found cousins term it, is fixed by a letter from my Mother to her dearly beloved cousin Annie Broûn, which that cousin's daughter sent to me—in it my Mother refers to "this *abominable* FUSS," declaring that it shall make no difference to their affection. But little girls of fourteen or fifteen are not entirely masters of their own destinies, and in fact small Annie and small Marie were, bit by bit, very effectually separated by the quarrel between their elders—the correspondence gradually died away, and it was only thirty years after my Mother's death that I ever heard the name of the cousin she had loved best of all. Now Annie's daughter has sent Marie's daughter a girlhood picture of young Annie, which I have put with a youthful photograph of little Marie; at last those loving cousins are reunited, at least in some measure, by their two daughters.

Such were my Mother's grandparents, James and Hannah. At some point Captain James left both the Great Lakes and New England on behalf of his lungs and went South, and there my Mother's father was brought up, and met, and married in 1836, the beautiful Quakeress Sarah Eliza Armitage of Baltimore. Her portrait shows a long, calm face, with a mouth of great decision; round the white neck a lace collar lies richly on the black silk dress. The Quaker influence on my Mother was strong, both in behaviour and in dress. When discoursing to us on the horror of ever wearing imitation lace or machine-made embroidery, she was nevertheless sharp enough to have hit on, and point out, the reason why Quakers were so enormously fussy about wearing

37

beautiful lace and materials of the richest quality. They were limited to three colours, black, white and grey; and they could only ornament their monochrome dresses with white collars and cuffs; but what Lyons silks, she would say, furnished the black, the white and the grey!—and for the cuffs and collars, *Point d'Alençon* and *Point de Venise* were practically the minimum.

My Grandmother knew a great deal about birds and flowers— my Mother picked that up directly from her—though she was not, I gather, very active in the modern sense. She entertained, she directed her household; first of slaves, later of freed slaves— who to begin with stoutly refused to accept any wages. But she never bustled, was never put about by the goings-on either of her popular and rather unduly dashing husband, or of her lively and high-spirited sons and daughters.

"Why are your children always so obedient, Mrs. Day?" a friend once asked her wistfully.

"I suppose because I never ask them to do anything I think they wouldn't like," the Quakeress replied tranquilly.

This deliberate digression from Cuthbert Slocomb and his wife, besides giving some idea of the Days' family background, helps to explain their double connection, with the North as well as with the South—a duality which strongly affected my Mother's life during the Civil War. In this Uncle Cud served with notable gallantry, and we will now return to him.

In fact he did a good deal more than just serve. The Slocombs were a wealthy New Orleans family, presided over at the outbreak of the Civil War by Cuthbert's mother, the widowed Mrs. Cora Slocomb, a lady seemingly as dominant as her daughter-in-law, my Aunt Abby. It is, alas, too late to find out how those two very tough ladies got on with each other—my guess would be, not too well. When the Civil War broke out—indeed, rather before—the Washington Artillery, a New Orleans formation which had "languished to thirteen members," was taken over by James B. Walton, who had married a niece of my Grandmother's, as Commander; he "built it up to a full company . . . splendidly

uniformed and equipped . . . by private funds." A very large proportion of those private funds were supplied from the Slocomb
fortune, eagerly devoted to this purpose by my uncle, who disposed of the family's wealth. It was the Washington Artillery
which took the Federal Arsenal at Baton Rouge in January, 1861,
three months before War was actually declared between North
and South; the first serious act of hostility by Confederate forces
to the Federal Government.

Cuthbert Slocomb was "mustered" as a Second Lieutenant in
May of that year, when he was simultaneously appointed a Staff
Officer and Quarter-Master—this last a very suitable assignment
for the man who was supplying so much of the "Q" out of his
own pocket. By September he had been promoted to First
Lieutenant, but before the year was out he resigned and left the
regiment up in Virginia to return to New Orleans, "on business
of the greatest importance"—which was nothing less than financing and organising a 5th Company of the Artillery. This was
intended as a reserve from which supplies and fresh drafts could
be despatched to the front, and with typical modesty the ex-
Lieutenant re-enlisted in it as a private; however, he was soon
"elected" a Lieutenant again, and the new Company, burning
with zeal and tired of drilling in New Orleans, offered their
services "for ninety days, or the war," to General Beauregard—the
offer was accepted, and early in March, 1862, they left for the
front. They soon saw active service, and in the battle of Shiloh
on April the 3rd Slocomb was badly wounded by a shot in
the breast. He made a quick recovery, and by June was a
Captain, promoted for valour, and now commanding his battery.

Much of this must read rather strangely to modern ears. A
regiment raised and equipped by private funds; an officer resign-
ing, re-enlisting as a private, and being "elected" Lieutenant; the
reserve company asking to be allowed to go to the front, receiving
permission, and covering itself with glory, as my uncle's battery
did not only at Shiloh but at Chickamauga and Missionary Ridge.
To understand it one must recall the American scene in those

days, when half the various States had what amounted to frontiers giving onto Indian, or at least quite lawless, territory; Louisiana was practically next door to Mexico, and the Washington regiment, from which the Washington Artillery derived, had fought in the Mexican War. And it is necessary also to remember the American character. "Rugged individualism" has come to-day to connote principally a free hand in business enterprise, but in the first half of the nineteenth century it meant, to Americans, primarily self-help in all things, defence included. So the existence and even the creation of semi-private military formations is not really so odd. The Southern Army had almost more of an amateur status than the Northern; the gay, deep-drinking, straight-riding men who so largely composed it just turned to soldiering, when they saw themselves threatened, as they ordinarily turned to any other job of work or sport—and very well they did it. Most of them knew one another—many were related, as was Colonel Walton to Captain Slocomb; their wives were first cousins.

But the Southern Army suffered a good deal from its semi-amateur status. A parallel in our own day is the Poles confronting the Germans. There was the same reckless and often wasteful gallantry, the same wild courage in actual onslaughts, the same cruel losses, the same touching dependence of rankers on their officers. Many years afterwards, at a reunion of the survivors of the Washington Artillery, one of them thus recalled the pitifulness of the battlefield: " 'Tis McGregor, 'tis Winston, 'tis Beggs, 'tis Billy Sewell, with his last breath whispering in Slocomb's ear—'Captain, haven't I done my duty?' "

All this epic of chivalric self-sacrifice, high courage, lost endeavour and ultimate defeat filtered through to us as children in a hundred anecdotes, exchanged between my Mother and our aunts—the whole "climate" of the South during the Civil War was part of the most intimate furniture of our young minds, and was linked especially to the figure, beloved at second hand, of Uncle Cud. But there was one story in particular which we thrilled to, though so far as I know it does not occur in any of the books of war-time reminiscences which the Southern officers, again like the Poles, poured out so freely after the war was over; it throws a certain light on my uncle's gentle character. During the last big battle of the war, when the two armies, after facing each other for months from lines of entrenchments several miles long, covering Richmond, at last went into action, the Confederates were in poor case for supplies—in the Washington Artillery Slocomb was the only man who had a fit charger left, and he was asked to take some urgent despatches to General Lee, at the far end of the front, himself. The entrenchments were in considerable depth, and Slocomb, springing on his horse, started to gallop down the open space of no-man's land between the opposing armies. At first he was fired at from both sides; then both lines roared at him to stop; he merely galloped on, oblivious alike of shots and shouts, and long before he reached the further end both armies were cheering the solitary rider. When he had handed over his despatches to Lee he fainted and fell, badly wounded. Aunt Abby was nursing in the military hospital behind the front, and presently found her husband among her patients; when she asked him what had induced him to do anything so mad as to gallop down the battle-front he replied: "Did I? I just took the only open space I could find." It was a story that as children we could not hear often enough.

If Uncle Cud Slocomb did a lot to finance his regiment *sur place*, my Grandfather Day also took an active part in the vital matter of supplies for the Southern armies, from further afield. As we know, his father had gone South, where he himself presently took up a business career. Captain James, a seafaring man, and his mother, that old sea-dog Elisha Hinman's daughter, had pressed their son to adopt a career in the Army or Navy, but this the younger James stoutly refused to do; he had decided, rightly, that he had a gift for business; into business he went, and prospered exceedingly. But New England, the first home of both his parents, exerted a strong pull on him, and in 1851 he built as a summer residence Walnut Grove at Stonington, the house which to the end of her life my Mother loved more than any other spot on earth. "Stonington" she always called it, using the name of the sea-port near which it stood rather than the more fanciful appellation of Walnut Grove. Actually it was known locally simply as "the Day place," and as a house always full—full of "clever women and accomplished men" and "gay young people," among whom a contemporary local historian lists "Abby and Helen and Sallie Day," along with Williamses, Champlins, and Trumbulls, Bessies and Emmelines and Elizas. This lady records delightful nonsenses about some of the girls plastering their hair down round their foreheads, when flat hair was the fashion, with "the black pomade that comes in sticks," and how on a hot evening of dancing the stiff pomaded waves got pushed aside, leaving a sharply defined line of black round the white foreheads, "that occasioned much merriment." When I read now those long-ago recollections I remember how Pa T., years afterwards, used to refer to his wife and her sisters—all middle-aged by then—as "the Day girls"; his phrase takes one straight back to the big hospitable house above the lake, full of youth and fun and dancing and folly.

It stood high, half hidden by the wild walnut-trees which gave it its name; they were thick along the banks of the stream—a favourite playground of my Mother's—which came tumbling through a confusion of glaciated rocks to feed the lake below, and in one place extended right down to the shore of an inlet from the sea known as "the cove," where the young people went bathing and boating between low reedy boulder-strewn shores. At certain tides the lake was connected with the cove, and it was possible to pass by boat from one to the other; but whatever the state of the tide boats could slip in at night from the ocean and anchor in the cove—whence it was a simple matter either to row up the lake with muffled oars to a point close below the house, or to scramble up direct from the cove under cover of the great trees, and tap on the french windows of the library, where Mr. Day always sat in evenings. During the Civil War boats constantly did so slip in, bringing news from the South—news, especially, of what was most urgently required down there; and taking back supplies of such things as medicines, tobacco, and that rare and precious commodity coffee. Wakeful children leaning from their windows at night might hear the faint sound of oars, however muffled, down on the lake, or the crack of breaking twigs in the undergrowth, and then the murmur of voices in the library; might overhear, next day, scraps of the longed-for news which the nocturnal visitors had brought—but they learned never to ask questions, nor to speak of what they heard.

My Grandfather of course had none of these convenient assets in mind when he built the place, years before the war; he little dreamed then that the lake and the inlet would presently afford free communication between North and South during a period when all normal channels were closed completely. He was only thinking, then, of an escape for himself and his family from the exhausting heats of summer in New Orleans. Moreover, he had acquired an interest in the New York, Providence and Boston R.R. Co., of which he was President from 1857 to 1867; and he had invested in the building of the railroad from Stonington to New London, chartered in 1852—later it became the "New Haven, New London, and Stonington Railroad Co.," and completed the first through route from New York to Boston. For all these reasons it suited him to be able to live in the North for part of the year; but when war broke out he was caught up in Connecticut with his wife and his younger children, including my Mother, and there he had to stay, for the next four years. It cannot have been a very pleasant sojourn: his son-in-law Cuthbert Slocomb and his niece's husband, Colonel Walton, were both in the thick of the fighting, as were most of the friends of a life-time; his eldest daughter Abby nursing in an Army hospital, and his business interests in New Orleans gone, probably, to glory. Being the man he was he took all this very philosophically, with his habitual quiet good-humour, and his equally habitual cigar. He had a fine taste in cigars and imported the very best for his own use, and for guests of his own age and standing; for the young men who frequented his house, whether in the North or in the South, in pursuit of his bevy of fine daughters, he kept boxes of inferior brands which he called his *Intimidados*—a young man who was seen surreptitiously disposing of an *Intimidado* rose high in Mr. Day's esteem.

But isolation and anxiety for those he loved—and he was a man of an immense warmth of heart, glowing always with affection and appreciation—were not the only disagreeable circumstances attending his enforced sojourn in the North. His neighbours, all dyed-in-the-wool Yankees, regarded him with the utmost suspicion—quite rightly, actually; here was a man of good old New England stock who had married South, made a fortune South, and then come back only to make no secret, when war broke out, of his Southern sympathies. Tarring and feathering was a common form of "rough justice" in those days, and it was a process almost as dangerous to life as it was humiliating and horrible; it never happened to him, though he was threatened with it more than once, but life cannot have been at all agreeable for my Grandparents in Connecticut during those years of Civil War.

All the same it was not merely to escape unpleasantness that James Ingersoll Day made his trip to Europe then. From the couriers who slipped into the Stonington inlet by night and tapped on his library window after dark he knew very precisely of what the Southern forces stood most in need, and presently he set out for the Old World to procure them—arms, ammunition, supplies of every sort. What is more, he did procure them, and got them shipped across to America. Wealthy, immensely cultivated, agreeable to the point of charm, he went everywhere, and everywhere made purchases for the Armies of the South. One of his oddest contacts was the Czar of Russia!—though exactly what he hoped to get from him, or got, I have no idea. Wherever he went, agents from the North dogged his footsteps—without, however, being able to put any serious check on his activities;

the supplies got in in spite of the attempted blockade. I cannot help wishing that my Quaker Grandmother, so beautiful, so quiet and staid, had accompanied her husband to Europe and met the Czar too; she would surely have been something quite new for him, in her close-bodiced full-skirted black or grey faille, with the little triangular Quaker shawl of fringed silk—I have it still —round her shoulders, and the matchless *Point de venise* collars and cuffs.

However, she did nothing of the sort. She remained at Stonington, housing under her roof, in summer especially, a perfect menagerie of old and young, black and white. Besides her own younger children, Jim, Rob, and little Marie, there were always for the summer seven little Broûns, the offspring of my Grandfather's sister Abigail, all shepherded by another sister-in-law, Mary McEwen, with her small daughter. The Broûn parents had gone down to South Carolina to look after some property there, leaving the children in Mrs. McEwen's care; but like my Grandparents they were caught by the Civil War, and had to remain in the South for four whole years, as the Days had to remain in the North. Some time before, Mr. Broûn had freed "his two most valuable slaves," William and Castalia, his butler and coachman; but when he sold his Alabama plantation and moved to New York they insisted on accompanying him—so they too had to be carted up to Connecticut in the summers along with the little Broûns, who with their cousins boated, bathed in "the cove," and rambled through the walnut-woods at "Uncle Day's."

My mother, Annie Broûn and my Uncle Jim were in those years inseparables—they were among the younger of the cousins, and hung together. The presence of William and Castalia helped at first to make the Broûn children feel at home in the strange house, but "Aunt Eliza," my Grandmother, very soon did more —"She was wonderful to them, and they all adored her," Annie Broûn's daughter notes. Over and over again in those three families, in spite of war and separation, comes the refrain—"those four happy summers at Stonington"; and from my Mother herself I always heard the same note of enchantment. Happy children, under their Aunt Eliza's loving and tranquil rule—no doubt she never asked her Broûn or McEwen nephews and nieces to do anything she thought they wouldn't like, either! "The beloved cousins" is another phrase from Annie Broûn—a sort of light of love and happiness lies over those long summer days in New England, nearly a century ago.

Chapter 4

*A*ND now at last, in those summers of the Civil War, we come to my Mother herself; at this point her own life, apart from the background furnished by her family and forbears, emerges. When the War broke out she was eight or nine years old; a buxom child, with brilliant, rather light brown eyes, a high colour in her round cheeks, her little nose not sharpened to its later aquiline neatness but still blunt with youth, and a perfect mop of auburn-chestnut hair. We have her portrait painted a couple of years earlier, leaning over the shoulder of that forbidding and learned old Quakeress, her Aunt Mary Baldwin, another of my Grandmother's sisters—a woman with a massive body and a heavy face, rather sour, in spite of the look of power and intellect about mouth and brow. There was no intention originally of having my Mother painted, the portrait was simply to be of her Aunt Mary; but during the sittings the little Marie and her young brother Jim kept coming in and playing about—so Aunt Abby told me—and the artist was so beguiled by the two pretty children that he insisted on painting them too. So there they are on the canvas to this day, the delightful little creatures, draped round that mountain of a woman with the unamiable expression; Uncle Jim wears a little velvet suit with lace collar and cuffs, *à la* Lord Fauntleroy, but my Mother—to her intense disgust at the time and ever afterwards—was taken out of her normal clothes and swathed in tinsel and muslin, to show off her small

47

white neck and her round chubby arms, by the artist's wish. Her distaste for this "dressing-up," even then, was intensely characteristic; already to her childish instinct it was slightly bogus—in fact "inaccurate." She hated that picture to her dying day, but loyally kept it for Great-Aunt Mary Baldwin's sake; and I cannot but be glad that she did, for it takes one back with a profound immediacy to that far-away child, wild and winsome, and even at that age appearing a little detached, a little disdainful of all these goings-on. To be disdainful about having one's portrait painted at the age of six or seven may seem rather exaggerated; but my Mother's disdain—seldom unjustly expressed, I must say —was throughout her life something to be reckoned with.

The War, then, found her up at Stonington with her parents. Stonington already had for her all the charm of a summer home, a place where in the holidays the disciplines of daily life were relaxed, and one led a carefree existence in unwonted surroundings, with strange birds, different flowers, a whole other world of natural delights. In the woods there in spring was that incredible natural miracle, the wild American dogwood, a tree rising sometimes to as much as sixty feet and covered with large white flowers, whose upcurving petals make them look like little white baskets. (When I myself saw it in the New England woods, with my Mother already twenty years in her grave, I realised what it must have meant to her when she saw it for the first time— as a child, with a child's intensity of perception—eighty years before.) And in those same woods, under the dogwoods and maples and hickories, grew the wild trilliums—the deep magenta and the white, with their squashy stems and foliage and their exquisite three-petalled flowers. The woods of New England in spring are a quite shattering experience for those who can be shattered by the things of nature.

But my Mother's sojourn in the North during the Civil War was not all joy for her, any more than it was for my Grandfather —and she had not the resource of smoking cigars! She had to be educated, and was sent to school; at first daily to the village school, where boys and girls alike were drilled either by the local schoolmaster, or the "school-marm," not only in the three R.s but in the elements of Latin and Greek, as well as other subjects; music and drawing she learned from a friend's governess. They must have been terrific, those New England schoolmistresses of a century ago: steeped in the classics, in love with learning for its own sake, ferocious disciplinarians, eager educators. It was of course "co-ed." even then; boys and girls studied together—but what would those bygone school-marms have said to the campus life of to-day? Or to the current educational standards? "We see very little of each other out of school hours," small Marie writes to Annie Broûn, apropos of the boys.

Of that part of her education my Mother loved every minute; then as later she had an unslaked thirst for knowledge, and a new fact, especially in the natural sciences, was like a nugget of gold to her. But when my Grandfather decided to go to Europe, her small private affairs took a decided turn for the worse. Uncle Bob was kept at home; there are stories of his innocently shouting "Hooray for the Yankees!" and of my grandmother forbidding anyone to check him, since it was safer for people to believe that at least one Day was *for* the Yankees. But the little Marie was deposited in a rather grand boarding-school. This of course was a school for girls only, another change for the worse; my Mother always liked boys, and liked doing the things they did, swimming and riding and boating and climbing trees and fishing and birds'-nesting; she abhorred girlish activities such as needlework, and was a bad needlewoman to the end of her days. (She never kept a doll in her life.) This athleticism—for it amounted to that—persisted; she was always a fine horsewoman, a strong swimmer, and a good oarswoman—greatly startling her English in-laws, when she appeared in Warwickshire in the middle of the Victorian era, by these two last activities.

Her swimming originally owed much to that quiet obstinate pertinacity about learning anything she wanted to learn. Mrs. Day did not think that girls needed to learn to swim; none of her elder daughters had wanted to and she forbade swimming to her youngest. Little Marie, always obedient, kept out of the water, but she coaxed her brother Jim to teach her her strokes, and for two whole years practised them assiduously in secret, lying on her stomach across the music-stool. A day came when Jim and Robert, accompanied by the little sister and a group of boys, probably the young Broûns, were fooling around at the docks at New London; someone gave Marie a careless push, and to their consternation she fell into the water—deep, and surrounded by high, slimy, unclimbable walls of dressed stone. It was a horrifying moment. The child went under, of course; after a few seconds she re-appeared on the surface, and to everyone's amazement struck out vigorously in a perfect breast-stroke, and swam about quite composedly till a rope was fetched and thrown, up which she climbed like the monkey she was to safety. After that performance my Grandmother gave in, and allowed her youngest daughter to go swimming with the boys.

But that was during the good days at Stonington—at her boarding-school she had a hard time. My Grandfather's reputation as a Southern sympathiser, and an active one at that, had preceded her there; she was surrounded by little Yankee girls who taunted her with being a slave-owner's daughter, rejoiced at Federal victories, and crowed over her on occasions of Confederate defeats. She sought consolation in working hard at her lessons, and carried off a good many prizes—I still have a little silver locket and chain, presented to her for the typically New England merits of "conscientiousness and proficiency, particularly in general knowledge." I have also a copy-book full of her essays, beautifully neat and quite well expressed, but for the most part as dull as the subjects set; in one, however, a genuine lyricism breaks out—"On which season of the year I prefer, and why." My Mother chose the spring, and in spite of the rather elaborate and stilted style which the other essays show to have been imposed on the girls, her knowledge and love of spring in wood and field in New England emerge with a note almost of passion. It did not get very good marks.

So the days, the weeks, the long months of the child's isolation dragged on; birthdays came and went—she was ten, she was eleven, she was twelve (just nine days before the armistice or capitulation was signed in the Court House of Appomattox), but without any of the delightful family celebrations of birthdays to which she was accustomed. In the summer holidays she went back to heaven and home, but in term-time the little girl was left clinging rather miserably to the odd opportunity of doing chores for the kind school-mistresses, of whom she became very fond. Consolation of one's private troubles by service to others is usually a rather maturely Christian thing, and I think it gives some measure of my Mother's character that she had learned to practise it before she was twelve years old. (In hard times in later years she often quoted the words—"The world is our schoolmaster, to bring us to Christ.")

At last the war ended: there was the expectation of complete reunion with the beloved family, made to seem doubly precious by the constant separations. But that hope too proved to be hope deferred. Her Father was still abroad, talking to the Czar, or to someone or other; her Mother went South, where Sister Abby was nursing her husband back to life, after the desperate wounds he had got in that insanely gallant ride. So those Easter holidays too passed at school, relieved only by the blessed absence of her triumphant little Yankee schoolfellows. But they came back for the summer term, and crowed louder than ever while it dragged its slow length out. Towards the end of it came good news: the Slocombs at least were coming North, though alone, to the house at Stonington, for Uncle Cud to convalesce, complete with the familiar black staff whom my Mother loved only less than she did her own family.

Now comes the final irony of my Mother's schooldays in the North. My Aunt Abby—unpardonably, as it seems to me—did not drive over herself on the last day of term to greet and collect that homesick child: no, she was busy making the house perfect and putting flowers in the little sister's room—a wonderful example of putting last things first and first things last. Instead she sent her Mother's former butler, Old Joe, with his crinkly white half-whiskers framing his black chin. Small Marie Day stood on the great portico among the crowd of other girls, all in their flowing summer muslins; carriage after carriage drove up and disgorged loving parents, who embraced their offspring and took them off. But presently, but at last, a buggy swung up the gravelled drive carrying as a passenger just Old Joe, and my Mother, nearly as impulsive as Aunt Sallie, flew down the wide steps to greet the darkie butler—she flung her arms round his neck and hugged him, while he murmured, "Mis' Marree! Ain't you growed!" Whereupon the little Yankee girls, who had spent those three years scourging James Day's child for being a slave-owner's daughter, drew their muslin skirts haughtily aside, muttering audibly—"Well! before I'd kiss a nigger!"

I have no exact date for my Grandfather's return from Europe. That he was still not back at Stonington in November, 1866, is plain from another letter of my Mother's to her cousin Annie, gaily dated—"Walnut Grove. November I don't know what.—1866."

"You asked me if I was going up to Niagara?" she writes. "I don't know. Mamma thinks of letting me go, but it is nothing decided yet, and I hope she won't let me go because in the first place I had rather not go away from home as you know, and in the second place I don't think I ought to go and leave her all alone at home with Auntie" (this is Mrs. Baldwin) "and Bob. . . . Helen goes home a week from Tuesday and the house will be very lonely then."

Quite a respectably unselfish attitude from a fourteen-year-old girl always eager to see the wonders of nature—but she adds later in the letter: "I am nearly always out and full of mischief and badness. I behave so badly that I am ashamed of myself, and am going to try to do better." What this "badness" was I don't know. In a letter to the same cousin a year later she apologises for not writing, and asks to be forgiven—"for I might have had time if I had been self-denying enough to give up a row on the lake, or

52

James Ingersoll Day and his five daughters
Standing: Aunt Jane, Aunt Helen, J.I.D., Aunt Sallie T.
Sitting: Aunt Abby, the author's Mother

The author, aged 3

James Ingersoll Day, the author's grandfather

something, which I was not." Honest enough. And it cannot have been the boys—whose attentions began early in America, even then—for about them she had no inhibitions; later in the same letter she writes airily (though still honestly):

"Little Dick and I, as I suppose you know, had a 'fuss,' as *of course* such *foolish children* must, and last summer had very little to do with one another, and this summer he was not here; but I've been making up to his cousin Will Wilcox, who lives in the new house which Capt. Soper has built right opposite us, below Dr. Palmer's garden that used to be."

But this letter contains one definite item of information.

"Sister Abby has kindly offered to take me to New Orleans where I will have a good opportunity to learn French, and attend a nice school; and as I expect to study *very very* hard, I shall have but little—in fact almost *no* time to write. . . . I expect to go some time in November, and then oh! for the studying, with God's help."

This was in the autumn of 1867; my Grandparents only went South a year or so later. It is not always easy to trace the precise course of financial embarrassments, even when they are contemporary, and after the lapse of little short of a century it is almost impossible. An account of my Grandfather's life, published in 1905, states that "Mr. Day" had become a partner of some young men in New York "in whom he had absolute confidence"; that the war ruined them, and that he was involved in their disaster and lost everything. This does not sound at all like James Ingersoll Day; as a rule he had so little confidence in young men and their judgment that he gave them his *Intimidados* to smoke. The family's version sounds more probable; according to this he returned to New Orleans a wealthy man, and then "went on a note bond" for a friend of his own age and standing; this friend went bankrupt, my Grandfather of course paid up, and lost everything. What is certain is that he did lose practically everything, and moved—with the ever-unruffled Sarah Eliza—into a small house, and to be earning something "sat down on a stool in his son-in-law, Cuthbert Slocomb's, office."

Those are my Mother's own words, and I find them moving. But in view of the reckless way in which my Uncle Cud had expended his personal fortune in fitting out the Washington Artillery we may well wonder why at the close of the Civil War he was on such a sound financial basis as to be in a position to offer his father-in-law a job. Here we encounter once more that formidable lady Mrs. Cora Slocomb, his mother, whose money affairs are actually mentioned in some detail in his own autobiography by no less a person than the hated Major-General Benjamin Franklin Butler, who was appointed military governor of New Orleans after its capitulation—derisively referred to as "Tea-spoon Butler," for reasons which will appear presently. He states that her husband's firm owed a very large debt to a firm in the North; when the Confederate authorities, very naturally, issued an ordinance confiscating all debts due to Northerners (like the English "Trading with the Enemy" enactments in World Wars I and II) a summons was served upon her—I quote Butler—"to show cause why she should not pay into the Treasury of the Confederacy the amount of the debt due to the Northern creditors of her deceased husband. She answered the summons in person, and declared that her husband's estate owed that debt to the Northern firm . . . and that she must pay it where it belonged. . . . The Confederate authorities brought upon her some pretty harsh pressure to change her determination. She said: 'You may do with me what you please, but I will not disobey the dictates of justice and conscience.' And she did not."

Old Mrs. Slocomb was of course in a pretty strong position, so much of her family money having been spent already on fitting out what Butler himself describes as "the crack artillery company of New Orleans." The family version of this story has it that the debts were mutual, but the company in the North owed far more than what was owed to them; that they held up all remittances throughout the War, and sent down a colossal lump sum, representing the profits which had accrued during the war years. Anyhow, however it happened—and the two stories do not really contradict each other—Uncle Cud ended the war as rich a man as when it began, which was really quite rich. What is interesting is this testimony from an enemy, whatever we may think of the wretched Tea-spoon Butler. But he was evidently greatly impressed by old Cora. She got round him to the extent of getting a permit to go to her property in North Carolina, and not only not having her New Orleans house requisitioned, but his personal guarantee that it would not be interfered with—all this while refusing to take the required oath of allegiance to the United States! He describes an interview with her, and quotes their correspondence about the house, at full length: "Yours shall be the solitary exception to the general rule adopted, that those who seek protection must take upon themselves a corresponding obligation." No doubt a lot of this was put in to whitewash himself in both Southern and Northern eyes, by showing that he could be generous when he chose; but it is none the less evident that my Uncle Cuthbert's mother was what the country-people in England call "a one."

My Mother, then, settled down in New Orleans with the still wealthy Slocombs after the war ended; and she now saw the place with the sharpened eyes of an observant girl in her early teens. New Orleans, on any showing, is a charming city, rich in many places with the heavy Spanish richness conferred on it by the brilliant builder Almonaster—a sort of Georgian baroque, like that for example of the Pontalba Buildings, so beautifully enclosing their great square, full of the overflowing greenery of the Gulf, in mellow brick; full everywhere of graceful ample houses in gardens which flower as much from trees as from parterres— and still more, even in the gardenless streets, there is another flowering of *grillages*, on gates and balconies and window-boxes. The wrought-ironwork of New Orleans has to be seen to be believed. That apart, the architecture of Bienville's city would have charm, but no immense distinction; but its ironwork gives it a unique architectural prestige. Little is left, after the disastrous fire of 1788, of the robust simplicity of its French-Canadian founders—for in spite of the wholesale export of colonists from the France of Louis Quatorze, the frails and thieves, the Manon Lescauts and the Des Grieux—the city owed its foundation and original character much more to the energetic, spirited, and competent offspring of Charles le Moyne, the Dieppe innkeeper's son who went to Canada to seek (and make) his fortune, than it does to *le Roi Soleil*. The history of New Orleans is one of the most amusing and exhilarating in the whole tale of human affairs. Founded by French-Canadians, peopled at least in part by French transportees from prisons and houses of detention, at so much a head to the press-gangs who collected them; ceded by De Choiseul to the Spaniards, who left their unmistakable imprint; receded to the French under Napoleon, and only three weeks later bought by the Americans under the transaction known as the "Louisiana Purchase." There are other ways of forming an empire than by sailing the seas and capturing ports and islands, as the English and Portuguese did; it can be done just as well by economic penetration or by an outright buying of territory for cash down, as in the "Louisiana Purchase." The Americans, very characteristically, used both methods; but they have in general failed to recognise that historically and in actual fact an Empire is not less an Empire because it is all situated on one continent and acquired—Alaska is the most recent instance—by financial means rather than by force of arms. (The pen, signing cheques, is perhaps really mightier than the sword.

New Orleans lies low; like Shanghai it is built on a mud-bank—in this case a narrow strip along the north shore of the river, between it and the arm of the sea known as Lake Ponchartrain; except where this mudflat was artificially built up it was nowhere higher than sixteen feet above sea-level, and often very much less—where the Slocombs first lived the street was barely three feet above high-water mark. A really bad hurricane blowing into Lake Ponchartrain from the Gulf, fortunately a thing which rarely happened, would raise the water anything from six to fifteen feet, flooding most of the town; but even a heavy fall of sub-tropical rain would cause flooding in the streets, since the fall to the Lake was only about one foot per mile. (In that overflow land the actual banks of the river are the highest points.) So even in my Mother's day the built-up streets and squares were known among the Creoles as *islets*. All the drains in those days, whether for rain or bath-water or—in the less prosperous districts— sewerage, consisted of open ditches some two feet deep running down both sides of the streets, with flowers growing along the banks; as a sanitary precaution the sluices in the levee along the river were opened every evening, to flush these drains into Lake Ponchartrain. In front of each house a small wooden bridge led from the sea of mud which was the street across the drain, first to the banquette, a side-walk slightly above street level paved with bricks, or in the more elegant quarters with large English or German slate slabs brought back as ballast in the returning cotton ships; from the banquette one reached the gardens or "yards" of the houses, which had usually been filled in with river silt to raise their level. These bridges were furnished on both sides with small benches on which people sat during the hot summer evenings, to get at least the illusion of coolness created by the flowing water —and drainage. The principal means of locomotion, especially from the residential district to the shopping quarter, a distance of anything from half a mile to two miles, was by mule-drawn trams; to give the mules foothold cypress boards three inches thick and a foot in breadth were laid cross-wise between the tram-lines. They were not nailed down, since there was nothing but mud to nail them to, and when a rainstorm of two or three inches an hour produced a more complete flooding than that organised nightly by the municipality, these boards would come adrift and float loose in a foot or more of water; my cousins, with the other small boys, would rush out and cruise about on the cypress planks in a drainage sea, pretending that they were seamen on their great-grandfather Captain James Day's ships up on the Great Lakes. If such a downpour was accompanied by a "back-up" in Lake Ponchartrain from a "blow," things were better still, for then the water might rise till it was as much as three or four feet deep and those wooden benches from the bridges, known as "kiosques," were carried away as well, and wandered up and down the streets.

It all sounds incredibly unhealthy, but in fact people seem to have been well, besides being gay, in these extraordinary surroundings; I heard a lot as a child about this relation and that having yellow fever, but nothing of typhoid—indeed I believe it is a recorded fact that there never was a case of typhoid fever in New Orleans till after the water-works and sewerage system were installed. Such is the merit of anti-bodies! And up to the close of the last century an immense quantity of cray-fish could be had merely by lifting the street-gratings and fishing in the drains below them; an outcry was raised by the gourmets and *restaurateurs* when it was proposed to seal off this primitive and insanitary source of a delicious food. My own cousins used to amuse themselves by catching "crawfish," as they were called locally, in holes in the garden, where the underground water stood within three feet of the surface. But the whole city was not as dirty as it sounds: sixty inches of rain a year, when it falls three or four inches at a time, can clear up a lot of filth—it had to, and it did.

Cuthbert Slocomb, during the period that my Mother was living with him and his wife, Abby, occupied in turn two houses, both on Esplanade Avenue; the first was rather far out, almost in the country, a big square three-story block with balconies on each floor under wide projecting eaves. After a time my Uncle Cud, who was extremely fond of racing, sold this house to the Jockey Club, which he had helped to found, and moved in nearer to the centre of the city, where he built another house; not quite so big, but none the less large and luxurious—quite large enough for one whole room to be entirely devoted to my Aunt Abby's collection of fans. A cousin has described this to me: there were fans on the walls, smaller fans on display-tables, very large fans in fan-holders standing about the floor. It sounds very odd, but I am told that it was really rather pretty. In fact this house was almost a private museum: in the "parlour," on more display-tables, were ranged specimens of her very fine collection of silver spoons—including her grandmother Hannah Hinman's, made from British prize-money melted down, and also some of her great-grandmother Abigail Dolbeare's ancestral spoons, with the Prince of Wales's feathers, plus two more, as a crest. There are several of these lying about in the family still. In the large upstairs hall, where a little coloured boy—"in uniform, mostly buttons," as my cousin describes him—waited all day long to answer bells and run errands, there hung on the wall a great frame filled with specimens of the lace which Mrs. Slocomb had collected. Possibly it was the room full of fans which prompted old Mammy to spend the whole of her first year's wages, in her unwished-for freedom, on buying my Grandmother a lovely one made of guinea-fowl feathers—for when my Grandfather lost his fortune, Mammy was passed on to act as lady's-maid to Aunt Abby. But anyhow the ex-slaves ran in and out of the various family houses in New Orleans like mice, so Mammy was certainly familiar with the fan room even before she was transferred to my aunt's service.

My Mother was not the only child in this curious establishment, full of lace and fans and freed slaves. Uncle Cud and Aunt Abby had just one daughter—called Cora after old Mrs. Slocomb, her grandmother; there were only a few years between the two little girls, and they were brought up together, partly under Mammy's aegis. My Mother had a pleasant story of a day when the French dress-maker came out to the house on Esplanade Avenue to fit Aunt Abby with a frock: little Cora—like her mother a tremendous talker—was fidgeting about the room, making comments at the pitch of her voice; Mammy was in attendance on her mistress.

"Oh, what a chatterbox that child is!" Aunt Abby exclaimed, exasperated.

"She didn' buy it, Mis' Abby," Mammy, who had known my aunt at the same age, replied.

But those first few years after the war were hard ones. Uncle Cud might be rich, but practically everyone else was ruined, or nearly so; almost every family in New Orleans had lost sons and brothers, and over all hung the bitter sense of humiliation and defeat. The people of New Orleans, who throughout their checquered history had shown a vigorous independence of spirit, alike to France, to the Spaniards (whom in fact they came to like) and finally to their American purchasers, chafed wretchedly under the harsh and tactless rule of the Northern Governor, General Butler. He owed his ridiculous sobriquet of "Tea-spoon Butler" to his alleged habit of requisitioning, on one pretext or another, the table-silver of the Southern families who were now at his mercy; the citizens of New Orleans, with a witty recklessness that reminds one of the Viennese, produced little terracotta figurines of an officer in Federal uniform carrying a spoon instead of a musket over his shoulder—unmistakably they represented the General, but they were on sale in all the shops; seized by the Northern troops one week, they reappeared the next.

And more uncomfortable still for the Southern families was the problem of the darkies, the ex-slaves, now legally free. Not all were like Mammy, wishing to spend their money on buying costly fans for their mistresses; nor like my Grandfather's staff, whose behaviour to-day seems truly astonishing. When, some time after the slaves were freed, his friend's bankruptcy ruined him, Mr. Day summoned Old Joe, his butler, and told him to take himself, and to give all the other servants notice, as it was no longer possible for him to pay their wages. Joe said at once that they would all gladly work for "Mas' Day" without wages. Mas' Day was obliged to point out that he could no longer afford even to feed them, wages or no. This did set Old Joe back a bit; he retired for a below-stairs consultation—from which he returned to say that the staff all had "savin's," and would feed themselves. No doubt in those rich households there had been abundant perquisites and pickings, even for slaves—but it was a very delightful gesture. Undeniably, of course, all slaves in the South had not been treated so well, and there was a good deal of rather hysterical exultation and triumph at now being considered as good as the white man: the rich white man, that is—darkies in positions of authority in their masters' establishments, like Mammy and Joe, had long looked down with the utmost contempt on the "pore white trash," as the impoverished white labourers and share-croppers of the South were already called. But there was bewilderment as well as triumph, as there is among all groups of people too suddenly made their own masters, before they have learned the habits of independence and self-regulation; the darkies' side of the picture had its own pathos, as the African picture has to-day. All these elements in the attitude of the Southern Negro at the time of liberation emerge with particular clarity in yet another darkie song:

> *Say, darkies, did you see de Massa wid de mustache*
> *   on his face,*
> *Go down de road sometime dis mornin', like he's gwine*
> *   to leave de place?*
> *He seen de smoke way up de river, where de Lincoln*
> *   gun-boats lay;*
> *He took his hat and lef' dam' sudden an' I 'spec' he's*
> *   run away.*
> * De mastah run, Haha! an' de darkies say, Hoho!*
> *It mus' be now de Kingdom comin', an' de year of*
> *   Jubilo.*
>
> *De ober-seer he make trouble an' he chase us round*
> *   a' spell;*
> *We done gone lock him in de office an' de key's frown*
> *   in de well.*

Then comes the note of disillusionment:

*Dere's wine an' cider in de cellar, an' de darkies
  dey'll hab some—
I 'spec' dat all get confiscated when de Lincoln
  sojers come.*

Pitiably true. That pathetic stanza takes one straight back to my Mother's little Yankee school-mates, horrified at the Southern girl who would "kiss a nigger," and straight ahead to nearly a century of Negro disillusionment in the North. I have never been able to ascertain the exact date of this song, but it has a peculiar veracity, even to the comic detail about the Massa's huge size: "His coat so big he could'n' pay de tailor, an' it don' go ha'f way round." So also has Owen Wister's beautifully conceived novel *Lady Baltimore*, probably half forgotten to-day; the scene of it is Charleston, not New Orleans, but the problem of the "reconst'ukted niggah" though there presented of a period years later, was true of the whole South.

I did not hear of this aspect from my aunts or my Mother, naturally enough, in view of the attitude of my Grandfather's staff, an attitude which went for the Slocombs' darkies too; but Tea-spoon Butler was out to inflict any humiliation he could on the citizens of New Orleans, especially the more prominent ones, and he thought up something really good for my Uncle Cud, in spite of his self-recorded courtesies to the latter's mother, old Mrs. Cora. Under the new dispensation, introduced by the Northern victors, the freed Negroes had all sorts of rights hitherto reserved to white people—amongst others the right to sit on a jury; and when a case came on between a Southerner and some Northerner, General Butler summoned a black jury, and called upon Captain Slocomb to sit on it as Chairman. It was the most calculated insult that could have been devised; even to-day the memory arouses anger in the South. But Uncle Cud was not a Christian for nothing, and he was also extremely shrewd; he had taken Butler's measure, and wished to spare his fellow-townsmen as much trouble as possible; he accepted the task without protest. He went to Court and sat there among the darkies, in full view of everyone; he listened to the evidence; then, with these unwonted colleagues, he retired to the jury-room to consider the verdict. But even his humility was unable to resist repeating afterwards, with considerable relish, what there took place.

"Well, gentlemen, what is our verdict to be?" Uncle Cud asked the eleven darky jurors.

"Jez's you say, Mas' Slocomb; jez's you say," they replied in chorus, grinning broadly.

He recounted blandly later that he gave the verdict against the Northerner, "on the facts."

My Mother returned to the South soon enough after the War was over, and at a sufficiently intelligent age, to get a vivid impression of what the conflict had meant to individuals, especially to women. Oddly enough most of this first emerged for me in 1914, at the outbreak of the first World War. My eldest child was born a few days after August the 4th, 1914, and my Mother, following the immemorial tradition of "seeing a daughter through her first," had come to stay with us in Lexham Gardens. As I lay in bed in my big pretty room with the silvery-blue striped wall-paper, in tired and relaxed idleness, shot through with anxiety about that unknown thing, war, half listening to the hot dusty rustle of the plane-trees in the square below, she gave me maternal advice; but in the hot weeks of that particular August the advice she gave took on an unwonted tone for such an occasion, and matched the secret anxiety.

"If you and Owen have to bury your silver, my dear child," she suddenly said one day, *àpropos de bottes*, "remember that it is no use to bury it near a building or a tree, and count on that as a landmark—because trees and buildings get blown up. Bury it near some quite large cross-roads; roads always run pretty much in the same place, whatever happens." Or, sitting large and calm in her grey summer dress, with her hands in her lap—my Mother never sewed or knitted, but also she never fidgeted; she had a most tranquillising capacity for stillness—she would give me detailed instructions for roasting barley if coffee should run out, and just what proportion of roasted acorns to add "if Owen likes chicory in his coffee." Owen doesn't—but I listened almost awe-struck, for I realised that I was hearing the voice of one of the very few people in England at that moment who had first-hand experience of actual war from the civilians' point of view. Her experience was so near first-hand as to make no matter; what she was telling me she had heard from her aunts and sisters and cousins so soon after it had taken place—and when she spoke of picking old sheets for lint, or roasting barley to make coffee, somehow she always succeeded (probably without any deliberate intention, it was just the way her mind worked) in giving me a perfectly clear background to these activities, since she had her-self seen that background so very soon afterwards. There in London, in those long hot quiet days—punctuated by my hus-band's return at all hours from the Foreign Office, where the young men were working round the clock in eight-hour shifts—I was carried by my Mother's words straight back to the deep South and the atmosphere of those other long hot quiet days, fifty years before, when her last war had been going on.

There was, in particular, one plantation house out in the country where much of the lint-picking and barley-roasting took place. Like many other such houses it was square-built, with deep verandahs all round on each floor to keep the cruel sun from reaching the rooms; even so, in the great heat of full summer it was the practice of the ladies of the household to sit of an after-noon in the big central hall for coolness, and there do their sewing while they chatted, or someone read aloud. To this house—I wish I could remember to whom it belonged, but I cannot; it was one of the innumerable relations, of course—my Mother went for a long visit during her first summer in the South after the war; and as they had done throughout that war the ladies sat in the big hall, with doors opening off it all round, and young Marie Day sat with them. Now to this very house had been sent during the war a young Northern officer who had been taken prisoner; he had lost the use of both his legs, and being permanently disabled he was despatched there to be cared for, since the hospitals were overflowing with sick and wounded. He was a charming boy, always courteous and uncomplaining though in constant pain, and his enemy hostess went to the trouble of procuring for him one of those new wheeled chairs which could be self-propelled by an outer band along the wheels, so that he could move about by himself; he was also given a bedroom, converted from a sitting-room, on the ground floor. He stayed on the plantation until, after several months of devoted care, he died—but it was summer for part of his stay, and it had become his habit, during the long hot afternoons, to wheel himself to his bedroom door, open it, and propel his chair out into the hall, where he sat a little apart from the group of women at their war-time tasks of picking lint or rolling bandages, listening to the reading or the soft Southern chatter, silently securing companionship.

My Mother knew nothing of all this, and she was surprised when, as they sat there, one of the doors off the hall opened of itself, and remained open; this happened several times, and on one occasion she got up to shut it.

"Don't do that," said the mistress of the house; "it's Lieutenant So-and-so. And if he was happy enough here to want to come and sit with us when he was a prisoner, and dying, he shall come and sit with us now, if he cares to."

Chapter 5

I *SAID* earlier that the child sees its mother as a child, and the
girl sees her as a girl; but I find it much more difficult to envisage my Mother's later girlhood than I do her childhood. There
are I think two reasons for this. Women—at least women of my
Mother's generation and my own—are apt to be much more
expansive to their children about their childish exploits than to
their growing daughters about their own young men and flirtations; moreover children growing up in the country, about their
childish ploys, seem to vary as little from continent to continent
as from generation to generation—wherever it is, whenever it is,
it is a single territory, and the Golden Age.

But when I try to form a picture of young Marie Day growing
up and coming out in New Orleans, there is the widest difference
imaginable. She came out in a small, old, lively and elegant
society, of which her sister was one of the leaders; I emerged into
something very different, the almost Forsyte-ian stodginess of
rich upper-middle-class London—until I gradually broke away on
my own account into more entertaining circles of mountaineers.
Nevertheless, I got some sort of picture of that other world of
hers largely through the directions which, like a good mother,
she gave us in regard to behaviour. She had an admirable technique for this, praising us for what we did right rather than
blaming us for what we did wrong—though she would often
criticise sharply other young women whom she saw falling short

of her standards. And occasionally she would throw in an anecdote from her own younger days, by way of an illustration of behaviour; this delighted me whenever it happened, and I always tried to lead her on to tell me more, though she was apt to keep her own counsel. But she would always respond to a direct question about an actual problem, and I learned to use this lever unscrupulously to prise up the lid of the past.

There was for instance the matter of presents from admiring young men; this prised the lid up in a most satisfactory manner, for it induced a whole flood of reminiscences about the great Carnival balls culminating on Shrove Tuesday, "Mardi Gras," during which the young men were supposed to—and did—give to their "call partners," quite respectably, "favors" which might be anything from a simple brooch to a pearl or diamond necklace, and could with equal propriety be accepted by the girls—since their partners were masked and therefore anonymous.

This practice, in one of the most rigidly formal of societies, correct with a French sense of correctitude, perhaps deserves some explanation. The Carnival parades and balls were organised by three clubs bearing the names of the three "Kings" whom they presented annually in their pageants: Rex, Momus and Comus; Rex was a half business half municipal organisation, and stood for civic or political achievement; the other two were purely social; all were very exclusive and very expensive. Each club elected a fresh "King" every year—their identity was in the old days a closely guarded secret beforehand. We knew even as children that both our Grandfather and beloved Uncle Bob had been Rex, and Uncle Bob Momus and Comus too. Immense social prestige attached to being Kings, as also to being the "Queens" of their choice; these were usually débutantes from the inner ring of that exclusive society of the old Creole families and the "accepted" American ones. Revels of one sort or another were more or less non-stop from Twelfth Night to Shrove Tuesday, when they reached their culmination in superb parades through the streets, staged on great floats, all representing some episode or epoch;

67

the costumes were magnificent, and all was done regardless of expense; all the performers except the three Kings and Queens were masked. The whole performance terminated in a vast ball at the Opera House, of which the stalls—or *parquet*, as they say in New Orleans—had been floored over on a level with the stage, where the actual dancing took place.

This ball was the great occasion when the young men could pay off their social debts to the matrons who had entertained them during the past year, and the girls who had caused them to be entertained. Each member of each club was entitled to give fifteen invitations, four of which were for the first four dances, the "call" dances. The girls who had received, anonymously, invitations to call dances—a great honour—sat at the back of the parterre; the rest of the company in "the horseshoe," the amphitheatre stalls immediately above. In the presence of the three Kings and their Courts, complete from Queens down to tiny pages, these fortunate young ladies were called out to dance with their masked partners, and then received their "favors"; after the first four dances the rest of the company descended from "the horseshoe" and dancing became general, going on till four or five in the morning. Needless to say, this was the only occasion on which girls could accept jewels from men—and then only because the identity of the masked donor was supposed to be unknown.

All this mumming and miming was carried through with most elaborate ceremonial. The Kings wrote to the young ladies whom they invited to be their Queens in language which could not be too flowery or exaggerated, and the young ladies replied in kind. Here is what one of his Queens wrote the day after the Mardi Gras festivities to my Uncle Bob:

New Orleans. Wednesday, February 11th, 1891.

To His Majesty King Comus

Was it a dream, or is it reality that you, like King Cophetua of old, stepped from your royal throne to choose me, the Beggar Maid, as your Queen?

Ah no, 'tis no dream! These glittering jewels gleaming before me remind me too vividly of my one brilliant night of Royalty. Was ever Queen favoured with so gracious a King, so royal a reception, so cordial a welcome?

Like the Beggar Maid, words fail me with which to thank your Most Gracious Majesty for your exquisite homage, and for all the beautiful gifts you verily showered on me.

There is the letter before me, in the delicate, rather spiky hand on the stiff glossy paper; not at all a bad effort on the part of a girl of seventeen, or even less—for in New Orleans in the old days some girls made their début as early as sixteen. I have also a letter from Momus—then my Uncle Bob—dated "from Our Royal Flagship *Belisarius*, off the mouth of Pearl River" to "Our most noble and dearly beloved Cousin Comus" which after making "to our mighty and very dearly beloved Cousin" the usual assurances of "Our profound respect, high regard, and affectionate esteem" states that it is "with much felicity that We delay our homeward voyage to accept the gracious invitation to attend, with Our Queen and Court, the glorious festival of Comus on Mardi Gras night. By the King himself:

Momus."

How much seems to have arisen out of the matter of presents from young gentlemen to young ladies! It was rather remote from my own modest problems; I never went to masked balls, and the most valuable present I was ever given was an ice-axe, which completely flummoxed my Mother. (The giver was a rather fatherly member of the Alpine Club.) But I remember raising with her the question of books, which some of my more academic young men proffered. Looking a little amused, a little surprised, rather pleased, my Mother agreed to books; it was clear to me that books had no more been among her own problems than ice-axes. But whatever might be given and taken on Mardi Gras night, the question of presents evidently remained a formidable one in New Orleans, for Southern men were tremendous givers. Years later I heard a story about one of my Mother's great-nieces, a very handsome woman, who for years was greatly admired by a man much her senior. One evening at a party she happened to say to him casually what a pity it was that her parents had no white lilac in their garden; it was almost her favourite flower. She woke next morning to find half a dozen large bushes of it standing in tubs below her windows in full bloom.

All the romantic part of life in New Orleans—which has been so much publicised by writers with few Southern connections, or none, that a delightful reality has been turned into something slightly spurious—my relations took completely for granted, as people do who live a thing instead of merely writing about it. The reality was quite amusing enough, without being glamourised into a sort of verbal technicolor. Of course, as children we heard endless talk about Mardi Gras, and how Uncle Bob was Rex this year, and Momus or Comus that, and Cousin Cora had been Rex's Queen—which she was in 1880. We got concrete evidence of all these goings-on in the stars and orders, of glittering paste hung on brilliant ribbons, which the aunts and cousins brought over to us; they lived, with other properties, in the "dress-up trunk," a genuine Saratoga with a barrel top lined in flowered glazed calico, with a series of trays covered with the same material, fitting in one above the other the whole way down; we took them out and wore them for charades. Altogether we derived a delightful picture of a whole city at play: the little children, in masks and fancy dress, running about the streets in the morning, fooling and playing practical jokes—followed later in the day by the great processions of splendid floats, carrying the Kings and Queens and the "spectacles," belonging to whatever incident or period was chosen for that year.

After Mardi Gras came Lent, when everyone relaxed from the labours connected with rehearsals and the preparation of those terribly expensive costumes, and took things easily for a few weeks —going out to stay on their plantations or at one of the resorts along the Gulf Coast, or to visit friends at Mandeville, where many of the Creole families had "summer cottages"—very comfortable cottages, too. At the mouth of Bayou St. John was the old Spanish Fort, round which nestled a fishing village; from this a paddle-steamer—known locally as a side-wheel steamer— took off across the Lake to the low ridge of higher land on the north shore known as Mandeville. Mandeville has been unfashion-able these many years, but as recently as thirty years ago going out of town to anywhere along the coast was still spoken of as "going cross the Lake for a few days."

I love to know the daily time-table of any society, so I eagerly learned that of New Orleans in my Mother's time. The average Creole—and by my Mother's day the American families in New Orleans tended to adopt the same régime—rose early and took a cup of coffee, as we in England take morning tea; about 9:00 A.M. there followed a substantial breakfast, after which the men went down to their offices, and the women pursued their more leisurely avocations. Somewhere between 4:00 and 5:00 P.M.—according to how fashionable one wished to be—there was dinner; then the theatre or the opera, or a dance in someone's house, if it was not Lent. In the summer after dinner people sat in the afore-mentioned kiosques over the running gutters, where the young men came and visited the girls, heavily chaperoned by their mammas or aunts; when the mosquitoes got too bad everyone went indoors for music, or to play cards—and if the dinner had been early, there followed a light supper before going to bed. But there was a good deal of variation about this, depending on the hour of dinner; unless there had been cards or dancing, supper became less and less usual as the Creoles came to adopt the later American hours.

It was a gentle quiet life, particularly suited to the women and the elderly. There was horse-racing, to which Uncle Cud was passionately addicted, and at certain seasons yacht-racing on the Lake. Over and above these amusements the young men let off steam by gambling and drinking—the last not only in their clubs but in the dives along the river-front (the New Orleans water-front was said to bear strong resemblances to that of

Marseilles), where sailors from the five seas foregathered with trappers from the remote West; here shooting and knife-fighting were freely indulged in, and the well-known Dr. Richardson (whom the Richardson Memorial Building at Tulane University long commemorated) had quite a collection of such knives; not as a result of his own contests, but given him by patients who had used them and subsequently come to him for repairs. He married Uncle Cud's sister Ida, so he was regarded as an uncle. He was a great botanist and entomologist and spent much of his time exploring in the Andes and along the Amazon, and introduced many new plants; among them unluckily the Water Hyacinth, now such a pest to navigation in the South—a less bracing monument to his memory than the Memorial Building. It was Dr. Richardson who first coined the crack that on Shrove Tuesday there was only one Rex, but by Ash Wednesday there were hundreds—hence the "going across the Lake" to recover.

The social structure in my Mother's time was complicated. It consisted of the rich American merchants and landowners and a few of the well-established doctors and lawyers who were accepted, with certain slight reservations, by the earlier inhabitants, the Creoles, or families of pure French or Spanish descent—many of these were still great landowners, albeit for the most part much impoverished; some, usually rather better off, were themselves merchants. But they were without exception very Parisian in outlook, very clannish, and very proud—except when it was too hot even to be proud, or when a too rigid exclusiveness became boring.

It was only after I was married, and had visited and travelled a good deal, that I realised what a wonderful table my Mother kept, for a child takes everything in its own home not only for granted, but as the norm. But in time I came to recognise that our food had been wonderful, and to understand the reason. In New Orleans food was a great preoccupation—food prepared by French-Negro cooks who possessed both the fine French culinary sense, and the quite extraordinary acuity of taste of the Negro.

No other land has ever produced cooks of this class—not even Peking, where the Chinese kitchen-boys learned eighteenth-century French cooking from the chefs brought out by the great diplomats, and handed it down from father to son; it was still in existence when I was in China, and most excellent it was, but it cannot compare with the New Orleans cuisine, especially in the old days. And what raw materials those Louisiana cooks had to work on!—vegetables grown on the most fertile soil, in the mildest climate in the world; game of every sort, and superb fish and shell-fish. The people of New Orleans had every excuse for taking the interest they did in their food; it would have been almost blasphemy to do otherwise. But those of us who enjoy and praise New Orleans cooking to-day are missing the supreme quality of that earlier time; the true perfection of the flavour of most fish and shell-fish cannot survive refrigeration, and even in New Orleans the ice-box has become the rule.

My Mother had the true Southern attitude to food. She laboured under certain drawbacks: my Father's extreme distaste for "made dishes" as opposed to the good solid roast, for instance, and the lack of her home materials. But she did what she could, getting sugar-corn seed sent over from the States, which she grew in trenches and had watered extravagantly with liquid manure, so that even in our brief chilly English summers we could usually enjoy corn on the cob, most delicious of foods; she imported Barataria prawns, put up in tins lined with muslin by two impoverished old French Creole ladies, to adorn her sauces and salads. She kept a huge manuscript recipe book of her favourite dishes; on almost every page are pinned letters from my aunts and cousins, giving directions for making some especially heavenly cake or sweet which they had encountered here or there. Of course she got over an ice-cream machine which, filled with coarse salt and crushed ice, and ground by hand like a coffee-mill, produced heavenly ices at a period when ices were a rarity in England even in restaurants. Water-ices were her great speciality—lemon, orange, black-currant, and raspberry—in summer we hardly ate anything else as "pudding." She had her waffle-iron too, so that in winter we could eat waffles, filling the little square holes with dabs of butter, and then sprinkling the whole with castor sugar and ground cinnamon—my mouth waters now at the thought. She was indeed a very good *maîtresse de maison*.

A New Orleans writer of the end of the nineteenth century quotes "the English traveller, Buckingham," who visited the city in 1839 as saying that contact with the Creoles in New Orleans had caused the Americans living there—among whom I must presumably reckon my relations—to lose "much of the stiffness which characterises the New England States"; he praised the "self-possession, ease and elegance" of the Creole women, whom he found "frank, warm-hearted and impassioned." All this rings quite true to me: anything more frank, warm-hearted and impassioned than for instance Aunt Sallie or my cousin Cora Slocomb I find it hard to imagine. And as a girl I was struck by my Mother's uninhibitedness about certain things; she was frankly disdainful of the more puritanical taboos obtaining in England in late Victorian and Edwardian times, for instance that concerning the use of powder by young women.

"If a girl is dancing, she *needs* to powder her face," she would say firmly. "In New Orleans a man who knew how to behave would take his partner, if she was shy and inexperienced, on his arm to the dressing room door, saying, 'I am sure you would like to put on a little powder.' It is absurd not to use powder at balls." However she was much too sensible to make us use it, since no one else in London did.

She had a very strong sense of elegance and *skill* in all social matters, and in conversation; any awkwardness or clumsiness was certain to bring out her famous disdain, and I still remember her scathing comments to me when an English girl once failed in this respect. This unfortunate young woman had been with us during a stay abroad when we had seen a good deal of a delightful middle-aged couple, the wife handsome and witty, who were travelling with what had once been the third point of the triangle, as one might call it, still attached, though now quite unobtrusively and correctly. On our return, at a dinner-party, this girl was prattling away innocently to the much older man beside her about how charming the X's were. "Oh—I thought there was a tragedy there," he said. The young lady faltered, blushed, and stammered out something about "not really knowing," which only made matters worse. My Mother heard it all.

"Unpardonable," she said to me afterwards. "Whatever she knew or didn't know, she should have said, 'If there was tragedy, it has left no scars.' "

Those were the standards with which her upbringing had left her; she minded much less about the past existence of a triangle than about present clumsiness in dealing with the subject.

Everything we used to hear about life in New Orleans sounded much more amusing than that which we ourselves led, and small wonder. My Father—for an immensely honourable reason, which shall be told in its place—had become a strict teetotaller, and had persuaded himself into regarding drink in all its forms as the direct creation of the Devil; cards also were the Devil's books, and we were never allowed them, even to play Racing Demon or Beggar-My-Neighbour; as for the theatre, it was forbidden absolutely; we were never even taken to pantomimes. How different was the world on which my aunts' lively chatter opened our eyes! That forbidding old lady my Great-Aunt Mary Baldwin had several sons, who were brought up in the atmosphere which according to "the English traveller" so diminished the New England stiffness —only in her case the stiffness was Quaker, and hailed from Baltimore. These young men led an extremely gay life, no doubt by way of reaction from her sternness. I have an old photograph of them, taken drinking with one of my uncles: a top-hat and two or three beavers are piled in a sort of Eiffel Tower on the floor, and a semi-recumbent man in an armchair is being dosed with Burgundy and champagne from two bottles by his friends. In spite of the obvious posing, the whiskers and the queer clothes, unmistakably they are having a tremendous time. One story in

75

particular about the Baldwin boys delighted us. They, with my Uncle Bob and some friends, were driving home from a carouse when they suddenly realised that one of their number was missing. With tipsy meticulousness they counted themselves and one another, over and over again, but still they were one short. Eventually they discovered that they had their feet on the missing man; he had passed out on the floor of the carriage.

Into this picture of post-Civil War New Orleans my Grandfather presently re-emerges, in a manner hardly less exhilarating than the proceedings of his Baldwin nephews. Not through anything my Mother told us; her filial piety would have forbidden any such repetition, even if she had ever heard these stories, which I don't believe she did; they reached me from other sources. James Ingersoll Day did not remain a poor man for very long; he presently became chairman of a big insurance company, and suitably wealthy—he really had the Midas touch. So the round of dinners and theatre-parties and the opera began again. Theatre and opera flourished tremendously in New Orleans; from early in the nineteenth century there was both a French and an American theatre, assiduously attended—and by no-one more ardently than by the old slaves, who were expert critics, especially of character parts. Actors and singers of world-wide reputation thought it worth while to appear there; among the latter was Jenny Lind, who came before the Civil War, in 1854; between her and my Grandfather there then arose a very agreeable flirtation. She gave him a daguerreotype of herself, in a heavy velvet and metal frame; she looks sweet. There is another of her peering through the open spokes of a giant fan at least six feet across—after nearly a century her glance is still gay and seductive to a degree. She must have been a charmer, and I can't help being glad that she and my Grandfather had such fun, a hundred years ago. (Jenny Lind was Don Gregory's grandmother, God rest his soul; no doubt it was from her that he got his taste for lively company, but it is queer and amusing that he should have become so much mixed up in our lives more than eighty years later.)

I have sometimes wondered whether that giant fan came from Aunt Abby Slocomb's fan-room, but I rather think not. Aunt Abby lost less of the New England stiffness than most of her sisters; she remained an acerb critic of other people's behaviour all her life, and she disapproved violently of her father's goings-on, possibly not altogether without reason. It wasn't only Jenny Lind —whom my Mother, now I come to think of it, always cited as an outstanding example of a singer who was of a completely moral and decorous life, so perhaps she *had* heard some of the stories, after all. After the Civil War, certainly, the middle-aged gentleman with the noble forehead and the splendid beard, who had been such a charmer all his life, had innumerable friends, respectable and less respectable; it was a commonplace in New Orleans that he would send home an affectionate note saying that he was detained at the office, and could, alas, not get back for dinner, and then give an exquisite little supper to some lady or ladies, often with a whole group of friends. His wife, Sarah Eliza, seems to have applied much the same technique to her husband as to her children; she never made a fuss—Quakers, so wisely, don't. My Aunt Abby, however, positively revelled in making a fuss. One night, when she was at the French Opera with a flock of young girls, Mr. Day appeared in a box across the house, escorting a beautiful creature who was all too well known in certain circles. The Opera was a great social occasion, the men in the entre'acte circulating about the "horse-shoe" or visiting the boxes, where the ladies firmly sat, waving their fans; on this evening every opera-glass in the house was promptly turned, first on my Grandfather and his companion, then on Mrs. Slocomb's box. My aunt, who was not Abigail Hinman's great-granddaughter for nothing, hastily scribbled a note and sent it round to her parent, saying that if he did not leave the Opera House at once, she and her party would. My poor Grandfather, presumably recognising that he really had gone too far this time, removed himself and his lady, and Aunt Abby sat the opera out in indignant triumph.

My aunts, including Aunt Abby, did not frequent the Opera

purely on social grounds; they were genuinely musical, played and sang themselves, could criticise performances with real knowledge and were always eager to entertain singers and musicians—my Grandfather was not alone in his hospitality to Jenny Lind. There were frequent musical parties in the big house on Esplanade Avenue, Aunt Abby and Aunt Sallie singing along with the visiting professionals, or just with their friends. Some of my Mother's happiest recollections were of such occasions, when on hot summer nights, with all the windows open, a quite considerable crowd would gather on the banquette in the street outside to listen; the young Marie Day, leaning out into the warm darkness, watched the listening figures, their faces illuminated by the soft light from the big chandeliers in the great drawing-room, and heard with happy pride the subdued and discreet applause that followed her sister Abby's rendering of some operatic air. To me this is a quite charming picture out of the almost forgotten days when people made their own music—the ladies singing for their pleasure, their opera-minded fellow-citizens standing in the dark to listen and applaud.

Many years later I got even more of a close-up of this Day attitude to singers from my cousin Louisa Townsend, Aunt Sallie T.'s daughter. She too attended every opera within reach, though she did not sing herself. I have a vivid recollection of her sitting at my side at the Wagner-Fest in Munich in 1910, a score on her knees, mouthing over every syllable, every note. And she would recount endless stories of Jean and Edouard de Reszke when they used to come and stay with her in her house next door to her mother's on Long Island, during their seasons at the Metropolitan Opera House in New York; Emma Eames (to whom my cousin accorded the same certificate of decorum as my Mother did to Jenny Lind) came too, and young Anton van Rooy—then at the beginning of the fame brought him by his instantaneous success as Wotan in 1897, and sustained subsequently by his glorious voice and his consummate artistry. Van Rooy used to be greatly amused by Jean de Reszke's nervous shyness. The older man felt the cold of the New York winters, and habitually wore a rather noticeable fur cap, with ear-flaps tied under the chin; as they drove about in my cousin's open carriage people saw the cap, recognised the famous singer, and cheered and waved—whereupon the wretched De Reszke would cower down in his seat, complaining bitterly that even in the country one had no privacy, no peace. The young Dutchman, in his heavy Teutonic French, rather brashly exhorted his senior: *"Jean, twaw tu es trop nerveux. Si les gens veulent me regarder, qu'ay-ce que çah me fait?"*

As quite a young girl, too, I got my own personal impression of the grace and courtliness of New Orleans manners when our relations came over to stay with us, which some of the huge tribe did every summer. If we were at home they came there, to the big, unbeautiful, but exceedingly comfortable Victorian house overlooking the Thames Valley; but if we were in Switzerland—which became our favourite summer haunt after everyone got tired of Dorset—they followed us, and stayed wherever we did. On the first of these migrations—to Brunnen, on the Lake of Lucerne, when I was thirteen—among the American troop that followed us was Cousin Walton Glenny (called for his grandfather, Colonel Walton of the Washington Artillery). Cousin Walton was tall, dark, handsome and dignified; he had the usual beautiful Southern voice, he smoked very fragrant cigars, and my sister Grace and I admired him beyond words. One afternoon—he was amazingly kind to us—he decided to take Grace and me for a row across the lake to visit the Rütli, the tiny open meadow set in the dark pinewoods where the Swiss made *their* Declaration of Independence six centuries ago. We had to wait a little while on the quay for the boat, and he lit one of those immensely expensive cigars. Almost immediately afterwards the boat drew up; Cousin Walton flung his newly lighted cigar into the lake, before removing his Panama to hand two schoolgirl cousins into the boat.

It was a number of episodes like this which enabled me to realise for myself, concretely, what Southern manners and

Southern life were like. I was accustomed to hearing stories about it from the aunts, told in their beautiful voices; but here was a real live man, young, handsome, and amusing, my Cousin Walton, demonstrating for us in his own person that social climate—and it was a delightful revelation. (When, rather later, my Cousin E. C. began to come to Europe the experience was repeated.) All this helped me to envisage later on, when I was grown up and coming out, the world in which my Mother had grown up and come out—and to understand her sometimes rather critical attitude towards my and my sisters' young men.

But when all is said, how is one to-day to recapture the essence of a life so magical and so remote? The dignity and elegance of the balls, masking the equally elegant flirtations; the gaiety and splendour of the Carnival; the Opera night after night, and the evenings of singing with the visiting stars; the perpetual visits to the theatre. It was indeed a very different world from that to which my Mother went when she married my Father.

And what was she like, then, herself? One or two rather modest little photographs survive; they show the young, sweet, rather serious face, and that immense wealth of hair, but little more. A lovely portrait in an evening dress with a bustle, and a "waterfall" of curls falling down onto the pretty neck and shoulders has alas disappeared—that gave much more of the high spirits, the beauty and charm of which my aunts so often spoke, and about which my slightly older contemporaries, her second cousins, write to me even to-day. Thirty years after her death the legend still persists. "She always had that sweet lovely way with her," my Cousin Louisa told me; and from her and Cora di Brazza I gathered a vivid impression of the lovely eager girl: a beautiful and tireless dancer, an intrepid rider, a companion before whom boredom fled. "If I was sitting next to a dull man at dinner, and *he* wouldn't talk, I just used to talk to amuse myself," she told me once, "and he generally ended by getting amused too." I don't doubt it! In all families there is usually one who is the flower of the flock, the *Wunderkind*, and in my Grandfather's rather large flock the flower was Marie. Her very name became an evocation. She was the first of the Day family to be christened Marie—no doubt because of the French influence in New Orleans, for there had been Mary Days in plenty, including her aunt Mrs. McEwen, who nourished the little Broûn children all through the Civil War. But in the next two generations not less than five other girls among her immediate relations were called after her: Marie Day this, Marie Day that—and all are proud of being one of "the six Marie Days."

And now, suddenly, into this remote scene of life in New Orleans there enters, with a tread that shakes the stage, even down the years, my Father.

Chapter 6

*T*HE visitor to Tavistock in Devon, which lies tucked in
so snugly under the great bulk of Dartmoor rising to
the east, will be very likely to eat his lunch at the town's principal
hostelry, the Bedford Hotel. This building has a curious history,
even more intimately connected with my father's family than with
that of His Grace of Bedford—though in no very admirable
fashion. In the year 1716 one Jacob Saunders, or Sanders—he
signed his name now one way, now the other, in the easy fashion
of his time—took from the Duke of Bedford a lease of a portion
of the site of the ancient Abbey of Tavistock. The Abbey ruins
then still stood, but Jacob promptly pulled down the Chapter-
House, the Cloisters, and the old Frater, or monks' eating-room
(called, delightfully, the Saxon School)—and on the foundations
of the last proceeded to build himself "a pompous dwelling-
house," at a cost of over three thousand pounds. This was a pre-
posterous sum to spend in those days (to-day it would represent
something like sixty thousand pounds) on a building erected on
leasehold, not freehold land; and down to this century it has been
known familiarly in the town as "Sanders' Folly." On the death
of his son John in 1766 the site, with all the buildings on it,
reverted to the Bedford Estate, and the pompous dwelling was
incorporated in what subsequently became the Bedford Hotel.

This iconoclastic Jacob Sanders—I prefer the spelling always
known to me from my Grandfather's days, and still familiar in

Tavistock—was a man of substance. He was a prosperous clothier, as the term was then understood: i.e., he manufactured woollen cloths and dealt in them wholesale. (From mediaeval times wool was one of the bases of Devon's prosperity.) He or his wife, Prothesia, also owned land in Plymouth which he left to his Uncle Isaac; his Tavistock property went to his son, and a "Survey" made in 1755 shows it to have been considerable. John Cunningham Sanders—styled "Esquire" in the survey, so the clothier's family was coming up in the world; "Esquire" had some meaning then—owned thirty-one "houses and enclosures" in the Borough of Tavistock, which gave him control of thirty-one freeholders' votes in Parliamentary elections; however, they too reverted to the all-powerful Duke in 1766.

Exactly what relation my great-great-grandfather, Richard Sanders, was to the wealthy and foolish Jacob I do not know —the family tradition has it that they were brothers or cousins. My great-great-grandfather is also mentioned in the Survey (though with no "Esquire") as owning a house in West Street for which he paid a Chief Rent of 8d. a year to the Duke of Bedford. It was a modest rather than a pompous dwelling; his son John lived in it after him, and there in 1810 my Grandfather, another Richard, was born—he and his forbears dwelt in it, first and last, for over two hundred years, generation after generation (including my Father) being born in the same room, in the same huge bed with the posts built into the ceiling. My Grandfather owned some other property in the town, but not much, and between generosity and muddling there was little enough left, by the time his second son, James, was approaching manhood, to launch his children in the world. His circumstances were still further reduced by the cranks of his wife, a staunch Plymouth Sister, who had forced him to dispose of some long-standing and quite profitable family holdings in tin-mines in Cornwall, because she held either tin or mining, I am not sure which, to be sinful.

This old Mrs. Sanders, my Grandmother, played a considerable rôle in my Mother's life when she came to England, and for that reason I must give some account of her. She was Mary Brooking of Yelverton, six miles out of Tavistock, a charming old house which I once saw as a girl, covered outside with overlapping slates, a more durable form of the American wood-shingled house. Behind it lay an enclosed herb-garden; on the lawn in front stood a sundial; the latter was regularly patrolled by white peacocks in Mary Brooking's childhood, and when I was taken to see the place they were still there, the spreading splendours of their tails so strangely chaste; but the house had long since passed into other hands by then. The Brookings really belonged at Newton Ferrers on the River Yealm, where they owned oyster-beds, a much more desirable possession than tin-mines, we thought when we ate the oysters on that spring pilgrimage to my Father's birthplace—they were smallish, but of a very delicate and yet intense flavour. James Foster Brooking, my great-grandfather and the Admiral's brother, was Lord of the Manor at Newton Ferrers, hence his rights over the oyster-beds; the family tombs are in the churchyard, and when I helped my Mother to pull the ivy off the crumbling iron railings and scrape the moss out of the lettering on the stones a great beech-tree overshadowed them.

There they all lie, those long-ago Brookings, right back to Caleb, my great-great-great grandfather, who was born in 1688, little more than half a century after Robert Day sailed from Ipswich for the New World; but while the Days across the Atlantic were living in Connecticut and spreading outwards to the South and West, making fortunes as they went, and the Sanderses were producing cloth in Tavistock, not many miles away, the Brookings were living the quiet lives of small country squires, except that they perpetually went to sea, in the Royal Navy. The Admiral was by no means the only one; his uncles and great-uncles and at least one brother were in it too, though in the more modest guise of pursers or sailing-masters. One of them, who died at sea, is buried in Sicily. They were a tremendous clan in the South-west, covering the face of the earth from Bristol to the Cornish border as far back as the fourteenth century; but my forbears were modest

Marie Louise Day,
aged 17

Aunt Sallie T., as a bride

Marie Louise Day, aged 15, with Cora Slocomb

Count Pierre di Brazza, *circa* 1896

folk, though armigers. I have several impressions of the big seal the Admiral always used, and his actual coat of arms embroidered in faded silks on a worn piece of satin mounted on a wooden oval: "six cross crosslets" on the shield, to denote a Crusader; the crest is the pilgrim's scallop-shell, and the motto is one I like very much —*Crux fidei calcar.*

I have no idea why my great-grandfather, James Brooking, moved to Yelverton from Newton Ferrers—where their house was called, delightfully, Brooking Close, a name perfectly suited to the deep quiet of their lives; perhaps it was too small for his thirteen children, the last twelve by one wife. (I have a rather dull little Livesey portrait of him, with Yelverton in the background.) My Grandmother, who was born there, loved the place, and gave my Mother a very vivid account of it as it was in her youth. As children their favourite walk with their governess was down the avenue to Roborough Down, where they used to play on a great boulderous outcrop called "The Rock," to them much enhanced by a stunted hawthorn-bush growing out of it—I saw that bush in 1905—and a "hidey-hole" in a crevice; the hidey-hole was later put to good use by the eldest sister as a post-box for her love-letters to the young man she ultimately married. Another most agreeable feature to the Brooking children in the eighteen-tens and eighteen-twenties was the Plymouth Leat, which carried water from somewhere up on Dartmoor, by Burrator I think, down to the city in a deep-cut narrow open channel which ran through the grounds; Mary Brooking, when quite a little girl, coaxed a maid-servant one summer's day to take a pail out and dash the running water over her small body as she stood stripped on the bank—a thing she never forgot; later on she used to go alone, secretly undress, slip in, and be carried down by the flowing current, and then race back and dress again.

She remembered, too, the tailor coming once a year and making a long stay to fabricate garments for the whole family, and the solemn peregrination once every two or three years in the great family coach to Buckland Monachorum, the parish church for

Yelverton, when two or even three children would be baptised at once; the Brookings were Church-people, not Presbyterians like Jacob Sanders, but Buckland Monachorum was many miles away, over extremely bad roads, so they economised on these baptismal trips—however they went to church fairly regularly at Meavy, which was much nearer. And family prayers were a daily affair, attended not only by all the indoor servants but all the outdoor men as well, including an individual whom my Grandmother referred to as "the Hind"; a "hind" in Devonshire parlance, then as now, meant a working bailiff or farm manager, who lived on the farm, but my Mother did not know this, and it was many years before I found it out for myself. James Brooking had a special prayer which he used on these occasions; it was written out in his own hand in the Family Bible.

One other detail has come down to me from my Grandmother's childhood, through my Mother. Mary Brooking was the Admiral's favourite niece, and she was often bidden to visit him; he never married, and his widowed sister, Mrs. Mary Dolling, kept house for him. I was called after her, because she was held to be a most saintly character; but I have always disliked both the name and this, the only thing I know of her. Small Mary was her godchild, and if she showed herself stubborn on these visits—as I am confident she often did—the pious Aunt Mary would stand her against the wall and stroke her down the front, saying, "Go down, proud stomach—go down." Horrible!

But these are not the sort of confidences that a mother-in-law would make to her daughter-in-law unless they were on very happy terms indeed, and I think it is a rather remarkable tribute to my Mother that old Mrs. Sanders should have come to feel so warmly towards someone who, when she first appeared, must have seemed to her puritanical eyes practically the Scarlet Woman in person. I cannot remember my English grandparents, any more than I can the American ones, but from my English aunts and my older cousins, her own family, I know that "Grannie Sanders" was regarded as a good deal of a holy terror, in every sense of the word. Tiny in person, savage in convictions, obstinate, prejudiced, overbearing, she had the solid qualities of immense physical strength and boundless energy and efficiency, coupled with a sort of naïve effrontery which amused and rather disarmed my Mother, accustomed as she was to the suppler courtesies of a milieu so different; she—and we as children—loved this story which her tough little mother-in-law cheerfully told against herself. Mrs. S. was a tremendous walker, and used to drag her children, even when quite small, on trudges of miles and miles. On one such occasion she had a whole gaggle of trots with her beside her own, twelve or fourteen all told; but to her dismay and impatience, when far from home they showed signs of breaking down. They were near a village, so she led her troop to the baker's shop, went in and commanded buns all round; when she came to search her pockets she found that she had no money with which to pay. She explained this to the baker's wife, told her name, and promised to send the money by the carrier's cart next market-day; the woman raised no objection, saying that her penniless customer had an honest face, and she would gladly trust her. Whereupon my Grandmother said that the children should have another bun each!

I never managed to get hold of the precise stage at which Mary Brooking forsook the Church of England to become a Plymouth Sister—I suppose that when I might still have learned it I was not sufficiently interested to find out. I do know that it was connected with a certain Mr. James L. Harris, who was prominent in the movement and a great friend of hers; James was a regular Brooking name, but it was principally in honour of this worthy that my Father was called James Harris Sanders. But nonconformity was entirely in the Devon, and particularly in the Tavistock, tradition. It is one of the curiosities of religious history in England that Devonshire, which in 1549 had risen in revolt against the Protestant dispensation, angrily demanding the re-establishment of the monasteries and contemptuously likening the new prayer-book to a "Christmas game," should a century later have become a hotbed of puritanism, and within the next hundred years the scene of bitter opposition even to the Anglican Church. Francis, Earl of Bedford, an unpleasing character, took a notable hand in this; he was a friend of Peter Martyr, whom he had met in Geneva, and when he was appointed Lord Lieutenant of Devonshire, in 1558, he threw all his weight into the Protestant scale: purging the Cathedral Chapter of Exeter, and either directly or through his religious nominees pressing for the abolition of Saints' days, and of "all curious singing, and playing of the organ," as well as of the use of the cross in baptisms. Others carried on the good work; one Ignatius Jourdain, when M.P. for Exeter in the seventeenth century, promoted a bill to punish the sin of adultery with death.

These dissenters—during the seventeenth century they began to be called "presbyterians"—having gradually broken down even the Anglican Church, proceeded to create as an alternative to episcopal discipline a scheme of provincial assemblies meeting every six months. However, this did not last very long—when the Commonwealth fell the presbyterian dominance fell with it; at the Restoration there was a strong Anglican reaction, and the dissenters, and particularly their ministers, were driven underground.

But with the departure of James II and the arrival of Dutch William they poked up their heads again. The Toleration Act of 1689 allowed them to have their own places of worship and preachers, and they availed themselves of this privilege to the full —Protestant nonconformity henceforth enjoyed, in the widest sense of the word, legal recognition, and it has enjoyed it ever since. In Tavistock, always under the aegis of the puritanical Bedfords, it throve exceedingly; and in 1701 the second Duke gave a lease of the misericord, or dining-hall of the infirmary of the ancient Abbey, to the presbyterians as a meeting-place. Godliness was enforced, "worldliness" proscribed—and worldliness included not only dancing (as we knew to our cost two hundred years later) but even playing bowls. But all this dreary strictness seems to have done little for morality, as indeed was only to be expected—if people may not dance or play bowls openly, they will do other things in secret. "Vice bears such an head here, I imagine no place more corrupt," wrote Mr. Jillard, one of the presbyterian ministers at Tavistock, dolefully in the early eighteenth century—"The poor very numerous and wicked, and the rich far from being exemplary Christians." The parish registers corroborate him. The proportion of bastard to legitimate births, which had been one to sixty-eight in the seventeenth century—high enough, in all conscience—was one to eighteen in the fifty years between 1736 and 1786.

But to return to my poor, gentle Grandfather, so trampled on by his fierce little Brooking wife. His easy-going generosity was rewarded, all of a sudden, in a way very unusual in this world. He had allowed two old ladies to live on very easy terms, indeed finally rent free, in one of the small houses which he still possessed. In due time they died; whereupon there suddenly swept down from the north a certain Mr. Tennant, their nephew, to clear up their affairs. Learning how matters had stood, this gentleman called on my Grandfather to thank him for his kindness to the old ladies, and asked if he could be of service to him in any way? He was in business; there might be openings; any boys to be placed, for instance?

Yes indeed—there were three; and placed my Uncle John, the eldest son, at once was, most advantageously—for this individual was no less a person than Mr. Charles Tennant, of C. Tennant, Sons & Co., with an office in Manchester—then the centre of the metal trade in Britain, as Liverpool was the centre for cotton; he had also an office in Glasgow for the iron side of the business, and the Tarshish mines had just been opened in Spain. (If people had spoken of industrialists as "Kings" in those days, which in England we didn't, I suppose Sir Charles Tennant, Bart., as he became twenty years later, would certainly have been called The Copper King.) My Uncle John was accordingly planted down in Birmingham, to sell the good Tennant copper to the manufacturers of brass bedsteads and brass trays there, and a very nice living he made of it, later taking his youngest brother, Sam, into partnership.

All this delighted my poor Grandfather, as far as his wife allowed him to take any pleasure in "worldly" things; he always retained a lurking fondness for metals of any sort, after that frustrating business of the sale of the tin-mines. But my Father was not the eldest son, and no ready-made place was found for him; his individual success-story was much more lively. Fired by what he had heard of the metal trade, he somehow, when not yet more than twenty, managed to borrow a hundred pounds; he went up to Manchester, where he bought a ton of copper—not on paper, but in the solid lump; this he proceeded to sell, making a handsome profit; and thereafter, without ever looking back, he went on to make his fortune. I rather think, from something he once said, that it was from Charles Tennant himself that he borrowed the hundred pounds; anyhow, presently he became closely linked with Tennants, making frequent trips to their mines in Spain. By the time that he went to New Orleans in 1873, only eight or nine years later, and was invited to my Uncle Cud's house on Esplanade Avenue, he was very well off indeed, with his own office in Birmingham. Though not quite thirty he was already a member of that small group of merchants who carried on the business of shipping, financing, and distributing metals; four years later they established themselves in London as The London Metal Exchange Company—the parent body of the present Metal Exchange. Indeed I have heard that along with Charles Tennant and others he had a good deal to do with the switch-over from Manchester to London as the centre for dealings in metals.

I am tempted to branch off here into a fuller account of the Metal Exchange and its origins: of the early meetings of these still unorganised but enterprising men who foregathered informally in the Royal Exchange or—later—at the Jerusalem Coffee House in Cowper Court or the News Room in Lombard Street to discuss their affairs, and of some of the people concerned—in particular Charles Edward Mathews, a close friend of my Father's and one of the founders of the Alpine Club. Mathews tried in vain to persuade my Father to take up mountaineering and join it: how I wish he had succeeded!—my own beginnings as a mountaineer would have been much easier than they were if climbing had been a thing my Father cared about. Among his intimates Mr. Mathews was always known as "The Young Pretender," because of his Christian names. But I must resist this temptation and return to New Orleans, and my Mother's surprising marriage.

Metal undoubtedly furnished the link between my Father and the Slocombs, though from Birmingham to New Orleans may seem a far cry. Their family fortune, which old Mrs. Cora had so stoutly bolstered up during the Civil War, was based on iron, and iron was still the concern in which Uncle Cud had given his father-in-law a temporary job when the war was over, while young James Sanders was already interested in iron and steel as well as in copper. So it came about that the son of Admiral Brooking's favourite niece met Elisha Hinman's great-granddaughter.

Photographs apart, it is to one of his English sisters-in-law that I owe the picture I gathered of my Father at this period of his life, rather than to the American aunts—who I think always remained, secretly, a little hostile to the young Englishman who swept the lovely and beloved little sister off her feet, and carried her away to Europe from under the noses of her troops of local adorers. Very tall, very fair, blue-eyed; strangely graceful both in posture and movement, with the pink-and-white complexion which he kept all his life, he had also a sort of innocent beguiling zest for the joys of living that triumphed perpetually over his rigidly narrow religious views—and he had a most glorious baritone voice. I have always suspected that it was his singing which got him the entrée—or kept it once he had got it—to my Aunt Abby's drawing-room; she would do anything for a fine singer, and my Father's voice was superb. Moreover he had considerable practical knowledge; he and his brothers, my Uncle John and my Uncle Sam, always practised with the local glee-clubs, especially in Birmingham, and as bachelors they used to go round in masks before Christmas, singing carols in parts outside people's houses, that lovely English custom of "the waits"; in theory they did this for the benefit of some local Cottage Hospital, for which they raised fantastic sums, but in reality I am sure they did it just for the unique and exquisite pleasure of singing in harmony, and being heard. These performances of theirs were in fact Mrs. Slocomb's musical evenings in reverse: the singers in the dark outside, the listeners in the light within.

Here then was this big, Nordic, impetuous young man, his wealth and his success all of his own making, with his home background of provincial puritanism, launched into my Mother's tranquil and established circle of related families, tied together in their close and intimate friendships—for New Orleans society then was one of the most tightly-knit in the world. Nor was it in the least provincial; on a small scale it was a capital city. What did she make of him, so tall and blond, so impatient, so eager, so efficient? Alas, one of the things a child can seldom come at with any closeness is its parents' emotional life. A letter of my Grandmother's written to her niece Annie Broûn on her engagement in 1868 shows not only that marriages, which almost came to a standstill in New Orleans in the first years of ruin after the Civil War, had begun again by then, but that my Mother took a rather tepid view of them. "Marie says it will seem strange to her to meet Annie as Mrs. Singleton at first, but she supposes that she will get used to it in time," Mrs. Day writes, adding that Marie is in bed with "a dreadful cold," but will write later—meanwhile "she sends her very best love and congratulations." And a day or so later Marie did write herself, wishing her "dear Annie" and her husband "all the world's blessings and greater, and that you may be as happy as this world permits." Tepid indeed! She goes on more naturally:

"It seems so strange Annie to think that you are to be married *tomorrow*. . . . Give Mr. Singleton my hearty congratulations. I know Annie how *his* house will be kept, and oh! *won't* there be lots of good things! May God bless you and your husband, Annie, and keep you both with His might."

But that was more than four years earlier. By now Marie Day

had been out for some time, and had her ample share of admirers —she never made any bones about having had troops of young men—and must inevitably have come to look on marriage less tepidly. One very revealing thing she did let fall about my Father when she was getting to know him. He asked her to go riding, and she agreed. Riding in New Orleans then was for women not such a usual pastime as it was in the North; partly because the Creole girls were too lazy, partly because on that swampy low-lying terrain there were only two places to ride: "the Bayou Road," out along Bayou St. John to Spanish Fort, which followed the line of old tow-path and finally crossed the marsh to the Fort, and the Gentilly Road which ran from the far end of Esplanade Avenue out along the stretch of firm ground known as the Metairie Ridge (it was only about six feet above flood-level), between the river and Lake Ponchartrain—in those days a wild and lovely place, with huge virgin cypresses and live-oaks growing in the swamps on either hand, and fields of wild irises in the clearings, where on hot days it was not unusual to meet alligators or water-moccasins sunning themselves, frightening the horses badly. However, my Mother was a first-generation American, not yet infected with the Creole languor, and she always loved riding; but in the easy casual local fashion she took her time about dressing and coming down on that particular day, and kept her escort waiting for at least a quarter of an hour. To her amazement, when they had mounted and ridden off he scolded her sharply for this—it was very wrong to be unpunctual and waste other people's time, it was discourteous, and generally there was no excuse for it. My Mother had never heard such ideas in her life—though she was to hear plenty about punctuality for the rest of it—young ladies always kept young gentlemen waiting; and she admitted rather quaintly that this attitude on the part of a man who made no secret of his admiration for her created a deep impression.

Which of the two rides they took on that occasion I don't know. But he fell head over ears in love with her, punctual or unpunctual, and she, at nineteen, preferred him to anyone she had met; presently they returned from another ride together, engaged. (It was typical of her, I always feel, to have got engaged on horseback.) And then nothing would do for that masterful creature Mr. James Sanders but that they should get married forthwith, so that he might take her back to England with him when he went. This was a thunderbolt to her family—but I gather that Marie Day, in her quiet fashion, was as insistent as her fiancé that so it should be. Presumably my Father was able to satisfy old James Ingersoll, who had married three daughters already, that he could maintain a wife "in the circumstances to which she was accustomed"—he could adduce a house on the outskirts of Leamington, with a pleasant garden and saddle-horses in the stables; she would have her own carriage. I cannot see Uncle Cud himself showing much interest in the financial details, but his firm must have been fairly well acquainted with my Father's status in the business world, and presumably they satisfied old Mr. Day, who would most certainly have looked into such things with some care. In the letter of my Grandmother written to her niece Annie in 1868, already referred to, she quotes her Marie as saying that twenty-one young couples were to be married in Trinity Church before Lent—"all very young. It seems they despair of better times, and so do not wait for them." But even five years later there were still not so many solid *partis* in the South—it was all a good deal better than poor Helen, whose Mr. Starkey was already letting her feed the pigs.

Aunt Abby, however, was horrified at such haste—and also genuinely distressed, I think, at letting her little sister go so far away, for good, with a man whom they had known for so short a time. And what was to be done about the trousseau?—a bride's outfit *could* only be got in Paris. Fortunately Marie had been in Europe on a tour only a year before—seeing the Grindelwald Glacier and other mountain wonders, which pleased her much more than any capitals; she had had some dresses made at Worth's, and they had kept her *toile,* the pattern of a client's figure cut out in calico or thick muslin, which Paris dressmakers preserved from year to year to enable them to fulfill long-range orders. So it was fairly simple for Mrs. Slocomb to write to Paris for a sumptuous outfit to be got ready with all speed; and young James Sanders agreed to pass the last few days of the honeymoon there, to collect the frocks and "buy bonnets." (What effect all these confections produced in Leamington shall be told in due course.) I have a couple of those long-ago trousseau dresses still; one of the deepest red Lyons silk with a huge pattern of blazing parrot-tulips—I contrived to annex this when I got married myself, and had it arranged to fit me; as a *robe de style* it was immensely decorative, and went on for ever. Many years later, when *Peking Picnic* and its successors had made it possible for me to get clothes from Worth's myself, I took it to Grosvenor Street to show to M. Jacques Worth; he was greatly entertained to find one of the firm's productions still being worn, after nearly seventy years.

I realise that such things as old dresses are trivialities, but in a way they bring me strangely close to my Mother's marriage —these, and a photograph of Aunt Abby's house, a large **L**-shaped building, very flat on top, with steps leading down to the street from a narrow portico. (It is now in ecclesiastical hands.) Down those steps she went to her wedding, in the dress of white *poult-de-soie* trimmed with scores of tiny bows and enriched with some most lovely Duchesse lace which one of my sisters still has. And then she sailed away to England, only to return once, in all her life, to New Orleans and to the home in New England which she loved so well.

> *Oh, Shenandoah, I love your daughter,*
> *Away you rolling river,*
> *I'll take her 'cross yon stormy water*
> *Away I'm bound to go. . . .*

That old sea-chanty has always, perhaps absurdly, recalled my Mother's wedding to me.

Chapter 7

I SHOULD never have learned anything from my Mother herself about her arrival in England, her impact on her new relations, and those early days of her married life— never should, and never did. But fortunately there was a very observant witness to it all, who was more than ready in later years to talk to me with the utmost freedom about my Mother, whom she loved dearly. This was my Aunt Isabel, my Uncle Sam's wife, who had married the youngest of the three Sanders sons some years before, and already had a growing family of beautiful blond children. She was born Isabel Brodie, of a Scottish family settled in Warwickshire, and to her dying day retained the agreeable, uninhibited, racy speech of English county folk; she really did say ridin' and huntin' and shootin' and fishin', and much more in the same style. She was a statuesque figure—very tall, with a marble-pale skin, a haughty subaquiline nose, and most exquisite ash-blonde hair; and she somehow managed to combine a quite genuine piety with the most cheerfully realistic, not to say hard-headed, outlook on life. Under her influence Uncle Sam, who was anyhow born with a gay spirit, had broken free already from the puritanical trammels which shackled my Father all his life, and when she went from her home at Snitterfield to visit the new American sister-in-law at Leamington she went with her usual tranquil sensible curiosity, and an open mind.

She liked what she found. The Worth dresses were of course

something quite astounding in the residential purlieus of Birmingham, as were the gay Paris bonnets; but they were beautiful, and Marie looked absolutely charming in them, my aunt said. All the same, that vivid creature with her soft warm voice, her impulsive affectionate manners and those clothes, came as a shock; and the "business associates" and their wives were by no means all as readily admiring as the former Miss Brodie, with her fearless background. Also my Father was nervous about his new acquisition, and his nervousness made him harsh—at lunch one day in summer, with all the windows open onto the sunny garden, a hornet flew in and zoomed round the table. "Oh, what is that big bug?" my Mother cried, using her native idiom for an insect. Her husband rebuked her sharply for using an improper word. Aunt Isabel never quite forgave "Jim" for that.

The first two or three years of married life are never easy; for my Mother I think they must have been exceptionally hard. She had wealth and every material comfort, and an adoring husband, in spite of his hasty nervous impatience; but she had lost so much to which she was used—there was no theatre, no opera, no cards, no nearest and dearest running in at all hours to chat to her and love her, nearest and dearest whom she had known always; and anyhow to exchange New Orleans—climate, flowers, food and all—for the English Midlands in the Victorian era would constitute a very odd experience. She had her riding, and sometimes there were rowing-parties on the Avon, when to everyone's amazement she pulled away in the double-skull or the randan along with the men. "You will blister your hands," they said—but she wore soft leather gloves with *Pomade Divine* inside, and got no blisters. Those expeditions could of course only take place when my Father was free on a Saturday, for to go boating on a Sunday was unthinkable. But all in all her life in England undoubtedly seemed both strange and lonely to her at first. One of her minor difficulties was such a simple thing as to get water to drink when she was entertained at dinners as a bride; she was not accustomed to wine, and never liked it. But drinking-water was practically unknown as a beverage in my Father's circles; there were not even tumblers to drink it from!—she had to drink it from a wineglass, and see her husband frown at her fussiness.

However, she had known difficulties and loneliness before, when she was a little girl at school in New England; and the child who had learned by the time she was twelve to console herself for her private unhappiness by showing help and kindness to others knew well enough, at nineteen, where her remedy lay. Diligently, dutifully, she set about cultivating her husband's sphere of acquaintance, and in particular his immediate relations, immensely odd as most of them must have seemed to her. Isabel Sanders was from the outset her great support, but she soon had her reward, for they all came to adore her, and to be on her side—I know this from the older cousins, as well as from Aunt Isabel. Her spirit of course bubbled up unquenchably in response to her brother-in-law Sam's jokes and nonsense—which made my Father jealous and reproving; but her dignity, patience, and sweetness commanded their admiration, while she herself won their hearts.

Even that of her tough little mother-in-law. I don't know when they first met, I presume during the Leamington period; the old people must obviously have come up from Tavistock on a visit to greet the new daughter-in-law. But after a couple of years in Leamington my Father found that he needed to be nearer London, as the epicentre for dealings in metals began to shift there, so he took an old house in Twickenham on the river, quite near the Bridge—and there my two eldest sisters, Cora and Therese, were born in 1875 and 1876 respectively. This move was an immense improvement from my Mother's point of view, quite apart from having two charming babies to occupy her. Below her windows was always the companionable river, moving gently through pleasant gardens; a short walk up the hill brought her to the open space outside the Star and Garter, and that marvellous view away towards London; London itself was within reach for shopping, with shops much more like those she was accustomed to, at home or in Paris, than the Birmingham ones. London was reached by train to Waterloo, the shops by a four-wheeled cab—a hansom cab was then highly improper for a woman alone; but unless my Father could come down to the West End to give her lunch a day's shopping was a starvation affair, for my Mother had as yet no circle of acquaintances in London—and how strange *that* must have seemed, a city where she knew no one—and there was no hotel, Café, or restaurant to which a respectable woman could go unescorted for a meal. The big shops none of them had dining-rooms as yet; Fuller's was of course not thought of in the eighteen-seventies, let alone Lyons or the A.B.C.; nor did Gunter's or Searcy's at that stage cater for hungry solitary women. She often told me of those exhausting days, when she was reduced to buying buns in a pastry-cook's and eating them in a cab! How thankful she and many others like her were when a respectable luncheon-place was opened on one of the streets leading from Nash's Regent Street to Hanover Square—Elphinstone's, it was called.

Best of all at Twickenham was the close proximity of Richmond Park. There my Mother could get her riding in lovely surround-ings—on Saturdays with my Father, otherwise with a groom; and there presently she began to take her two little girls for them to play in warm weather; she showed them the deer and the wild-flowers, she made them listen to the songs of birds. My sister Cora was always a sweet biddable child, but Therese had a full share of the Brooking stubbornness and temper, even as a dot of a thing. On one occasion, there in the Park, my Mother forbade her to touch the picnic-things, because she had already upset the milk—"If you touch them, I shall have to whip you," she said. Time and again the naughty little thing approached with out-stretched hand, keeping a wary eye on her Mamma; at last she did touch them, and my Mother took the little fat hand and slapped it. She always kept her word.

"I hate you! I'd like to whip *you*!" the furious little creature sobbed. Sarah Eliza's daughter held out her hand.

"Very well; there you are; whip me," she said. The child hesi-tated, then took the outstretched hand in both of hers, held it to her cheek, and kissed it.

Which seems a much more satisfactory way of dealing with a

cross child than Great-Aunt Mary Dolling's "Go down, proud stomach."

That sojourn in Twickenham furnished the first really prolonged contact between my Mother and her mother-in-law. My English grandfather died in the summer of 1878, and his widow and her unmarried daughter, a difficult character, sold the house in which Sanderses had been born and lived for more than two centuries, and moved up to lodgings in Richmond, to be near the adored Jim, who doted on his mother to the extent of writing to her every day—if he had no time to write a letter, he simply sent her the envelope, to show that he was alive, and loved her. (Very nice in its way, but a formidable complex.) As old Mrs. Sanders was by now getting on for seventy, though still a stout walker, my Mother took upon herself the duty of escorting her every Sunday to "Meeting," fitting in her own religious observances as best she might. (Why my maiden aunt did not shoulder this task I don't know—as I say, she was difficult.) To the Brethren's conventicle in Richmond "unbelievers" were not admitted, so rain or shine my Mother had to stand in the exiguous porch, or walk up and down outside, till the prayers and manifestations were over, when she led the little old lady home to a delicious Sunday lunch; all cold, of course—hot food on Sundays was another sin. But these faithful attentions ended by causing a strong affection to spring up in the fierce old lady's breast for the erstwhile "Scarlet Woman" from across the Atlantic, and it is to that affection that we owe those details about a very early nineteenth-century childhood in Devonshire.

One of my oldest cousins, a son of Uncle Sam's and quite a shrewd lawyer, as a middle-aged man once said to my sister Jenny: "My Father could *keep* money, but he could never make it; Uncle John could neither make it nor keep it; it was only Uncle Jim who could *make* money." I think that was true. My Father maintained fairly close links with his brothers in Birmingham even after he had his own office in London, and put them in the way of a lot of business as his own prosperity increased; but he exacted from them—and especially from his brother John—some form of promise that there should be no speculation or investment without his concurrence. However, while he was away on one of his trips to Spain poor Uncle John forgot his undertaking, did some deals on his own account, and crashed completely: to save him from bankruptcy my Father had to raise, and pay out, very large sums—sums so large that his personal position was crippled. The carriage, the horses, the pleasant house at Twickenham all had to go—what is more, Marie Day's rather meagre marriage-portion was taken too, to meet this emergency; and as she had been married before the Married Women's Property Act was passed in 1875 it never occurred to my Father to replace it when he was in funds again, so that to the day of her death my Mother never had a penny to call her own. In fact she faced much the same situation as her mother had faced when old James Ingersoll Day so ill-advisedly went on that note bond for his friend, some ten years before. It was decided to move to Tunbridge Wells, and a house was leased there in Neville Park; all those Victorian houses still stand in pretty gardens with wide views. Unluckily my Mother was pregnant when this disaster overtook them, though she was still riding regularly on a quiet horse; now she had to cope with the labours of a move, with retrenchment (never an easy thing to her, any more than it is to me), with a new district and new tradespeople. As a result she had a miscarriage. The doctor who attended her was a percipient person; at one point he said—"If you had still been riding, Mrs. Sanders, everyone would have said that that brought on your miscarriage; but *I* say that if you had still been riding you would not have had it."

As far as I can place it, Uncle John's crash occurred about 1879; a third child—again a girl, to my Father's dismay—was born in the spring of 1881 at Tunbridge Wells. But he, like James Ingersoll, was not a man to stay down for long. Working ceaselessly, with almost savage energy, within two or three years he succeeded not only in setting his ruined brother on his feet again, but in completely retrieving his own fortunes. He was of course lucky in that he was already firmly established in the metal trade, which in the eighteen-seventies and eighteen-eighties saw an unprecedented boom. Railways, shipping lines, metal consumers of every sort were expanding in all directions; and late in 1881 or early in the following year he was in a position to buy a large and beautiful country place in Hertfordshire—Porters, near Shenley —where at last a son was born to him in the autumn of 1882.

For my elder sisters and my brother Harry, Porters remained throughout their lives the same sort of enchanted land that Stonington had been to my Mother and her cousins—the golden scene of a happy childhood, where everything was more perfect, held more delight than anywhere else. Even to me an aura of magic hung about the very name from the way they spoke of it, though as we left it six weeks before I was two I can naturally remember very little of it myself.

Even from the most objective point of view it was a beautiful house, in parts very old; it owed its curious name to the fact that in John of Gaunt's day it had been the porter's lodge to "Good Duke Humphrey" of Gloucester's castle in the valley below—the castle had vanished except for its moat, which still surrounded "Belgrove's Farm," nearly a mile away across the park. A real subterranean passage had once run between the two houses; it was no longer in use, but it had a way of caving in from time to time under the weight of grazing horses or cows, to my Father's vexation and the children's delight. Externally the house was late Georgian, with a pillared portico and a pretty pediment on the garden front; inside it had amusing features. The flue of the drawing-room chimney had been made to run sideways to enable a window to be set over the fireplace, a feature occasionally found in houses built or altered around the year 1800; the dining-room, nearly fifty feet long and part of the original structure, was separated from the rest of the house by walls ten feet thick, pierced in three places by entrances with doors at each end—these, my sisters told me, were perfect for playing "robbers" or hide-

and-seek, but dreadfully frightening to a small child who had been naughty at meal-times and was shut up there by my Father to repent in the dark.

At Porters my Mother had her first real opportunity of enjoying that peculiarly English pursuit—gardening. There were four acres of walled kitchen-gardens, ranges of hot-houses full of peaches and nectarines, and vineries producing superb grapes; behind the house two big cedars overshadowed a shaven lawn, and all about were borders—beds with roses, with lilies, with pinks and carnations and delphiniums and Canterbury bells, all the mixed Tennysonian loveliness of an old-fashioned English garden. This was nectar and ambrosia to my Mother; she flung herself with enthusiasm into the delightful business of adding to its beauties and experimenting with new ones, and presently she became an exceedingly learned and skilful gardener. Altogether all her special gifts—for entertaining, for housekeeping, for gardening—had full scope at Porters, and fully flowered; after Stonington it was the place she loved best on earth, and during the years she spent there her life in England reached its apogee of activity and happiness.

There was plenty of activity. She arrived in Hertfordshire with three children, and five more were born there; soon there had to be a schoolroom as well as the nurseries. The place was self-supporting to an extent incredible to-day, and all its manifold activities had to be supervised and kept running smoothly. The water-supply for the house derived from an old well in the yard, and was pumped up by an aged donkey called Nellie, who walked round and round for hours every day performing this duty—in summer, when she was not pumping, she drew the mowing-machine about the lawns, shod in four neat leather boots so that her small feet should not leave prints on the turf. (I can remember Nellie and her boots myself, for she came on with us to Surrey; pensioned off at last in a paddock, she was finally "put to sleep" at the fantastic age of nearly forty.) Gas for lighting was made on the estate, in a corner of the park; the machine was worked by "Old Palmer," a white-haired man who couldn't read; however he could make gas all right, and he also presided over the ice-house, brick-lined vaults hollowed out under a mound—when the ponds froze, as soon as the skating was over the ice was broken up and carted into the ice-house, where by some primitive methods of insulation it was preserved all through the summer.

Then besides the kitchen, the dairy, and the laundry, each with its appropriate staff, there was the bakehouse, the game-larder, and the ham-and-bacon room (where everything for the use of the entire household was cured and stored); the brewery, where beer was made for consumption in the servants' hall—servants then expected beer with their meals. My Father saw to the stables and the horses, but my Mother kept an eye on the cow-houses, to ensure cleanliness at milking-time, and she took a passionate interest in her poultry, especially the turkeys and ducks. When I came to keep poultry semi-commercially myself I found that there was nothing she couldn't tell me about dipping boluses of meal in olive-oil to make them slip more easily down the gullets of fattening birds, or opening the crop of a crop-bound hen with a razor, removing the obstruction inside—again with olive oil—and sewing both skins up with a curved needle and dental floss silk.

Such a self-contained unit was of course in constant need of running repairs and carpentry jobs of every sort. These were carried out by Thresher, the estate joiner, another old man who, like Palmer, could neither read nor write; but he did beautiful carpentering, taking his measurements by putting knots in bits of string, and he alone understood all the ramifications of the chimneys in the old house, which had been altered and added to so many times—when they were swept he always had to preside over operations. Both Thresher and Palmer remained about the place, "man and boy," for sixty years, and had something of the proprietary freedom towards their employers of Old Ben and Old Joe; my Mother got on with them famously.

In some ways this life, with its manifold practical activities, reminds one of great-great-uncle John Day and his wife Lydia in Ohio, sixty-odd years before—but there were vast differences, of which not the least was the presence of English servants in large numbers. The English servant in the Victorian era was a species all to itself—and one of the most spoilt and extravagant species *humani generis* that ever existed. There was a positive hierarchy of grades, of uppers and middles and unders; my Mother, accustomed to the enthusiastic willingness of Negroes, was filled with disdain for the detestable phrase—"That is not my work, Madam." However, by the time she went to Porters she had been in England for eight or nine years, had learned her way round, and had come to terms with the species; as I said earlier she spoiled them in some ways, but she already commanded their respect. Their extravagance she would not stand for. The French-crossed darkies of New Orleans had inherited French habits of frugality, and such practices as the cook exacting a commission on all orders from the grocer and butcher, and selling the dripping from the joints she promptly put an end to. She got her groceries in bulk, straight from the old Haymarket Stores in London, always ordering and often choosing them herself; I went there with her many times as a girl, and I well remember the obvious deference of the elderly men at the linen or grocery counters for her care and knowledgeable thoroughness about her purchases. One episode delighted her; any of the more ludicrous manifestations of English pomposity always amused her New England mind. She had gone to complain about the flavour of the last lot of coffee; the grey-haired Mr. So-and-So who always attended to her wants was not there, and a rather slick young man was in his place. My Mother made her complaint—with great courtesy, as she always did. "Madam," said the slick young man, drawing himself up, "if there is any adulteration, it must be in the bean!"

It is interesting to me that the slave-owner's daughter should have found herself in revolt, not only against the waste and extravagance prevalent among English servants, but far more against the treatment of the younger ones by their superiors. At one point, when the babies and the miscarriages, of which she had more than one at Porters, were coming thicker than usual my father insisted on her employing a house-keeper. That did not last long. The quality of the food went down while the bills went up; but neither of these things caused the final débâcle. My Mother learned one day that some lesser being, a kitchen-maid or under-house maid, had transgressed the iron rule of "in by nine" on her day out; the house-keeper had waited up for her and turned her out of the house next day, without wages, and without a character. The house-keeper when tackled about this cheerfully admitted it; it was always done, it was the only way to keep young girls in order—but she herself, to her intense astonishment, was sent packing at twenty-four hours' notice, with a month's wages "in lieu." Moreover my Mother traced the girl, and put her in a decent family on the estate till she could find another place for her. She had had no previous experience of house-keepers, or she would certainly have followed the wise custom prevailing in most large English households by which the mistress never allowed man or maid to leave until she had interviewed them alone, so that if there had been any injustice she could deal with it.

As with cross children, so with silly young servant-maids she had her own methods. A foolish little fifth or sixth housemaid, left alone one day in "the mistress's" bedroom, was tempted by some equally silly silver bangles and a little locket, gifts from a governess or someone, and stole them. My Mother made enquiries of Mary, the middle-aged head-housemaid; there was a search, they were found, and the culprit was brought, weeping and trembling, to confess her guilt and receive sentence. When she had done so my Mother dismissed Mary, and spoke to the child alone.

"I *give* you these," she said. "You are to wear the locket and chain *always*, under your dress; then you will remember never again to take what doesn't belong to you. The bangles of course you can only wear at home, or on Sundays—but they are yours now." Then she ordered round the carriage and drove off to a lady living some fifteen miles away, whom she knew to be in need of a young maid. After the usual courtesies she electrified her hostess by saying—"I know you want an under-housemaid —will you take a little thief?" And swearing the mistress to secrecy, she got the small sinner the job.

I have always admired my Mother for that episode—not only for the highly imaginative penalty, but for taking that long drive. She had plenty of other calls on her time and strength.

But those bygone English servants had their merits, ferociously training the young ones to be as efficient as themselves, and preserving their own peculiar traditions with rigid faithfulness. Mary, the old head-housemaid afore-mentioned, once furnished a charming example of this. It was her duty to bring her master and mistress their morning tea at 6.30 A.M., since breakfast was always at a quarter to eight to enable my Father to catch an early train to the City. While they took their tea in bed Yah, the nurse—not so old then—was supposed to bring in the adored little son, so that his doting Father might enjoy his company. On one occasion the small boy, still under three, failed to materialise, and my Father, furious and as usual impatient, sent the white-haired Mary to the nurseries with a fierce reproof for the nurse. Mary reappeared herself, with the child in her arms—the nurse had overslept, and was not yet dressed.

"What did Mary say?" my Father asked the small creature, wishing to know whether his message had been duly transmitted.

"She said—'Gentlemen mustn't kiss the maids,'" the child replied. My Mother was enchanted. The scene on the way downstairs was easy to imagine: the innocent arms thrust round the old woman's neck. Oh, no—gentlemen mustn't kiss the maids; not in those days.

In Hertfordshire my Mother got a very different welcome from that accorded her in the business circles of Leamington, on her first arrival in England. The pretty eager woman, always so gay and gracious in spite of her perpetual pregnancies, was gladly accepted by the country gentry round about; this brought her a source of pleasure that she had long missed, congenial neighbours and friends. Delightful and cultivated people lived all round; they liked her and she liked them; they gardened and she gardened —and this easy society, full of common interests, was an immense relaxation after her dutiful efforts with less congenial people. There were the Dashwoods down in the village, who had children about the ages of her own; they played together constantly. There were the four Miss Durants, all her good friends, who married agreeable men; later their children became friends of my own. The keenest gardener, and for that reason a person she saw much of, was Vicary Gibbs; Aldenham was within driving distance, and she loved going over to see his treasures and his latest acquisitions, from all over the world; he for his part considered her thumb to be exceptionally green, and when some new rarity reached him he would often take a spare root, twig, corm or bulb of it over to Porters, for her to see what she could do. She was not, of course, in the least in his class as a gardener, but she was fast becoming a very good one all the same, and spent every moment she could spare out of doors—some of her neighbours thought that perhaps she spent more time in her garden than she ought. Vicary Gibbs himself teased her about this, when he went over one day to Porters to lunch, and she took him out to see the new beds she was making near the cedars, behind the house. "Is this where you *really* are, Mrs. Sanders, when we are so often told that you are out?" he asked. Of course it was, and to him she gaily admitted it.

I like to think of my Mother during those years: happy, busy, useful years, but full of enjoyment too—the happiest years of her married life. I like especially to think of her being able to "spread herself" over her garden in a way I have never been able to afford to do—making rose-gardens, making pergolas, planting shrubs (on Vicary Gibbs' advice), showering bulbs in unconventional and unexpected places. She did literally shower them: she taught her gardeners, and later she taught me, that the only way to plant bulbs with a natural effect is to throw them on the ground in handfuls, and dibble them in where they fall. There is no fuller expression of the human personality than a garden, especially if its creator really has a free hand, and at Porters my Mother's hand was blissfully free. To keep up a large garden, let alone to develop it, costs a lot of money—but in those happy years of the eighties money for her really *was* no object, in spite of the school-room and the ever-expanding nurseries. My Father's business was expanding even faster than the nurseries; he once told my husband that during most of the time that he was at Porters his income was seldom less than £80,000 a year. This with income-tax at under a shilling in the pound! No wonder my Mother had a free hand in the garden.

One thing that she created there sticks in my mind, because *I remember it*. This may seem impossible, since we left the place, as I have said, six weeks before my second birthday, and I never saw Porters again till the late nineteen-thirties, when it was being built over and I was middle-aged. But it is the fact. Long after I was married I said one day to my Mother that I seemed to remember rolling over and over down the smooth grass paths of a hollow full of red roses; paths intersected the rosebeds fanwise, and converged on a round grass-plot at the bottom, where my fat little body came to rest. Could this be true?—and if so, where was it? My Mother smiled delightedly. Yes—she had had an old hollow full of rubbish cleared out at Porters; she planted it with beds of crimson roses, and had turf laid on the paths between the beds. Now I was two in the middle of September, and we left Porters the last week in July, when those red roses would be out, but probably rather past their prime—so I remembered some-thing, clearly, that I last saw at the age of twenty-two months.

I have another example of the same sort, going even further back. My Mother often told us how frightened I used to be of the turkey-cock at Porters, till I was sick of hearing about a rather shameful episode in the farmyard, when the great bird came strutting and gobbling towards us with outspread tail and wings brushing the ground, all his wattles aflame with the ingorged blood, and I fled to her in terror; whereas my sister Grace, only two years older, confronted him boldly, strutting herself, and gobbling back at him—I clung to my Mother, it seems, crying out, "The turkey-gobbler will *eat* her!" Now it so happened that one Christmas during the first World War my Mother was staying with us in London, and old Yah, our ex-nurse, was looking after my oldest child while her own nurse was absent—over nursery tea the two old ladies, friends of nearly a lifetime, were recalling the past, as old ladies will, and this tale of the turkey-gobbler came up. I said to my Mother then—

"It's a curious thing, but you know whenever you tell that story, I *see* the place, as plainly as anything. The farmyard is cobbled, and lies on quite a steep slope; there are buildings round the lower sides, but not at the top, and there are two gates, not in the middle but rather high up, on each side. There is a pump down in one lower corner, too."

My Mother didn't quite realise the import of this at first; she just said, yes, that *was* exactly what the farmyard at Porters was like. But I was interested, and pursued the point.

"I can see Grace, too. She is wearing a little navy-blue coat of some rather knobbly woolen stuff, trimmed with grey lambskin; and she has on a little navy-blue bonnet trimmed with lambskin to match, turned back in the corners behind the ears."

Yah pricked up her own ears at this—anything to do with our clothes always thrilled her.

"They had those coats new that winter, Ma'am, Miss Grace and Miss Cottie; and we had to let them down next winter when we went to Eastbourne." Her peasant memory had it all taped out.

"And when did we leave off our winter coats, Yah?" I asked.

"Beginning of May, Miss Cottie, usually, or if it was very warm, end of April. Of course you had your spring coats to go into, before the summer came on."

My Mother joined in, and they worked it out. Neither could remember for certain quite *how* warm it had been that year, but both were positive that Grace could not have been strutting about in that little blue reefer with the lamb's-wool facings later than the first week in May, and I was only two in the second week of September that year. Turkey-cocks begin to strut and droop their wings and gobble as early as February; but putting it at its lowest, I had here conclusive proof of an exceedingly sharp visual memory going back to a moment when I was at most a year and seven months old.

Such proofs must surely be rare—anyhow I find the fact interesting.

One might have supposed that between her growing family of children, her large household, her garden, and her neighbours my Mother had enough to do at Porters; but not so—she presently embarked on a further activity. She had soon come to the proper "Big House" terms with the two neighbouring villages of Radlett and Shenley, so that anyone who was ill or in trouble in either at once turned to her for help. (So curious and interesting in an American, one would think to-day; but I am sure that there was a true, a *feudal* sense of responsibility about those who had owned slaves in the Southern States.) Anyhow, the still young Mrs. Sanders soon came to hear of any children and young girls—sometimes orphans, sometimes not—whose home circumstances were unhappy or even placed them in moral danger, and she decided to rescue as many as she could. "The Radlett Lodge," the gate-lodge at the end of the drive which led to Radlett, fell vacant; it was anyhow large and my Mother coaxed my Father into adding to it, installing a Matron, and then filling it with ten or a dozen of these unfortunate children, who were educated, trained in household tasks, and eventually well placed in private service. I myself knew all about "Mother's orphans," as I innocently called them, because when we moved from Hertfordshire to Surrey the whole outfit was carted along with us, and planted down in a house close by.

Perhaps it was her memories of her own intensely happy childhood under Sarah Eliza's gentle rule that made my Mother so revel in giving pleasure to children or young people; anyhow she did, and no trouble was too great when that was the end in view. There was for instance the matter of the Christmas-trees. These were unusual in England in the eighteen-eighties, but the first governess who was installed to teach my eldest sisters at Porters was a German, a devout Lutheran called Fräulein Gerlach; she naturally insisted on a tree, and promptly converted her employer to the idea; soon my Mother was having supplies of coloured glass balls, great and small, and all sorts of delicious glittering objects like bunches of silver grapes shipped over from Germany. (I have a surprising number of the survivors still—they have been twice round the world with me, furnishing forth Christmas-trees from Peking to Lisbon, via Mexico and Budapest; they now do so in the County Mayo.) To begin with there was just a tree in the house, to which "the cottage children," my Mother's protégés at the lodge, and the offspring of tenants and employees on the place came; but before long my Mother had started a second one in the village school at Shenley, which was attended by every single schoolchild, and many more too young or too old to go to school. Enormous boxes of fondants, "penny chocolates" (as we called the little round flat chocolate pastilles of my youth), acid-drops and so forth were sent down from London; Miss Copus, the sewing-maid, ran up scores and scores of brightly coloured muslin bags on the machine, and snipped gay ribbons to tie them with; then my Mother roped in her own younger children, my sisters Jenny and Helen and my brother Harry, to mix the sweets on big japanned trays and fill and tie the bags. My brother was a liability rather than an asset at this task, because he ate so many sweets; when my Mother remonstrated with him he said—" 'Thou shalt not muzzle the ox that treadeth out the corn,' " and went on gobbling as before, leaving her helpless with laughter. (This was one effect of the daily family prayers which my Father, like his Grandfather Brooking before him, said regularly, plus a long reading from the Bible, before catching that early train to Liverpool Street; as a result we all knew the Old and the New Testaments practically by heart.)

But the sweets and the oranges for each child were only a side-issue; as well there had to be the "proper present," boots or shoes or a frock or handkerchiefs, and a book or toy as well; to avoid repetition my Mother, helped by her invaluable amanuensis Louisa Hesketh, kept huge ledgers in which each child was re-corded, with its age and a note of what presents it and its brothers and sisters received each year, so something appropriate could always be chosen. And then ordered in London, from huge ruled lists; unpacked, re-packed in bright paper, labelled, and finally presented. A herculean task!—but my Mother delighted in it.

These are my sisters' recollections; when most of this was going on at Porters I was not yet born; but trivial as they are in themselves, they do, I think, convey a certain idea of my Mother at the plenitude of her activities and powers. And they are the vivid personal memories of young children, *her* children, who themselves filled the bags of sweets, and peeped into the ledgers to see which child was getting what, and finally helped with the distribution under the lighted tree in the village school. It all still went on in Surrey, when I can remember it myself, only on a slightly smaller scale; there the tree in the high open hall of the house was lit over and over again—for the family, for the children of neighbours and friends, for "the orphans" and the village children, and for the choirboys, who came to sing carols first, and then to receive sweets and oranges and be regaled with cocoa. And all those long-ago children gazed at the Teutonic wax angel topping the tree, in the soft light of the many-coloured candles, and shook the pink-and-white glass bells on the lower branches to hear them ring, as my own grandchild and my steward's children do to-day; and showed one another the glass icicles—suspended magically and invisibly on black cotton—and the silver cardboard bird with the plumed tail of pink feathers. (The moth got at that tail at last, but I have made him a new one, of shredded crimson paper.) A vanished world—but a world of much happiness for countless children, evoked by the tireless love and labour of the daughter of Sarah Eliza Day, who had made so many children happy away across the ocean, years before.

Chapter 8

I THINK it is time that I should now devote rather more attention to my Father than I have hitherto done, for his temperament and way of life, so different to her own, inevitably affected my Mother.

He was not an easy character. He was arbitrary, energetic, and very impatient; quick, competent, and thorough himself, he was remorseless in hounding down slackness or incompetence or stupidity, with wounding words and a voice frighteningly loud—to me anyhow. If anyone about him, whether an employee or a child, failed to carry out their orders he had only one reply to any excuses about difficulties, or not having understood: "The way to do a thing is to do it." (I have found this an admirable motto to carry one through life—so simple, really.) On any deliberate failure in duty he had no mercy at all. One of his most curious traits—for physically he was extremely brave—was an acute nervousness; and to safeguard his precious family at night, particularly during his constant journeys abroad, he employed at Porters a night-watchman, whose business it was to circumambulate the house hourly till daybreak, lantern in hand. One night there was a fall of snow; my Father, looking out at 1 A.M., saw that it had ceased. After his morning tea had been brought by old Mary at that unearthly hour of half-past six, and he had taken it, as he shaved and dressed he threw open the window to gulp in the early air, and looked out on the whitened lawns and the boughs of the cedars, bending beneath their lovely load. But in the faint light he also looked immediately beneath his window, where there should have been tracks in the snow left by the night-watchman on his rounds. There were none. Before leaving for London and his office at 8.15 A.M. he had interviewed the culprit, and dismissed him on the spot. (He brought another back with him that night.)

He always had, and retained, an enormous and innocent enjoyment of his wealth, which he owed to no one but himself; but he put it to uses that seemed to him good, and he was admirably open-handed, I think, in the way he let my Mother throw it about on her rose-gardens and her orphanages and village Christmas-trees. His own uses for it were not ignoble, either. Like many men of his generation he had conceived an almost idolatrous admiration for Mr. Gladstone and his policies, and became an ardent Liberal. It was natural enough, one can see, for a man who was making eighty thousand a year out of importing and exporting metals to think highly of Free Trade as a policy; but there was genuine idealism there too, and my Father was prepared to back his ideals in hard cash. In those spacious days restrictions on the personal outlay of parliamentary candidates were not as rigid as they are to-day; more or less, a candidate spent what he chose, or had. And on no less than four occasions my Father stood for Parliament in the Liberal interest—not in the least because he wished to enter politics, for which he had neither the taste nor the time, but to please his idol Mr. Gladstone. They were all safe Conservative seats, complete forlorn hopes; but Mr. Gladstone did not want them to go uncontested, so my Father readily spent his time and money in contesting them. He was rather a good natural speaker, and I am sure he enjoyed himself very much. In 1886 he stood for Leicestershire, and also—a by-election—for Kings Lynn; in 1887 he stood in Somerset against a Mr. Alsopp (a son of Lord Hindlip so presumably a brewer); the *Somersetshire Gazette* for April the 20th of that year amused itself by delving into the genealogies of both families, and discovering that the rival candidates were remote kinsmen, through a Sanders-Alsopp marriage in the eighteenth century. I have no record of where the fourth election was. Anyhow my Father cheerfully lost them all, and each time returned—still cheerful, his duty to Mr. Gladstone done—to making money in his office in Lime Street, and to his country Sundays with his family.

I have an idea that it was these by-elections which were to some extent responsible for the two four-in-hands. My Father really enjoyed driving more than riding, and a four-in-hand must be one of the most exciting things in the world to drive; he soon started one at Porters, and then presently there was the second. A candidate driving about to his meetings in a four-in-hand anyhow created a very fine effect, but one who produced *two!*—rosettes with the Liberal colours on the men's liveries, and bows of them on the whips; it was all very dashing indeed, even though it didn't win the seats. Mr. Gladstone was pleased, too; he came and spoke for the devoted henchman, and shook his pretty little girls (who adored the elections) by the hand; my sister Therese for years preserved religiously in her "treasure-drawer" a pair of gloves, of which one had touched Mr. Gladstone's hand. As for my sister Jenny, who was deliciously pretty and as brave as a lion, she was sometimes perched up on the box as they clattered into some town or village (the coachman at her side) holding the reins herself—which drove the crowds to frenzied applause. It must all have been great fun, and I wish I hadn't missed it by not being born.

The odd streak of nobility in my Father's character emerged most clearly of all in the very peculiar business of his becoming a teetotaller. He was accustomed to drinking wine at all meals, and enjoyed it; in fact he gradually developed a rather fine taste in wines, and by the time he went to Porters he had collected quite a good cellar—he generally contrived to pass through France on his trips to and from Spain, and would delay a little to pick up choice lots of Burgundy or champagne or liqueurs, here or there. He went several times to the Grande Chartreuse itself, before the monks left for Spain in 1901, to buy the yellow, the

Marie Louise Day, aged 25

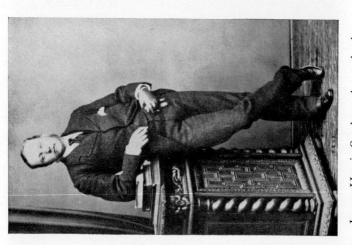

James Harris Sanders, the author's
father, at the time of his marriage

The author in court dress, 1930

green, and the rare and extremely potent white, the famous Élixir des Pères Chartreux, direct from the Abbey. I think this was probably the happiest contact he ever had with the *real* Scarlet Woman, the Church of Rome; he liked the monks very much, he once told me.

Now at Porters there was a young under-keeper of whom my Father was very fond. The young man was clever and energetic, brilliant at raising pheasants, a magician at handling ferrets; he had married a nice young woman from Shenley village, and had a fine baby boy. But he drank. On Saturday nights, his wages in his pocket, he would go down to the village pub, and drink and drink—and he was one of those unfortunates who drank himself not silly but savage. One Sunday morning an appalling tale was brought up to my Father:—the night before, the young keeper, returning home in an alcoholic frenzy, had snatched his baby out of the cradle and put it on the open fire; the child was dead.

My Father, horrified, went down to the cottage after Church to interview his favourite employee, who had done this awful thing, hoping to persuade him to "take the pledge." With astounding brass, as it seems to me, the young man said—"You take your glass of wine at dinner, Sir—why shouldn't I take my glass of beer?" In my Father's place I should certainly have pointed out that I had never yet put any of my six children on the fire as a result of drinking wine at dinner; but my Father did nothing of the sort. Without the smallest hesitation he said:—"I never will again, if you will take the pledge with me." And after the local magistrates had let the young father off with a derisory fine, master and man went down to the village together, and together "took the pledge"—i.e., became teetotallers.

They both kept their pledge—the young keeper was redeemed, and my Father fore-went wine for the rest of his life. It cannot have been easy for him: he was in his middle forties when this took place; he was accustomed to wine, and enjoyed it; he was as always working extremely hard, and felt the need of the stimulus. But he gave it up to save another soul—and never went back on his vow; tiresome as the results seemed to us later, I cannot but applaud him. (It was also a typical piece of Brooking exaggeration on moral questions, but I love him for it.) Uncle Sam made rather a fuss when he and Aunt Isabel came to stay—usually with troops of their children—because for some years my Father did not like even the sight of the forbidden thing on the table; moreover, the shock of that baby's death produced in him an almost genuine conviction that alcohol in every form was evil in itself. (We were all brought up as rigid teetotallers.) But my Mother got round that somehow, with port or sherry served in the morning-room; she spent so much of her life smoothing over her Jim's idiosyncrasies that she became very good at all that.

After I had started climbing myself my father once told me that he never took up mountaineering, as Charles Edward Mathews constantly pressed him to do, because he was already so fond of stalking and fishing; if he was going to toil up a mountain, he said, he preferred there to be stags on it. He was a tolerable shot at pheasants, though I believe never much good at driven grouse, the one form of sport he never cared about; but he was deadly at rabbits, knocking them head-over-heels, and practically never using a second cartridge. We were all made to shoot from the age of ten, with .410s, and rigidly drilled in field manners: a child who failed to open the breech of its gun when climbing a fence had it taken away for a week. Also he taught us all to wring a rabbit's neck as quite small children—until we could do this we were not allowed to handle a gun.

But his passion was for stalking. Exactly when he started I don't know, nor who introduced him to it—possibly his great crony James Ross of Montreal, the Highland-born engineer who took charge of the construction of the Canadian Pacific Railway westward from Winnipeg in 1883; Ross and my Father had known each other for some time before that, when the Scot was doing railway engineering in the States, where my Father was already involved with the steel industry—the two Jameses both used to say, laughing, that it was James Sanders who got James Ross his job with the C.P.R.!—but what really lay behind that story I don't know. James Ross was also mad about stalking and fishing, before his heart gave him the trouble it did later on, and for many years they used to rent a forest every autumn and shoot it together. Usually they took Kinlochewe, on Loch Maree, a most splendid place which my Father loved; the great hills on its sixty thousand acres ran up to over three thousand feet, and the stags were big as a rule, with magnificent heads—seventy was an average bag; the salmon in the Kinlochewe River and in the loch itself were fierce and sporting. In later years he used to write us detailed accounts of particular stalks—his eagerness and delight breathed from every line.

Anyhow, whoever or whatever caused my Father to take up stalking and fishing, by 1880 or thereabouts they had become the main pleasures of his life, and caused him to procure to my Mother one of the greatest pleasures in hers, when he decided to rent Gruinard, in Wester Ross, and to transport his whole family thither for four or five months. He did this for two seasons in succession, and two long, enchanted summers my Mother spent in the West Highlands. She had never seen anything in the least like it: the immense bare hills, their subtle tawny colouring muted by the soft aqueous air, and the long, late, rose-shadowed twilights; Gruinard lies far North, and even without "summer time," in June, up there, one could read a book by daylight at 11 P.M. Nor had she ever encountered any people in the least like the Highland gillies and boatmen, speaking their beautiful idiomatic English directly translated from the Gaelic—always so courteous, but so remote and withdrawn at first, so warm-hearted once they had accepted the stranger. Gruinard Bay is a broad shallow inlet lying between the two long narrow ones of Loch Ewe and Little Loch Broom; behind it and all round the hills rise to over three thousand feet; beyond the bay, across the Minch, stretches "The Long Island," Lewis and Harris, too low and flat to be much seen unless one climbs the hills; not far from the long white house the Meikle Gruinard, a sizeable river, full of salmon, brawls its way to the sea. To reach the place was quite an undertaking: the express to Inverness, a change, and on in a small slow train to Achnasheen, whence a drive of forty miles in various horse-drawn conveyances completed the journey. Plate and linen were sent in advance by a coasting-steamer to Ullapool, and fetched across in the fishermen's boats; supplies of groceries came up fortnightly from Glasgow in the same way. Groceries apart, shooting-tenants were expected to live off the place, and it was easy enough to do so with salmon, lobsters, sea-fish, and hares, rabbits, grouse, and venison in abundance; to my Mother's amused exasperation her English servants soon protested at being asked to eat salmon or lobster more than twice a week!—and venison at all; so she had blackfaced mutton killed for them, and she and the children lived on the delicacies.

But none of that worried her. She made it clear to me later that Gruinard had been pure bliss. (Can that be why I, too, have found a purer bliss in the West Highlands than anywhere else on earth, except in the Alps?) And I think it was there that she first began to take a serious interest in European wild-flowers, encountering the unknown flora of the West Highlands: Grass of Parnassus, the orange bog-asphodel, pinguiculas, mauve and yellow; and milk-wort, the insect-eating droseras, and the splendid bronze-blue fronds of Royal Fern. She had never seen anything like them in Hertfordshire, and of course she had to know what they were; she wrote "spang off" in her dashing, rather sprawly hand to Hatchard's, in Piccadilly for the best wild-flower book available—and wrote to Sarah Eliza, her mother, to say that she wanted this as a present. Hatchard's sent her the six volumes of *The Flowering Plants, Grasses, Sedges and Ferns of Great Britain*, by Miss Anne Pratt—and a very good choice too, since Bentham and Hooker only appeared in 1886, some four or five years after the family was at Gruinard. A thing I find amusing is the parallel between my American Mother in the eighteen-eighties writing hurriedly from Scotland to London for a British Flora, and her English daughter in the nineteen-forties—also suddenly confronted with something new to her, the astonishing wild-flowers of South California—ascertaining in Hollywood from Charles Laughton, of all people, what was the best book for the flora of the Coast, and rushing off to buy it. (I met John van Druten in the shop, which led to many delightful things.)

But wild-flowers were not the only thing to attract my Mother's attention at Gruinard. Before long she was going out with the fishermen in their strong, broad-beamed, chunky boats, and exclaiming at what the trawls brought up—star-fish, shells, sea-beasts of all sorts; she found other creatures and other growths when she took her children to paddle in the pools along the shore. So there were more letters to London, and more books arrived: Dr. Louis Figuier's *Ocean World* and *Insect World*, and some large tomes on sea-weeds and shells; she and Besa Hesketh covered them, Anne Pratt and all, in dark-green glazed calico, neatly stitched inside the covers—it is still on them to-day, with the faded labels gummed on the backs. She decided to make a collection of sea-weeds, since she found so many more than the good Dr. Figuier mentioned; neither Gairloch nor Ullapool could produce enough blotting-paper for her needs, so she telegraphed to London for that, and mounted her specimens with exquisite care. (When she got home she sent her collection to the Natural History Museum at South Kensington to be named; it earned much praise, being far more complete than anything hitherto sent in from those waters, and the Museum eventually kept it—as later Kew was to keep a hurried, and far less beautifully mounted collection of wild-flowers which I made in High Albania in 1936.)

There were not many visitors at Gruinard, except when my Father dashed up for a week or so at a time for a few days' salmon-fishing, or to crawl belly-flat over the great naked hills with the stalker, peer at the splendid distant stags through his telescope, and bring down, if he was lucky, "a royal" with his rifle. (A "royal," it should perhaps be explained, is a stag with six tines on either antler.) Gruinard was by no means as large a forest as Kinlochewe, his later love, it ran only to seventeen or eighteen thousand acres—but it was a splendid stretch of country, and carried some fine stags. When he came my Father occasionally brought a friend or two; otherwise, except for his children and the local people, my Mother was alone. She liked that—the place was her companion, as places have always been the best of companions to me. She gave me, long afterwards, a very clear picture of those long, happy, solitary days on the hill or out in the boat, with the austere splendour of the West Highland landscape—in Ross-shire more austere and more splendid than anywhere else—spread out all round her. It was a far cry from New Orleans, with its subtropical warmth and luxuriant vegetation, and its easy-going languid Catholic population, this countryside of naked hills peopled by rigid Presbyterians: she was blessedly able to be completely happy in both places. She busied herself in finding and identifying new flowers on land, and new sea-things as she sailed about the coast; soon she was taking out the boats simply to trawl for sea-weeds, regardless of the fish. No wonder she was happy; using her mind, filling it with fresh knowledge and new beauties—is there any more stimulating pleasure? That settling down with the bowl of flowers on the table and the book on one's knee, a pencil in one hand, the magnifying-glass in the other: reading, peering, comparing, and finally triumphantly jotting down place and date. Happy hours; triumphant moments—perhaps most triumphant of all when in the immortal works of the Abbé Coste one can write a place and date alongside the inspiring words: "*Une seule espèce.*"

It is strange to me now to think that my Mother and Osgood Mackenzie, that great—if destructive—nature-lover should have spent those two summers within a few miles' drive of each other, and never met. He was then in his early forties, a few years her senior, and was living at Poolewe. When I met his daughter, Mairi Hanbury, there forty years later, I realised how much they would have had to say to one another, and how thrilled my Mother would have been by his knowledge. But lairds did not usually bother to call on shooting-tenants, and anyhow the Mackenzies were tremendous xenophobes; Gruinard was a Mackenzie property, at that time let on a long lease by the trustees to some people called Murray, who sub-let it to my Father. The Gruinard family were Mackenzies of Dundonnell, and there were endless stories, which I learned after I got to know the district myself, about them. A Miss Mackenzie of Dundonnell married a Mr. Catton and got Gruinard as a marriage portion; the poor husband was not very "strong in the intellects," nor in his eyesight either, it would seem, for one day when he went on the hill after stags he shot two horses instead!—for which he had to pay their crofter owners twenty-five pounds a-piece. Moreover, after this episode his guns and rifles were taken away from him; the charitable country-people were very sorry for him.

But there are hard memories, even to-day, of the estate factor, or bailiff, of whom my Mother fell foul. It is always bad for a place to be under trustees: they are not on the spot, they may have no local interest, and the factor, who *is* on the spot, has far too free a hand; if he is hard and self-seeking, a money return is all he looks for. The complaint against my Mother was this—that since her servants refused to eat venison, and she and her three infants could not consume a whole stag, let alone two or three, by themselves she used to distribute the surplus meat among the crofters, particularly to those houses where there was illness, or a baby on the way. The factor remonstrated with her. She asked him what he expected her to do with all that good meat?—his reply was "Bury it." This was at a time when poverty in the Highlands was fairly acute: the crofters lived mainly on oatmeal and potatoes, with milk to drink and fish occasionally—many never saw meat from month's end to month's end, unless they managed to steal a cast ewe. There was, according to Osgood Mackenzie, a good deal of sheep-stealing at that time, and no wonder. However, my Mother did not bury her surplus venison; she went on giving it away, and salmon and white-fish too.

One entrancing story is still told about this factor. He was a "Skye-man"—from the Isle of Skye—and he was "wicked in that way," i.e., in the matter of oppressing the crofters. Now at Tournaig, not far off, there was a famous bard, "The Bard of Tournaig," also known as "The Last of the Bards"; he made poems in Gaelic about local occurrences and places, and then recited them—and he made a poem about the factor and his "wickedness." The wretched factor was proud to be the subject of a poem, and went down to the bard's house to hear it—"he died the same night"! (Long years afterwards I went and sat in the bard's kitchen, when he was a very old man indeed, and heard him recite another of his poems, "The Weaver's Threshold"; and then listened while he made an extempore translation of it into the beautiful pure English of the bi-lingual Highlander.) There is another story, still remembered to-day, of the factor who was so indignant with my Mother because she preferred giving food away to burying it. He accompanied his Laird, the poor batty individual who shot the horses, on a round of visits to various crofters on the estate; with proper courtesy some of the crofters offered Laird and factor "a dram," but all who did this had their rents raised, since they were rich enough to drink whisky.

When my Mother left Gruinard for the last time, driving along the rough narrow road at the head of that long procession of carts and carriages, the people from all the small houses, near and far, came out and stood at their doors, silently holding up both hands above their heads in blessing. It was a thing she never forgot.

One incident occurred at Gruinard which I think is worth recording, for the light it throws on individual freedom seventy years ago. At one point my sister Cora fell and broke her arm; the local doctor was sent for, and set it according to his lights. My Father hastened up from London on hearing of the accident; his natural nervousness always mounted almost to the point of frenzy where his children's health was concerned. He found the child running a temperature, in pain, and the arm swollen. Thereupon he telegraphed to one of the principal orthopaedic surgeons in London asking him to come to Wester Ross forthwith to re-set the arm, no matter what the fee, by special train. The surgeon agreed to come for five hundred guineas; a special train was laid on from London to Achnasheen, and another took the great man back afterwards. In effect, my Father's action was justified; the London specialist found that the arm had been set out of alignment, so that it would have been crooked, stiff, and shortened if left to the rather veterinary skills of the Highland doctor. But how delightful to be able to set *two* special trains in motion by telegram from one end of the British Isles to the other, without any tedious applications to Regional Boards or a Ministry of Transport. It did my sister a lifelong good, and did the public no harm. How nice our lost liberties were!

My Father's impatience during this episode—doing everything by telegram and by special train—however justified, was typical of him. It was thoroughly in keeping with his character that the registered telegraphic address of his office should have "Immediate, London."

It has always been rather a puzzle to me why only those two summers should have been spent in the West Highlands, seeing how much my Mother adored being there. It cannot have been from motives of economy, for in any case my Father took other stalkings every year with Mr. Ross, at Kinlochewe or elsewhere. My Mother never pressed her own wishes or preferences; and it may be that as her family grew, and she became increasingly involved in her garden and her friendships at Porters, she had less desire to go away. There was always a lot of cheerful family hospitality going on in Hertfordshire; it was nothing for a party of six or seven relations, American or English, to come and stay for a month or more; "the Snitterfield cousins," as we called the young Sam Sanderses, often came without their parents, because their mother trusted them with "Aunt Marie." Then there were the Wickhams, a considerable and a very pleasant feature in our lives. My Father's younger sister Hannah had married a rather dry, quiet lawyer called Ernest Wickham, and it was an understood thing that they always spent Christmas with us, a visit lasting a fortnight at the very least. Aunt Onnie, as we always called her, was a pretty woman with fair curly hair, fashionable clothes, and a gently spoiled, rather coquettish manner; she was surprisingly *mondaine* for old Mary Brooking's daughter, went boldly to the theatre, and made cool fun of her brother Jim for his puritanical ways. As for her husband, Uncle Wickham, he was simply her doormat, though he had ten times her brains, with a lot of learning added. I wish I knew where and how Aunt Onnie met him—it is maddening to me now, the child's incurious acceptance of its surroundings; how much I could have known if it had ever occurred to me to find out!

One of the many things I now do not know for certain is why we left Porters at all. Was there a "business recession" in the early eighteen-nineties? It can not have been poor Uncle John up to his deals again, for he had died some time before; though I believe that my Father had to bail him out at least three times, first and last. In any case the beloved place was first let for a couple of years, then sold; we spent one winter at Eastbourne, another at Brighton, and the intervening summers in two furnished houses, one on each side of Windsor Great Park—and ultimately settled down in what was to be the home of my own youth, a late-Victorian house called Ridgemead, at Englefield Green in Surrey. My Mother was uprooted from her garden, where the delightful labours of the last ten years were now bearing full and splendid fruit, and severed from her happy friendships in Hertfordshire; she spent two years dragging a household which included a nursery and—by now—two schoolrooms round from one furnished house to another, and ended by exchanging the almost mediaeval beauty and dignity of life at Porters for existence in a house large and comfortable indeed, but externally monstrous, and situated in a neighbourhood which, Windsor Great Park apart, was practically suburban. It was all typical of the restlessness and uncertainty of business life, and was the first of a succession of downward steps in the matter of houses and wealth: more than steps, bumps—bump, bump, bump—as will be told in due course. Like her mother before her, my Mother accepted it all with uncomplaining and unshaken tranquillity.

Chapter 9

I REMEMBER little of that interregnum between Hertford-shire and Surrey, except that at Eastbourne I first began to be taken to church. We went to Holy Trinity, because the parson there, Mr. Bathurst, was acceptably low-church; I enjoyed the hymns, because for them my Father always lifted Grace and me up to stand on the seat on either side of him; he had a theory that children could sing praise to God better if they were not muffled and stifled by stout adult backs. This was most agreeable; we piped as loud as we could, and looked round on the congregation at the same time. But in this unusual position we could not only see, we could also be seen—and seen we were by, amongst others, the members of my future husband's family. His grandmother lived in Eastbourne, and as the O'Malleys too were very pious and very low-church they also attended Holy Trinity. We did not know them, nor they us, but twenty years later one of my sisters-in-law told me how clearly she remembered the two little girls who used to stand on the seat during the hymns, one on each side of a tall blond man. We were stamped on her memory, she said, by the beauty of our clothes: pelisses of thick cream corded silk and "Victoria bonnets" to match trimmed with tufts of tiny ostrich-feathers, filled in round the face with endless ruchings of lace, and tied under our chins with big bows of ribbon. She described these to me minutely, and an old photograph with an Eastbourne firm's name on the back corroborates her—I can just remember those clothes myself, and I, too, thought them very fine. My mother-in-law had neither as much dress-sense nor, I suppose, as much money as my Mother, and her daughters greatly envied us our pretty outfits.

The house at Englefield Green is the first home that I remember clearly and continuously. A child really only remembers the things that were important to it—in the case of a happy child, as on the whole I was, this means mainly the things that brought it delight. Moreover, children seldom criticise their own surroundings, *as* children. It meant nothing to me that the house itself was externally monstrous: red brick and mock timber-and-plaster, with balconies, porches, bow-windows and flat leaded roofs in all directions; I thought it nice that there was hardly a bedroom from which one could not step into the open air in one's nightgown, and on the leads outside the room where for a long time I slept with Patty, the second nurse, I was able to make my pet snails creep races along the cold grey surface towards the lettuce-leaves which I spread out enticingly some feet ahead of them. The Victorian shrubberies were to us places of enchantment then, however odd I might think them to-day, except for the syringas and flowering cherries of which they were full; there we played our American games about Ethan Allen and the Green Mountain Boys, and European ones about the Graeco-Turkish and the Boer wars—we had our own names for each of the wildernesses of laurels and yews and lilac-bushes.

A great source of pleasure was the river. The house stood on a spur of hill four hundred feet above the Thames; from the terrace, flanked with standard roses, surrounding it we looked out on one side to Windsor Castle through a gap in the high line of beeches which fringed the lawn, on another across the flat blue of the Thames Valley to Harrow Hill, with its twin spires. Immediately below us ran the Thames, full and gentle between flat grassy fields and hedgerows—only a few minutes' scamper down Priests' Hill by the short-cut through the wood to Haines' boat-house, but, oh, what a long pull up again, burdened with the picnic-baskets! There we learned to row, to scull, and to handle the Canadian canoe, the first to reach England, brought over by Mr. Ross; in the spring and summer when Cora and Therese, now both at Oxford, were at home to take us we spent long afternoons on the quiet water, going ashore to have tea or to pick cowslips, looking up at the rounded heights of Cooper's Hill, next door to us on the ridge that overhung the valley, and—in my case, anyhow—conjuring up pictures of the gathering for Magna Carta as we slid down between the broad flats of Runnymede and the small island, set with great willows, where the charter was actually signed. At week-ends, when my Father was at home, we had out the randan and went much further—downstream as far as Staines or Laleham, upstream through Datchet with its house-boats to where Windsor Castle stood up quite close at hand across the Home Park. My elder sisters rather disliked these expeditions in the randan, with my Father drilling everyone about feathering and keeping in stroke, but I enjoyed going so far afield; I liked sitting on the comfortable padded seats in the stern, with their wicker backs, or perched up in the bows alone, peering at fish and waterweeds, while my Mother, in her cool grey dress under a broad sun-hat, and those soft gloves, swung strongly and rhythmically to the sculls with the rest, her back as flat as a board on the pull. She was never tired, and when we went ashore for lunch she quickly organised the unpacking of the eatables, and afterwards took us off to hunt for birds'-nests or wild-flowers.

Perhaps what most affected our lives in Surrey was the proximity of Windsor Great Park, barely half a mile away. This, though bordered on two sides by semi-suburban districts, really amounted to a big nature-reserve. The deer, of course, were introduced and unnaturally tame, but they led their own unfettered lives; during the rutting season, in late autumn, the deep angry bellows of the red stags came clearly to our ears as we lay in bed at night—a wild and splendid sound to hear in the dark barely twenty miles from London. Other creatures were completely wild. There was a heronry in a big stand of old Scots pine on a hill overlooking Virginia Water, which we used to visit in spring when the young were hatched; we soon found out that if we went on foot the old birds would fly off, leaving their hungry broods cackling disconsolately in the big sprawling untidy mess of sticks which served them for nests—but if we rode up on horseback they took us for animals, and ignored us completely; we could sit in our saddles and watch the great birds plane in and settle, with an adjustment of their big black-tipped wings, on the edge of the nest, to thrust fish into the gaping bills of their young. I remember how the rank fishy smell from the white-stained nests came down to us where we sat, conquering the aromatic fragrance from the carpet of pine-needles beneath our ponies' feet.

Both the Great Crested Grebe and the Slavonian Grebe— which before the days of Witherby we called the Eared Grebe —nested on Virginia Water; when I was rather older I used to persuade some adult to walk the four miles there and the four miles back with me (we were never allowed outside "the grounds" alone) to hunt for their nests, concealed among the reeds in little bays along the shore, where a thick growth of rhododendrons screened them, with a fringe of alders at the water's edge. When I had spotted a nest I would climb out along the horizontal alder boughs that overhung the water and watch the Grebes, literally under my very eyes, pulling the lengths of rush of which their water-logged nests were built over the eggs to cover them before they went off, swimming and diving alternately, for a meal. When I got home I flew to my Mother to report my observations; she was as interested as the most eager bird-watcher could wish, and would reach down a volume of Morris's *History of British Birds* to check on my reports. As with flowers and sea-weeds, so with birds: she always supplied herself with books—though why she never had Bewick I don't know. Perhaps he was very expensive; during my childhood economy, or attempted economy, was becoming a constant factor.

In the Great Park there were unusual wild-flowers, too. We

soon knew where to look for Spurge Laurel, and where to find the pale Helleborine under the beech-trees. There we walked on Sunday afternoons with my Father, who was just as fanatical about making very small children tramp for miles and miles as his small mother had been; but we loved it—especially in autumn, when we took bootbags stuffed in the pockets of our heavy fur-trimmed coats, and gathered Spanish chestnuts, rubbing the prickly husks gently under the soles of our stout buttoned boots so as not to bruise the brown shining fruit within, while the autumnal smell of fallen leaves and moist earth came up and filled our nostrils. When we got home we ate them boiled for tea with wafer-thin bread-and-butter, sitting round the long dining-room table—there was always "dining-room tea" on Sundays; and hungry and exercised as we were, those chestnuts seemed the most delectable of foods.

But above all, for us, the Park meant riding. Except in snow or hard frost we were expected to ride practically every day, however inclement the weather—before lunch in winter, after tea in summer. (One of our governesses used to say bitterly that the children were apparently kept to exercise the horses, instead of the other way round.) Of course we rode side-saddle, in tight-fitting habits with long riding-trousers under them, held in place by leather straps below the insteps. My Father had an idiosyncrasy about saddles, as about so many things; he held that if a woman always rode, as was the fashion, on the near side, i.e., with her legs to the left, one hip would get higher than the other—so there was a complete outfit of "off" as well as "near" saddles, and we used them on alternate days.

But at the time I took alternate side-saddles, like the ugliness of our house, for granted. What I still remember is the winter wind in my face as we galloped across the heathy expanse of Smith's Lawn, and the exquisite feel of the movement of my own chestnut, partly Arab, under me; the first stir of spring in the air in the cold empty woods round the Obelisk Pond; the smell of the sweating horses on hot summer rides, and leaning down out of the saddle to slap the horse-flies that clung to their darkened necks and sides, making them sidle and fidget. Windsor Park, tamed as it is, has great beauty; as a child that beauty drove deep into me, filling me with delight and with an intense desire to find words to express what I saw. I was always teasing away at words, out riding—indeed I was only ten when this curious habit gave me a fall. We were crossing the head of a glade of great beeches down which, miles away, the omnipresent mass of Windsor Castle stood up, its battlements tender in tone as a pearl in the autumn mist; I was seeking words to describe this when Hall, the coachman, who always rode with us, gave the order to canter. Lost in the view and that search for words, I never heard him; my pony bounded forward, and off I came on my head.

But riding led to one of the silliest episodes in my whole life; with a single exception, the one of which I am still most bitterly ashamed. I have already mentioned my Father's extreme nervousness on our account; where horses were concerned this became altogether exaggerated. Normally he bought aged trusty animals, ex-hunters with lovely manners, for his six daughters to exercise; but it so happened that when I, the youngest, needed to be furnished with something rather more active than Blackberry, our old Welsh pony, as a mount he was offered by a cab-driver in Egham the above-mentioned half-Arab chestnut, which had been parked with the cabby by a bankrupt race-owner, and finally left on his hands as a bad debt. The cabby, poor man, had little use for a blood horse whose only task in life hitherto had been to pace race-horses for flying starts; he implored my Father to buy it. My brother Harry took it out on trial, and carefully concealed the fact that it had kicked in the window of a four-wheeled cab in Windsor High Street—satisfied, my poor Father acquired the lovely creature and gave it to me. But at first I was only allowed to ride it on the leading-rein, a situation so humiliating to the led. Now about the same time a new cob was bought for my sister Grace, a stumpy object but a clever jumper, called Bravo; at first she too was abjectly led, but presently she announced her intention of asking my Father to let her ride off the leading-rein. Then, as ever, I was a great moral coward, and particularly frightened of my Father, so I begged her at the same time to ask if I might not also ride Lightfoot—what period names, Bravo and Lightfoot! —unled, and she said that she would.

She made her request on a Saturday, and I waited, palpitating, for the result. "What did he say?" I asked when she came out of the Moorish room.

"Yes," said Grace tersely, and went on upstairs. I asked for no details, I walked on air—henceforth I was to ride my lovely little horse in freedom. Expansionist and boastful, I told everyone —the maids, the governess, old Yah, the nurse, my sisters. But alas, alas, Grace had quite forgotten my request, at least she never made it; that "Yes" concerned herself alone. On Monday when the horses came round to the door, there was the hateful rein attached to the chestnut's bridle. "But I am to ride *off* the leading-rein," I expostulated.

"I've had no orders to that effect, Miss," said the groom stolidly; and on the leading-rein, fuming and helpless, I had to ride that day. When we got home I tackled Grace, who said rather contemptuously that if I wanted questions asked of Dad, why didn't I ask them myself?

"But you *promised*!" I remonstrated.

"Well, I didn't do it."

The humiliation, the disappointment, were more than I could bear; I decided to run away. I laid my plans not unskilfully for a child of eleven, as I was then. Before our afternoon lessons I had to lie down in the night nursery for three-quarters of an hour, during which time no one invigilated me. I secured one of the squashy rush-bags with handles in which we carried our provisions on river-picnics, filled it with food, a set of spare under-clothes, and a "better" dress—all this I hid under my bed. In my pockets I stuffed away such money as I had: about eighteen shillings and sixpence, mostly in new threepenny bits, to which I added my paltry little scraps of jewellery—my "bib-brooch," a bar of pearls

133

and coral, and a Venetian necklet and bracelet of pearls set at intervals on fine gold chains. Before anyone was likely to come and rouse me I got up, took my rush-bag, slipped down the back stairs and out through the french window which gave onto the terrace from the dining-room; no one saw me scoot into the shelter of one of those clumps of laurels, and I got clear away through a small wood and climbed the low iron fence which separated our garden from the grounds of Beaumont College. Here I was safe to meet no one but perhaps one of the Jesuit Fathers, strolling along reading his breviary. After half a mile along Beaumont's Beech Walk I crossed the road and got into Windsor Park.

I had decided to make for Windsor, and to ask for a job in a shop; before that, though, I should have to find a "respectable" room for the night. Windsor was a good four miles away by the shortest route, but this I did not take, for a rather pitiful reason— we often walked those four miles on Sundays to hear Matins in St. George's Chapel, and on those mornings I was always happy; now, though full of pride and anger, I was desperately unhappy, and I could not face that well-known track. Instead I made a detour by "the Copper Horse," the local name for the bronze equestrian statue at the far end of the Long Walk; there I encountered a group of boys from Scaitcliffe (the preparatory school attended by my brother Jack) escorted by a mistress—they were in quarantine for something and therefore "off games"; Jack was not with them. The young mistress, who knew quite well that we were never allowed out alone, asked curiously where I was going—I replied, unconvincingly, "for a picnic," and hurried away. It was a cold, grey afternoon, and as I plodded along my bag seemed to grow heavier and heavier, and my spirits began to sink. Should I get a job? Would my eighteen shillings and sixpence be enough for a room? When I got into the town and trudged up Sheet Street everything got worse and worse; people turned to look at the skinny little girl lugging the bulging picnic-basket— I for my part looked helplessly at the house-fronts, wondering behind which I should find the respectable room. I was getting hungry by now, and the light was beginning to fail; I decided— and when I did so I knew it was really a surrender, and that my brief revolt was at an end—to go and consult Besa.

Besa, my Mother's amanuensis—she who used to compile those lists of Christmas presents for the school-children of Shenley and Radlett—had expressed a desire for an independent career, and my father had accordingly set her up in Windsor as the manageress of a branch of Fullers, then a new and exciting institution which sold wonderful cakes, unusual sweets like Peppermint Lumps and Maple Sugar Drops, and superb ice-creams. Besa's shop stood on the steep street which curves round immediately below the Norman Tower, and was much patronised by the Eton boys. A niece helped her to run it, and when we rode over to Windsor to drop a note of invitation to dinner on one of the Canons (whose style and title—"The Most Honourable, the Reverend Canon the Marquess of Normanby"—never failed to entertain us) we invariably halted in the street outside the shop, and had our pockets stuffed with gratis candies by dear stout Besa, with her veined purple cheeks. To this familiar place, then, I betook myself—cold, weary, and discouraged—on that dismal evening. Besa threw up her stumpy hands in astonishment at the sight of me, alone, and at such an hour, but she brewed me a cup of hot chocolate with whipped cream, another Fullers' speciality, and held me in talk, munching her lovely cakes, while her niece slipped out on some unexplained errand. I didn't tell Besa *why* I had run away, I just said that I had left home. She examined the contents of the rush-bag, exclaiming at the thoroughness of my preparations, and presently led me through to her sitting-room at the back of the shop, where in her armchair in front of the fire I promptly fell asleep.

Meanwhile at home there was a great to-do—as I am afraid I had intended. Munna, our detested Polish governess, did not fuss very much when I failed to turn up for lessons at half-past three, but when tea-time came, and no sign of me, she went to my

Mother, and then enquiries were made. Quite fruitlessly at first; no one had seen me since I was sent to rest; and then that wretched business of hunting for a lost child began. The grounds were large, and contained two woods, in one of which was a small pond; I was always climbing trees, I might have fallen; and helped by the maids my Mother went all through the place in the gathering dusk, calling me by name, while the gardeners gruesomely dragged the pond. In vain. On her return to the house—in a despair which I can now imagine—a note was put into her hands: it was from Mr. Morton, the headmaster of Scaitcliffe; the young mistress had mentioned meeting me all alone by the Copper Horse, and he thought this so peculiar that he decided to report it. The next move seemed to be to notify the police of my disappearance, and a groom rode off to do so; on his way home he met the village telegraph-boy, whistling his way on foot across the Green, and hearing that there was a telegram for my Mother he very sensibly galloped back with it himself. The telegram was from Besa: that was the errand on which her niece had gone out—and my Mother, inexpressibly thankful, but still astounded, ordered round the brougham and drove off to Windsor to collect me.

I was still asleep when she arrived, and at first I hardly knew where I was or what was happening; but when I saw her face I realised for the first time what I had done. She kissed me and didn't scold me, but as I sat beside her in the brougham, cuddled up against the warmth and softness of her fur cloak in the dark, the pain and bewilderment in her voice as she asked me *why* I had run away told me, even more plainly than her face had done, exactly what sort of cruelty I had perpetrated. I stammered out, "The leading-rein!" over and over again; gradually, gently, she drew the whole silly story from me. But she never uttered a word of reproach, and all the time her arm was round me. It was an exquisite mercifulness which I have never forgotten—my Father's long sermonisings when at last I was back in my bed at home, his pathetic prayers for my soul's welfare meant nothing at all to me compared with that.

I was, of course, in fearful disgrace for a long time. I had to go on riding on the hated leading-rein, I was watched at every hour of the day; my pocket-money was stopped, my hoard of threepenny-bits taken away and, far worse, even my treasured scraps of jewellery were taken into custody. These were, of course, my Father's sanctions, and I think them as futile and unkind now as I thought them then; my Mother, though she was too loyal to say so, would never have done anything of the sort.

This difference between the moral climates in which our two parents lived coloured our whole youth. With my Mother, all was gentleness and ease; around my Father, in spite of his real merits, and his ardent love of his children, the air was always full of discipline or reprobation. This sprang mostly, I think, from his own character—which alas I inherit—but his upbringing and religious views had a good deal to do with it too. My two eldest sisters had never even been allowed to learn to dance; at Englefield Green, however, my Mother somehow coaxed him into allowing us to attend the great Mrs. Wordsworth's weekly dancing-classes held at Scaitcliffe. She gave all sorts of ingenious reasons: Cottie (myself) slouched, Grace was stout and clumsy, Helen needed exercise; it would be so nice for Jackie to see us there. Anyhow she triumphed, and we went—from which it was only a short step to our being allowed to go to the local children's parties at Christmas-time, attired in our best flounced frocks, to hop about in the polka and scoot across the floor in the "galoppe" and the "Washington Post." I was always a bad dancer, but I enjoyed these parties immensely; I was pretty enough to get troops of youthful partners—who probably danced as badly as I did, anyhow.

Nowhere did the contrast between the two parental climates show more clearly than in their treatment of Sunday. To my Father this was the Jewish Sabbath, "the day of rest": our normal games had to be put aside, as also our lay story-books—we might paint, but only texts, and read books solely of a religious character. When I was about thirteen I somehow got hold of Borrow's *The Bible in Spain*, that extremely un-edifying work; I reserved it for my Sunday reading, and triumphantly showed the title to my Father when he came round to see what we were at—poor man, he had never read it, and patted me on the head. (I was enraptured, much later in life, to learn that Robert Louis Stevenson had done exactly the same thing with *his* rigid parents, and got away with it.)

But my Mother made Sunday afternoons a pure delight to us when we were little, especially in summer. Yah and Patty, the second nurse, were sent out for the afternoon, and she took charge. If it was fine we went down to the small beech-wood where earlier in the year we had picked snowdrops, hundreds and hundreds of bunches of snowdrops to be sent up in hampers to the Homoeopathic Hospital and the Children's Hospital in Great Ormond Street; in this wood on a small steep mound stood those four tall poplars in which the starlings chattered on winter evenings, and slung between two of the great trunks was a hammock in which my Mother swung us in turns, hour after hour, while she sang the darkie songs that so re-created her childhood for me. Below the drooping boughs of the beeches, and beyond those same iron railings which I climbed when I ran away the small boys of the junior school at Beaumont were playing cricket; their white flannels gleamed in the sun, their happy cries came up to us. Sometimes the thought that (according to my Father) these cheerful little creatures would all go to Hell for such activities on a Sunday just pricked at my mind, but not for long; as I swung up and down, up and down, the soft delicious air reaching every part of my body through my thin frock, and those songs from far away in my ears, I was so happy, and so busy trying to imagine the notes of "de mocking-bird" and to visualise the darkies in the cornfield grieving for Massa, that I usually forgot all about Hell.

Winter Sunday afternoons were good too, under my Mother's auspices—but with her all was good. The place where she conducted her activities was called the Moorish room, because carved wooden harem-shutters enclosed the fireplace and panelled most of it. In the bow-window stood a heavy mock-Jacobean oak desk at which she dashed off her innumerable and rather illegible letters. There were a lovely squashy divan covered with sapphire-blue velvet inset with squares barbarously cut from silken Isfahan rugs, and many saddle-bag armchairs; we were allowed to pull out all the cushions, collect carriage-rugs from the oaken chests in the hall as roofs, and behind the divan create ships or royal dwellings or smugglers' caves at our pleasure. We constantly shouted out accounts of who we were and what we were doing, and received encouraging confirmation.

There was one other peculiar feature about our Sundays. Owing to my Father's sabbatical ideas all food had to be cold, except for tea and coffee, and potatoes baked in their jackets. A healthy child is normally rather greedy, and it is natural that food should figure in its memories; though physically fragile I was perfectly healthy and extremely greedy, and I remember our food at home vividly. As a period picture, a piece of social history, the side-table at breakfast-time on a Sunday morning at Ridgemead is perhaps worth recording. It stood in that bow-window with doors opening onto the terrace through which I escaped on my idiotic flight to Windsor; on it were ranged, week after week, the following: a ham, uncut; a glassed tongue mounted on a round spiked wooden slab, to ensure easy cutting; a *pâté de foie gras* six inches across; a lump of glazed pressed beef and, according to season, a pasty of either lamb, mutton, or venison. For luncheon and supper there were similar but larger cold joints, with cold birds and cold pies. I was actually responsible for introducing a new form of pie: after reading in Pepys about the "Turkey Pie" which he so relished I coaxed my Mother to have one made; Wattie, our stately Scottish cook, who could make anything, launched herself with enthusiasm on this unknown dish—it was quite as good as Pepys said, and thereafter we often had it. My Mother had almost as many cookery-books as books about flowers and birds; there was one called *Crefydd's Family Fare* of which I have a copy still, and I still follow its recipes for preserves—such as using red-currant juice in the making of strawberry jam so that it shall set.

The very word "pectin" was unknown in good Crefydd's day, still less could town-dwellers buy it in packets to set their jam with; but currants are full of pectin while strawberries contain almost none, and both my Mother and the Welshwoman knew empirically that to get firm jam, strawberries must be allied with currant-juice.

For children brought up in the country there always arises the question of their gardens, which by the parent's fault usually afford a record of dismal failure, in some root-robbed, over-shaded, hopeless corner. Our gardens were not in the least like that. My Mother sacrificed a considerable stretch of a twelve-foot border with a south aspect, the choicest spot in the garden, to our efforts; the ground was well dug and dunged, and paths laid out, giving us each three decent plots. Nor were we fobbed off with packets of seeds for annuals—the dull cornflower or the impossible mignonette, which drives every professional gardener mad; for our gardens we were given pansy-plants of good strains, and lovely little miniature roses; I remember with particular affection *Perle d'Or*, a tiny bush with intensely scented flowers of a coppery cream and tightly-curled buds—what rapture to cut sprays of this and put them in the nursery in the little sand-coloured Corfe-ware jars which we brought back from our annual visits to Dorset! As a result of this sensible treatment, Grace and I really worked at our gardens, and enjoyed them; we bought seeds with our own money, toiled at our weeding, and generally learned something of the joys and the disappointments of gardening. Always ambitious, I went so far as to construct a "hot-bed" with rather erratically-built brick walls; I carted the horse-manure for this along from the stables in my little wheel-barrow, and coaxed some glass to cover it out of Hastings, the head gardener. When this effort produced radishes for tea in March I was the proudest child in England. My brother Jack, however, was definitely allergic to gardening. He vaguely tended his plot with the pansies and rose-bushes in it, but the other two he simply dug up. One of the men on the place had a half-witted son called Mark, whom my Mother charitably caused to be employed as garden-boy; he was very little use of course, but he was a source of endless pleasurable occupation to us, because we used to bury him in Jack's garden. A grave would be dug with immense labour, and Mark bribed with our pocket-money to lie down in it, grinning, and be covered with earth up to his chin—when this ceremony had been gone through we had to fill the grave in again for fear of my Father. We called the poor cheerful youth "Mark, the Burial Lad."

Gardens belonged to nursery days; when Grace and I were old enough to begin regular lessons with Munna, our Protestant Polish governess, what with riding and French-speaking walks there was little time for them. But one phenomenon from Victorian nursery life continues to puzzle me—"naughtiness." Children to-day are never "naughty"; they have acidosis or fixations or something, and are treated for these complaints by doctors. But the English story-books of my early youth were full of the same misdeeds and punishments which defaced our childhood, showing that naughtiness, now non-existent, was common form in those days—and I wonder *why*. Looking back, I think that my own quite exceptional naughtiness ("Miss Cottie is more trouble than all the rest put together") was as much due to boredom and restlessness as anything else; always fizzing with surplus energy and dramatic ideas, when I either teased poor Jack to the point of murderous onslaughts on my person, or led him into crimes like climbing all round the outside of the house from balcony to balcony, transacting the gaps by ivy or rain-gutters, I may really have been trying to relieve the monotony of nursery life.

This monotony was itself mainly due, I now think, to the mentality of the Victorian nannie—so different to that of my own children's nurse, who battened on H. C. Cameron's works, and kept Lombroso's *The Delinquent Child* as a *livre de chevet*. What is more I have sometimes thought that those Victorian nannies, of little or no education, themselves suffered from boredom and magnified the tiny crimes of the infants under their care in order to have something to think about and talk about. I consider Yah, who lived in our household for over thirty years, and was head-nurse for half of them. She came when she was twelve, so she had not had much opportunity for schooling. Short and thick-set, she had a healthy red-and-white skin and masses of splendid golden hair worn in tight plaits round her head by day, which fell to her knees when she brushed it out in the mornings, stand-ing in her long-sleeved pink spencer in front of the chest of drawers in the night nursery. Jack and I were obsessed by this hair: we used to creep out of bed and steal across the floor to take the lovely crinkly shining stuff in our hands and hold it to our faces; but Yah, if she caught us at this, would turn round to deal us a proper welt with her hair-brush. She was completely conscientious, good at health according to the standards of her day, and she had an earthy peasant simplicity which was very wholesome. "Well, I used to like to go and see the lambs' tails cut off," I heard her tell my Father once when he asked her what she had enjoyed most on the Hampshire farm where she was brought up. She always talked broad 'Ampshire, as she called her home county; sometimes this led to confusion in our minds. When her corns didn't hurt and she was in consequence in a good mood, she would sing to us; our favourite song was one about the Crimea.

> Dark was the 'arbour, gaily song and story ran
> Round a British camp-fire, forty years ago;
> We were awaiting the word to fight old Inkerman,
> Burning to avenge past insults.
> Camped were we beside a friendly stream,
> Victory a theme, little did we dream
> That we were the victims of a Russian scheme
> To smash our brave defenders.
> But, it's—fighting with the Seventh Royal Fusiliers,
> The gay old Fusiliers, the gallant Fusiliers—
> Through deadly Russian shot and Cossack spears
> We carved our way to glory.

142

So sang Yah—whose peculiar sobriquet, by the way, represented some infant shot at her name Harriet—and we wondered a great deal about that arbour. Arbours were always dark and ivy-grown, so why *say* that it was dark? And how many of the gallant fusiliers could get inside it?—arbours in our experience were very small. Later I got Munna to read about the Battle of Inkerman to us, and then, informed, poked Grace up to ask Yah if the song really referred to the *h*arbour?

"Yes," said Yah complacently—"I *said* 'arbour."

To-day this song interests me for other reasons. It sounds like a typical piece of music-hall jingoism—but how came Yah to know the words and tune of a music-hall song?—since she came to Porters from the depths of 'Ampshire at the age of twelve. She said her father sang it, and I can only suppose that by, say, 1875 it had filtered down into the heart of rural England, to become a near folk-song.

We greatly enjoyed Yah's songs—so rare, and connoting benevolence: at one point we had a sandy-haired freckled Irish under-nurse who also sang to us, and about soldiers by a river.

Far far away, on the banks of the Nile
Three thousand miles from his own green isle,
A brave Irish soldier, a gallant dragoon,
Read his mother's letter, by the light of the moon.
He stole from the camp, that little note to read—
And the news that it brought him made his stout heart bleed;
For while Pat was fighting at the head of his band
His mother was evicted, by the laws of the land.
And the tears rolled down his sun-burnt cheeks
And dropped on the letter in his hand:
Then it's true, too true—
There's trouble in our native land.

I have succeeded in tracking down this typically sentimental piece—it is a Dublin street ballad, probably of the late eighteen-nineties. It confused us too, because the red-haired Eileen always sang "invicted": when we asked her what that meant she said it was something very cruel. We were familiar with the word "Invicta" in brass letters on the steam-roller which made the new road past our garden, and I envisaged the gallant dragoon's mother being crushed under one of these monstrous machines—I used to dream about it at night. (Perhaps I was not so far out, after all.)

But Yah's simplicity had its drawbacks. She loved us all; but with her, peasant-fashion, the male child came first, regardless of anything else. Grace could do little, I *no* right; but Jack, her own baby boy—had she not "taken him from the month"?—could do no wrong. This led to real injustice, a thing children recognise and hate, and I revenged myself for it by using my long tongue and deadly command of language on poor Jack, who really was not at fault, driving him nearly mad; or fled for comfort to my Mother in the Moorish room—a refuge from the storm, a shadow from the heat, when the blast of my private terrible ones, Yah and Munna, was as a storm against the wall. (If only one could write like the prophet Isaiah.)

But all in all we were very happy, especially out of doors. Yah's writ, owing to her corns, did not run much beyond the nursery—"I've got a bone in my leg" was her invariable excuse if we tried to get her to walk any distance. (We pitied her sincerely for this mysterious and disabling complaint.) Gardening with our little tools, hay-making with the men, birds'-nesting, watching the performances of ants with lumps of sugar or bits of chicken along the terrace walk, cutting pinks (to be sent, like the snowdrops, to hospitals) in the hot sun in the kitchen garden, or clipping lavender for the linen-room—in spring and summer at least, the greater part of every day was pure delight. I can remember now the ecstasy that pierced me, like an arrow, on spring mornings when through the dark-green bobbles that fringed the nursery blind I saw the sun brilliant on the sycamore and variegated ash outside the window, and knew that it was another fine day, in which to range about the garden, and hunt for bumble-bees' dark front-doors, or perhaps, in the afternoons, to be allowed to help my Mother pick the flowers for the table, or paint tar and beeswax on her conifers where the rabbits had gnawed them. When she was out in the garden on her own ploys, sometimes I heard her singing to herself; not darkie songs, or nursery rhymes, but old operatic airs—remembered no doubt from those evenings of singing, in Uncle Cud's house in New Orleans, so many years ago.

Chapter 10

*I*T *HAS* always been something of a mystery to me why my Mother with all her concern for our welfare should have been, occasionally, so unlucky in the matter of our governesses. Both she and my Father cared a great deal about education as such, he in particular holding that a good knowledge of modern languages brought in a higher personal dividend, in pleasure and interest, than almost any other possession; and they fairly hunted my two eldest sisters off to Oxford the moment they were out of the schoolroom. (A London season or any "worldly" wickedness of that sort was of course unthinkable, and I honestly believe that the idea of marrying off any of his six daughters simply never occurred to him. But they must be well educated.) There were certain limitations on my Mother's choice of governesses for us: they had got to be German, because Germans were always good Protestants, usually Lutherans, and perfectly moral; whereas Frenchwomen were probably immoral and almost certainly Catholics—which was worse. I can imagine now how these ideas must have struck my Mother, brought up in the Catholic, French-speaking, French-descended city of New Orleans; but she was a good wife, and obediently sought out German Protestants for her schoolrooms. Sometimes she was fortunate: the beloved Gerlach—Fräu as we called her—who came to Porters and started the Christmas-tree industry was one of those immensely able, highly cultivated German women, who finding little intellectual outlet at home came over to England to make their living by bringing up the female youth of Britain. They were something of a portent, those really first-class German governesses of the end of the last century; Fräu for instance taught my elder sisters to play the piano really well, and to speak and write French, German, and Italian as gentlewomen in those countries spoke and wrote them, besides causing them to read widely in all three literatures. These are not accomplishments with which girls to-day normally leave school, and I think the system of education at home was in many ways superior to girls' schools—while there were governesses of that calibre available, and large well-staffed homes in which they could be accommodated.

But all were not of that calibre. The woman who was teaching Jenny and Helen when Grace and I entered the schoolroom, a Protestant Polish Jewess, was not only incompetent as a teacher, but idle and ill-tempered as well; I think the reason that she lasted as long as she did, three or four years at least, was because my Father so highly approved of her—less on educational grounds than because she helped to maintain a Protestant Sailors' Home in Barcelona, that terrible papistical port, by collecting and selling stamps. We all had to collect stamps for Munna, and to help her to paste them onto sheets of paper in our lesson-time; in spite of this duplicity, she was far more emphatic than my Father on the certainty that the happy little Beaumont boys would go to Hell because they played cricket on Sundays. She was finally gotten rid of because she kicked my sister Helen so hard on her sturdy shin that she nearly broke her own ankle in the process, and had to have the Doctor; this could not be concealed from my Father, and Munna went—greatly, I am confident, to my Mother's relief. (I see it all so clearly now: that trying to hold the balance between the children's welfare and a husband's likes and dislikes—and the hatred of a change, and the desire for peace and continuity in the house.)

My Mother's next choice was unlucky too. She turned again to the family of dear Fräu, and engaged her younger sister, Miss

Marie Gerlach. But sisters are not necessarily alike, and Fräulein Marie was a flop. She had a square face the colour of decaying bone, surmounted by dark greasy plaits; she suffered from rheumatic joints, and sat at the schoolroom table massaging her knuckles with vaseline and sipping sour milk, which she stirred with a little wooden twiddler. The vaseline left greasy marks on our lesson-books and copy-books, and with a child's fastidiousness, this exasperated me; her breath always carried a taint from the sour milk, and altogether she inspired me with a profound physical repulsion—moreover she did not teach very well. Grace and I had begun to learn French with Fräu when we were five and seven respectively, sitting on a bearskin rug in front of the school-room fire while our sisters did their preparation, and spelling out the delicious unwonted syllables from the songs and rhymes in the *Éditions Haussmann*, with their charming illustrations; when we had learned a song by heart Fräu would rise from her chair and sweep across to the piano, her long full skirts, edged with fringed mohair braid, brushing the carpet, and make us sing it—"A la tour, prends garde," "Cadet Roussel," "Il était une bergère," or "Au clair de la lune"—all carefully bowdlerised for children's use. Lessons with Marie Gerlach had none of this benignant pleasantness; however she did not last even as long as Munna, and my poor Mother, on her next venture, really struck oil again, this time with that wonderful combination of snob, great scholar, and brilliant musician, Ida Bernhardt. Fräulein Bé, as we called her, came to us straight from the Asquith household, and like all governesses she lauded her late pupils to the skies, to emphasise the ineptitude of her current ones; but when in later life I met Lady Violet Bonham-Carter and Elisabeth Bibesco I recognised that for once a governess had not exaggerated.

Once in the schoolroom, even under Munna's inept rule, I was perfectly happy and very "good" in the Victorian sense of the word: i.e., I gave no trouble—which supports my private notion that what afflicted me in the nursery was mainly boredom. I could learn anything by heart at lightning speed, and remember it indefinitely; I adored these foreign languages—Miss Marie started us on German when I was eight or nine—and enjoyed nothing more than trying to speak with new tongues, or making translations into and out of them. In fact I was God's gift to any governess, and basked in the unwonted sunshine of approval. The one thing that I was always hopeless at was the piano, but I contrived to get much enjoyment even out of this—for hours and hours every week I was sent to practise on the Steinway grand in the drawing-room; this stood in a recess full of my Mother's books, and I used to prop *The Ceramic Art* or Mrs. Palliser's *Great Book of Lace* up in front of my music and read eagerly, keeping a faint tinkling going with one hand while I turned the pages with the other. This was quite enough for Munna, in the school-room away across the hall; she never came to look at me until the time was up. But when Fräulein Bernhardt arrived these readings came to an end; a superb musician herself, she very soon realised that I should never learn to play the piano, so I was taken off music and set to learning Latin instead, which suited me much better.

My translation from the nursery to the schoolroom must have been a great relief to my mother, with the sudden cessation of all those searing and uncivilised rows, even if I did still sometimes flee to her in the Moorish room. But she always had time for me, as she had for everybody. I compare my married life with hers, and wonder how she did it. I had only three children; she had nine, ranging in age and requirements from two daughters at Oxford down to babyhood. Of course she had all those troops of perfectly trained servants, but still I marvel. She helped us to pursue all our interests, however peculiar and inconvenient. My sister Cora, for example, having taken a First in Modern Languages at Oxford, went on to take another First in Science, and then settled down to do research work for Professor Poulton. One summer the task he set her was to study the variation in protective colouring of the pupa-cases of tortoiseshell butterflies:

he supplied the cardboard boxes, tinted in various shades from shell-pink to dark brown and black, for them to pupate in, we children collected the caterpillars in empty match-boxes and then, in those brown leather gloves which formed part of the Victorian child's outfit, gathered the nettles on which the crawling objects were to feed until such time as they reached the pupa stage, when Cora transferred them to the boxes to observe and note the results. But it was my Mother who produced the main essential for this experiment—two empty rooms with a South aspect, where caterpillars could crawl and creep at will, and gnaw away at nettles on a bare floor, leaving horrible little green rolls of excreta after them.

These efforts of my sister Cora's were of course "science," undertaken for a professor, and worth some trouble; but it was just the same when Jack and I wanted, quite pointlessly and un-scientifically, to check the travelling speed of tadpoles. After we had fished up the jellied spawn from that same pond in the daffodil wood which was dragged for me so lugubriously when I ran away, and had hatched out the swarming shadowy dot-and-comma creatures, a long glass bath, an inch-tape, and a stop-watch were produced for our idiotic purposes, and we were able to record the fact that tadpoles, if you agitate the water behind them with a twig, in fact swim very fast indeed.

When we went to Dorset in the summer she walked with us for miles, showing us birds and flowers; she took a boat round the Old Harry Rocks on a calm day so that we might see samphire and the original sea-kale, *Cakile maritima*, growing on the chalk cliffs. She swam with us, steady and powerful; she taught us to float, breathing deeply and regularly, with her muscles relaxed— we soon learned that if you stiffen you sink—and how to dive off the stern of a boat and climb in over the bows; on rough days she showed us the art of diving through breakers, the exact moment to pierce the curved glassy wall before the poised crest falls in a tumbling confusion which bowls the swimmer over, leaving him battered and exhausted. All these things she did herself, and we followed her example; but when she did them, including the very considerable muscular feat of heaving one's body over the bows and into a rowing-boat, she was a stout heavy woman approaching fifty. She was really very athletic.

My Mother encouraged not only such pursuits as racing tad-poles and swimming but also the making of friends, a thing at which she herself excelled. At home everyone brought their friends to stay, for weeks at a time. Cora and Tiss—so Therese came to be called; as a family we were inveterate about nick-names—brought their fellow-students from Lady Margaret Hall at Oxford: Nellie Hodgkin, the Quaker historian's daughter; Katharine Thicknesse; Lettice Verney from Claydon. As a very small girl indeed my sister Cora took me to stay at Claydon for a week-end, and on the Sunday morning I was led into a room where a very old lady, with a ravaged, majestically intelligent face lay on a sofa; she took me by the hand, and spoke kindly to me. This was Miss Florence Nightingale; the hand that writes these words has touched the hand of the Lady with the Lamp.

My brother Harry of course brought his friends from Win-chester too: Jack White, the Field-Marshal's son—who got into even more trouble at school than Harry did himself—and many more, of whom I remember best Cecil Palmer, because he used to maintain so stoutly that Huntley & Palmers never advertised, because they didn't need to; their biscuits advertised themselves. Also, he was much nicer to me than most big schoolboys are to the little sisters of their friends. In all these young creatures and their affairs my Mother took the liveliest interest; they in their turn developed a strong affection for her, many corresponding with her till her death. She would sit, placid and benign, in the drawing-room in the evenings among the soft blurred blue-grey cretonnes and the masses of flowers of her own arranging: in the Easter holidays lilac and apple-blossom in burnished copper jars, in which they look so lovely, and flowering cherry in polished brass ones—while the tide of talk and laughter and nonsense flowed about her.

Presently music usually flowed too. All my four elder sisters sang, but Cora's voice was outstanding for purity and sweetness, while Helen's was practically a true operatic soprano, of great power and range. I recall the drawing-room as seeming full, night after night, of young ladies in long evening frocks, clustered round the piano and singing from white throats above white shoulders, while young gentlemen, also in full evening dress, turned the pages for my sister Cora, who accompanied everyone with her pretty hands, gradually becoming battered from hockey at college. Donald Tovey often came to dine, with his aunt Miss Weisse, whose famous school was only a mile and a half away across the Green, and after dinner he would by her be driven to the piano to play to us, classical music or some of his own compositions; tall, loosely built, he always looked distraught with shyness as he made his way across the room, more often than not knocking into the furniture—but once at the keyboard all shyness was lost. There was a firm, cool, *scholarly* quality about his playing, however violent the music, which even then gave me a distaste for more lush interpretations. When the guests left, the masterly crashing of Tovey's chords still in our ears, we could hear his aunt's voice in the hall, reminding him to put on his overshoes.

Another person who played and sang to and with us continually was Dr. F. E. Hutchinson, the biographer of George Herbert; as a young man he was chaplain at Cooper's Hill College, just across the road from our house. Englefield Green was a curious mixture of the semi-suburban and the semi-academic: besides Cooper's Hill, a place devoted mainly to training young men for the Indian Civil Service, there was Holloway College, built out of pills and ointment; both institutions of course had their professorial staff. The Cooper's Hill professors lived in what the country-people called "The Villas," a row of stuccoed semi-detached houses built for their accommodation in the college grounds:

there dwelt among others Professor Marshall Ward, who composed—and sang—amusing settings to Lear's Nonsense Rhymes; Frank Kingdon Ward, his son, was a childhood playmate of ours; till she died, he always came to visit my Mother between his plant-collecting trips to Assam and the Himalayas. But it was F. E. Hutchinson who was the great delight of our childhood. Small, sandy, spectacled, with a rather monkeyfied face which gave him something of the air of a clerical chimpanzee, he would join Jack and me in our more lunatic pastimes, condemned by all other grown-ups, like sliding down off half-built hayricks or falling flat on our faces, our bodies held rigid, on the top of them. He helped my Mother to teach us to skate during the great frosts of the late nineties, when Virginia Water, the whole winding four miles of it, was frozen over for weeks on end. We used to drive there in the waggonette, our skating-boots stuffed with hot potatoes baked in their jackets which we transferred to our normal boots when we changed on the bank, and then ate on the drive home; on the ice we staggered about, holding on to the backs of kitchen chairs—my Mother, tall and stately, in a mantle of sable-tails down to her knees, would sweep round us in graceful circles, and then gather one or other of us up from our chairs to wheel away with her, arms crossed, in the Dutch Roll, to give us the feel of the outside edge. But F. E. H. would always come to look after those left behind, and instruct them himself —not tall, not stately, but uncommonly good on the ice—and beguile us with neat little jokes in his warm eager crackling voice when we fell down.

His singing voice was small and slightly crackling too, and rather harsh, but his performance had the same scholarly quality as Donald Tovey's playing, and was immensely pleasing. He introduced us to Arthur Somervell's settings of the songs from Tennyson's "Maud," which everyone was presently singing; but also to the more robust and grim humours of mediaeval ballads, like "Diverus and Lazarus"—I can see him at the piano now, his

eyes gleaming with amusement and satisfaction behind his thick
lenses as he mouthed out:

> Rise up, rise up, Brother Diverus,
> Rise up and come with me—
> There's a place prepared for you in Hell
> To sit upon a serpent's knee!

My Mother loved all this music, and it was she, primarily, who
drew these people to the house, though the younger ones often
made friends subsequently with my older sisters; my Father
enjoyed guests when they came, but had not the time to do
anything about bringing them. His contribution to our social life
consisted mainly of the people connected with his business—some
of them rather interesting—of whom we shall hear more presently.
But he was a genial host and a good if controversial talker, and
liked nothing better than to see his table spread—with an
abundance of plain but delicious food—for twenty or thirty
people. He liked music too, if it had tunes which he could remember, and much of what my sisters sang had this satisfactory quality.
I don't know how far he appreciated their *Lieder*: Schubert and
Brahms, the northern, ice-cold melodies of Grieg, and the wistful
lyricism of Franz—for German was not one of his languages.
But he had sung enough himself to enjoy singing, and he loved
the Mendelssohn duets, which like everyone else at that date my
sisters sang endlessly. Making one's own music had much to
recommend it, if the performers were sincere and careful—and
one could choose what should be sung. In our drawing-room my
Father, drawn by the sound of singing from his evening perusal
of *The Westminster Gazette* in the Moorish room, could stroll in
and ask for one of Arthur Somervell's settings to Blake's *Songs
of Innocence*—"Little Lamb, Who Made Thee?" or "How Sweet
Is the Shepherd's Sweet Lot"; my Mother, who retained her
early taste for French music, would suggest César Franck's
Mariage des Roses, or something of Gounod or Fauré—though
neither she nor I liked the rather bogus *fin-de-siècle* melancholy

of Hahn's "Chansons grises." Around the turn of the century people began to sing also the eighteenth-century *Bergerettes*, with their delightful, rather insincere affectation of country life and innocence, which brought the Petit Trianon to life in the mind; like everyone else my sisters sang these, and *Plaisir d'amour* too, the song which Marie Antoinette used to sing with Count Fersen. The Petit Trianon with a vengeance!

> *Plaisir d'amour ne dure qu'un moment*
> *Chagrin d'amour dure toute la vie.*

So love, the unguessed-at, could alter and fail and bring this delicate distress, we thought, listening in a charmed wonder, while across the lawn the light faded behind a line of trees as monumental as a Piranesi drawing.

There were many more English songs, Victorian in feeling if not in date, which I used to hear as I looked out on that darkling garden with the line of beeches beyond, beside the "Maud" lyrics, in which every young woman thought to recognise herself in Maud on a Sunday:

> *She came to the village church,*
> *And sat by a pillar alone;*
> *An angel watching an urn*
> *Wept over her, carved in stone;*
> *And once, but once, she lifted her eyes,*
> *And suddenly, sweetly, strangely blushed*
> *To find they were met by my own.*

They were really very lovely—first-class second-class music—those late nineteenth-century songs, all in the English-romantic tradition, strangely clear and pure. Somervell did a wonderful cycle called *Love in Springtime*, mainly to words by Tennyson and Christina Rossetti. And in that room, during those evenings of singing, there first began for me something of immeasurable importance in my life: the close association between music and visual and emotional experience which is the special privilege of the non-musical. When Helen sang—

A perfect sunlight, on rustling
forest-tips,

I saw again what I had seen that very afternoon as we paused to rest our horses on some high point in Windsor Great Park, a breeze-shaken sea of tree-tops under a summer sun—and song and sight became one for me, each enhancing the other. Sometimes words and music together brought arrowy intimations of things further outside a youthful experience even than love.

Underneath the growing grass
Underneath the living flowers
Deeper than the sound of showers
There we shall not count the hours
By the shadows, as they pass.

Youth and health shall be but vain,
Beauty reckoned of no worth.
There a very little girth
Can hold what once the earth
Seemed too narrow to contain.

As Helen's voice dropped on the last notes I chilled—sitting there in a soft chair in a pleasant room full of happy people—with an icy recognition of what the grave meant, that could engulf youth and beauty and genius.

These family friendships with the people who came to the house, and played and sang ought, I realise, to have been the main feature of that period of my life: the music should have been incidental to the personal relationships. In fact those personal relationships were incidental to the music, which was making its first, almost overwhelming impact on me. If there was an exception to this it was F. E. H.—"Little Hutch," as my Father used to call him. It was he who introduced me, when I was barely twelve, to S. Francis; he remarked to me one evening in the drawing-room, as simply and casually as if he were talking of two people he knew well—"Of all the human beings who have ever lived, I think S. Francis was *most* like Christ." This impressed me deeply, it was so very different to Spurgeon's sermons and my Father's whole treatment of religion; and on my next list of birthday or Christmas wishes I put down *The Little Flowers of S. Francis of Assisi*. In fact F. E. H. did something very important for me; though I did not realise it at the time he was, through all those years of my childhood and early girlhood, affording me my first glimpse of *to eu zén*—the good life, as the best Christians live it. Years later, when he was Chaplain of All Souls, one of my daughters boarded with him and his wife in Oxford, and she wrote of this to me, adding—"and it fills one with an indescribable sense of delight and reassurance." When his Oxford friends came to stay with him at Cooper's Hill it was an understood thing that he should bring them to tea or dinner, or to join us in our river-picnics—when he always wore his little pink Leander blazer, which we admired enormously.

It must seem surprising that children of twelve and thirteen should have met all these people at dinner. The reason lay in another of my Father's idiosyncrasies. He was the most intensely "family" man that ever lived, and since he left the house every morning at eight-thirty he insisted that all his children who were capable of walking up-and-downstairs should be present at the evening meal as well as at breakfast, so that he might see more of them. Dinner was accordingly put at the uncompromising hour of six-thirty, and this went for dinner-parties as well as for daily life. I realise now the immense social problems presented to my Mother by having to arrange the seating for a company which included six daughters, ranging in age from twenty-five to nine! —but I also now recognise how valuable this very peculiar form of entertainment was to us younger ones, since it allowed us to listen to the table-talk of intelligent adults, which is really one of the most liberal forms of education. And some of these adults were very intelligent indeed. Besides the Cooper's Hill professors there was Arthur Shipley, afterwards Master of Christ's at Cambridge, rosy and rotund, with his beguiling lisp; Dr. Ginsburg, the Sanscrit scholar, used to discuss Aryan roots with old Archdeacon Baly, Sir George White's father-in-law, and in spite of my Father's religious views Father Bampton, then the head of Beaumont, was a frequent and ever-welcome guest. Small, neat, courteous, he made himself enormously acceptable by his good temper and his ever-ready wit. *"You burnt Tyndale!"* Dr. Ginsburg thundered one evening when the talk had turned on Tyndale's Bible. In a flash—

"You did something very unpleasant to Our Lord Jesus Christ," the little Jesuit responded mildly to the Jewish scholar—"But our Heavenly Father loves you all the same, exactly as He loves us!"

Such episodes enthralled me; as I grew older, and had a room of my own, I used to write down any parts of the conversation that had particularly interested me when I went to bed, with descriptions of the speakers and their gestures and expressions, modelling myself in this as far as possible on *Wuthering Heights* and *Jane Eyre*, my two favourite books—which I read over and over again, year after year and often twice a year.

It must seem even more surprising that people should have been willing to come and dine at such an uncompromising hour as six-thirty, and sit among a bevy of children. Again, I think this was largely due to my Mother—though my older sisters were very pretty and lively and intelligent; her wonderful food probably came into it to some extent, and in summer at least there were other features, unusual but amusing. When the hay was cut and carried on the stretch of rough grass beyond the lawn a big circle was carefully left just where one could best see Windsor Castle through the gap in Beaumont's Beech Walk, with banks built high enough to lean back against, and a low sofa-height seat of hay all round the inside; on fine evenings we often left the dining-room by the french windows, strolled across the lawn, and went to take coffee in the squashy, sweet-smelling hay-circle.

Sometimes my Father would insist that one of those delicious ices of my Mother's should be served out there as well; we sat on while the light slowly faded, and bats squeaked and flitted overhead, listening to the night-jars churring in and out of the four poplars, till someone said that the dew was beginning to fall, and we trailed back across the lawn again and into the drawing-room —through more french windows—and my sisters sang, and Schubert and Grieg drowned the night-jars.

Old Archdeacon Baly had the cure of the small Chapel Royal in Windsor Great Park; he had a noble white beard and smoked cheroots, and exhaled a sort of vague benevolence; he used to express balanced opinions in carefully measured phrases—of his invalid wife's pet dog, a very blatant mongrel, he said when I asked its name—"We call him Fitz, because he is of doubtful birth." Whenever we could we escaped from the fundamentalist rigours of the hideous church in Englefield Green, St. Jude's, by walking a couple of miles to the Park Chapel, where the dear old Archdeacon preached learned, beautifully expressed sermons about nothing very much, and where we could watch Royalty, Prince and Princess Christian from Cumberland Lodge, in an adjoining pew.

But the sight of Royalty was a familiar feature of my childhood, with Windsor only four miles away. We could tell from the drawing-room windows whether the Sovereign was in residence or not by the presence or absence of the Royal Standard, floating above the Castle from the Round Tower, and Queen Victoria herself we knew by sight better than many of our neighbours. She liked driving all about the country-side in an open victoria with a single outrider, and on our walks or rides we constantly encountered the tiny old lady huddled up in one corner of the carriage, with her pouched severe face under the widow's bonnet, and wearing round her shoulders a little white woollen cape very like our own flannel petticoats—in fact, for a long time I thought it *was* a flannel petticoat that she wore! But then Queens could wear anything they liked, of course. On the box sat her Scottish familiar, John Brown, muffled in a thick scarf and wearing a most vinegarish expression; usually the old Queen looked nearly as sour as her retainer, but sometimes, when we laboriously manœuvered our horses onto the grass verge and bowed deeply over their withers, she would smile benevolently at us. And once the White girls caused her to laugh outright, a thing not usual with that sad old ruler in the late nineties. May and Gladys, Sir George White's daughters, spent much of their time with their grandfather Archdeacon Baly, and were close friends of my sister Helen and my sister Grace; all four girls walked together with their respective governesses. Theirs, who was French and whom they called Zella, was nearly as tedious as, but much less vicious than, our Polish Munna—Munna and Zella completed, in our private *argot*, the word Mademoiselle. But to return to Queen Victoria. The young Whites, like the young Sanderses, used often to drive about in that intensely period vehicle a donkey-cart—then generally known, how rightly, as a governess-cart—and on one particular occasion May, Gladys, and Zella, May at the reins, met in this conveyance the old Queen, outrider, John Brown and all. The Baly donkey was excessively stubborn, and when May tried to haul him to one side of the narrow road, he slewed round and stood four-square across it, blocking the way. Poor May, scarlet with embarrassment, tugged and beat at him in vain; Zella exhorted her in a torrent of futile French; Gladys laughed irrepressibly. The Queen's carriage perforce came to a halt; the stately outrider dismounted and took a hand at pulling the donkey himself, while the old Queen peered out to see what was happening—when she saw the nature of the obstruction she laughed quite as heartily as Gladys, and made John Brown get down and help to pull the donkey.

Those last years of Queen Victoria's life were overshadowed by the Boer War; for my Mother herself it brought fresh complications. Like many Liberals my Father was an ardent pro-Boer; in his case his Evangelicalism probably had something to do with this, certainly President Kruger was soon ranged alongside Mr.

Gladstone and General Booth (of the Salvation Army) in his private Pantheon, with W. T. Stead, who "plugged" the Boer cause ceaselessly in his magazine *The Review of Reviews*, as a runner-up. Feeling ran very high in England during those years, far higher than in the other two wars of my lifetime; to be a pro-Boer was practically to be a traitor in most people's eyes. My Father made no secret of his opinions; indeed he trumpeted them abroad, especially at his own dinner-table. This was extremely unpopular. Harry was still at Winchester, and we had no immediate relations in the Army ourselves, but for our neighbours it was otherwise—soon half the families in the village had someone "at the war." Arthur Shipley's brother joined the C.I.V. and went out with the first draft; Jack White, still practically a schoolboy, secured a commission and went off; his Father was already holding a command in South Africa. "Jingoism" was rampant (the word derives from the old music-hall song of 1878: "We don't want to fight, but by Jingo if we do, We've got the ships, we've got the men, and we've got the money too!") and was loudly condemned by my Father; nevertheless the maids and grooms were perpetually singing or whistling Kipling's words, set to a vigorous tune—

Cook's son, duke's son, son of a belted Earl,
(Fifty thousand horse and foot, going to Table Bay)
Each of them doing his country's work, and who's to look
     after the girl?
Pass the hat, for your credit's sake, and pay, pay, PAY!

This is not, I know, how the words are printed in the book, but it is how the country-people sang them at the time—they liked the horse and foot, and couldn't be bothered with the Lambeth publican.

But as the months and then the years of the conflict dragged on, and the losses grew, bewilderment and frustration at the unexpected length and difficulty of this war against an untrained civilian enemy—as far as the general public was concerned so light-heartedly embarked upon—increased, and the bitterness grew in proportion. Most people continued to come to the house, I think principally for my Mother's sake; but she had always to be steering the conversation away from controversy, or even making a clatter over helping herself to a dish when something particularly outrageous was said. It must all have been quite familiar to her—those years of the Civil War in New England held much the same situation; but none of her own younger children were as innocently tactful as little Robbie with his "Hurrah for the Yankees!" On the contrary, we were violently partisan, following the campaign in the *Daily Graphic* and on our school-room atlas; the Tugela and Modder rivers became familiar names, the Boer generals our current heroes; forgetting the War of Independence we turned to fighting out their battles in the woods and shrubberies. I was usually cast for the part of De Wet because I was the fleetest of foot, and could stage his astonishing get-aways and pouncing return attacks.

In this matter of partisanship I was far the worst, and caused a good deal of trouble. With my peculiar verbal memory I instantly mastered the more pithy of the anti-English verses which my Father read aloud to us from *The Review of Reviews*, and would recite them to our small acquaintances, especially at those dancing-classes at Scaitcliffe. This made things very hard for poor Jack, who was then a weekly boarder, coming home only for Sundays. He was a stoutly built, slow-spoken, rather reserved little boy; uncommonly sensible, except when I led him astray, and usually very calm—though with a formidable strength when roused, as I knew to my cost when I teased him past bearing. But for most of the war years he was one of the youngest in the school, and every boy's hand was against him. It was all very well for us, cantering past the football-ground to derisive shouts of "There go the Boer cavalry!" or for me quoting Mr. Stead's epigrams once a week at the dancing-class, and getting my sash pulled undone for my pains; for Jack, who from Monday to Saturday could not escape persecution, night or day, it was no joke. But he never once recanted his opinions, and his steadfastness won the admiration of all the masters. (His little tormentors could not of course foresee that within a few days of his twenty-third birthday in 1915 he would fall in the first gas attack at St. Julien, where he was fighting with the First Canadian Division.)

All this was torture to my Mother, who heard about it not from her stubborn silent little son, but from his headmaster, who was one of her many devoted slaves. But—perhaps remembering her own hard school-days in New England nearly forty years before, in another war where feeling was very bitter—she decided that unless his health suffered he had better stick it out; if he did, she said, it would stand him in good stead all his life. He stuck it out all right, but she, too, could not foresee how short that life was to be.

It was not only my reckless tongue which caused trouble; I did things, too. I learned, doubtless from the *Daily Graphic*, exactly what the make-up and colours of the Boer flag were, and coaxed out of Miss Copus, the sewing-maid, lengths of material in the appropriate green, white, brown, and so on, and then got her to stitch them together. Having thus procured an unmistakable Boer flag I went off to the wood with my hatchet and chopped down a ten-foot ash-sapling; this I trimmed, and with hammer and tacks literally nailed my colours to the mast; I got a length of wire from the tool-shed, and proceeded to climb the tallest tree in a belt of young larch which sheltered the kitchen-garden on the North, in full view of the road, and made my flag-pole fast to the top of the trunk. When I scrambled down and went to look at it from the garden it floated out, rather crookedly but in my opinion most satisfactorily, well clear of the green larch-tops. This performance produced a prompt and markedly unfavourable reaction; the tradesmen's boys stood and booed, people complained to the police, and presently an embarrassed but shocked constable arrived at the house to insist that it must be taken down at once. My Mother guessed who was responsible; she sent for Hastings to have it removed, but this was easier said than done, since I was so thin and light that no one else on the place could climb anywhere near high enough to reach it. So I was summoned, at last rather frightened by all the fuss and by the presence of the policeman, so large and blue and solid, and made to take the offending object down myself.

Why my Mother did not lose her temper with me on that and on many other occasions I cannot think, but she didn't—I was not punished or scolded at all. But her very restraint had the effect of making me realise that I had been an even bigger fool than usual, and the exhilaration of the grooms and under-gardeners at this latest example of "Miss Cottie's goings-on" failed to console me.

A rather odd situation arose for us during the Boer War from the occasional presence of the two White daughters in our midst. They stayed at Ridgemead more than once, but I remember particularly the last days of the year 1899, when Sir George, their Father, was being besieged by the Boers in Ladysmith, and all England was distracted by fears for his safety and that of his troops. Every morning at prayers after breakfast in the dining-room during that visit, May and Gladys, kneeling before their chairs, listened to my Father praying fervently, extempore, for the success of the Boer arms—this luckily amused them enormously, and they usually managed to stifle their irrepressible giggles fairly well.

May and Gladys White brought us glimpses of a larger world than our own; they could recount stories of India, where their father had been Commander-in-Chief, of a kind much more to our taste than that tiresome book, *Little Henry and His Bearer*—concerning Vice-regal garden-parties and social doings in Simla, and above all about their father's absentmindedness. Sir George was noted for this trait and his children, who adored him, revelled in the consternation it sometimes caused. One of their favourite tales concerned a certain official posted in a very hot station, who had a lively frivolous wife; she always left him there alone in summer, to pass "the hot weather" herself among the gaieties of Simla; Sir George disapproved. The unfortunate official presently died; his widow, abandoning her weeds with unusual speed, appeared at Simla as before, dressed in bright colours, and on a warm evening came sailing up to the C.-in-C., waving her fan.

"Oh, Sir George, terribly hot to-night, isn't it?"

Sir George had completely forgotten that the unhappy man was dead, and growled repressively:

"Nothing to where your poor husband is grilling now."

May White smoked, something excessively daring in those days, and my sister Helen followed suit; I used to keep watch for them as they strolled up and down by the high laurel hedge at the far end of the lawn on summer evenings, and fly to give warning of the approach of elders. May White was so beautiful, with her flawless milk-and-wildrose skin, her big expressive mouth, her greenish eyes and eyebrows and her mass of pale-gold hair. Her clothes and Gladys's, but especially hers, were far more fashionable than ours. But how, I wonder now, did little country-bred girls of nine or ten recognise what was fashionable and what was not? Anyhow we did recognise fashion when we saw it—perhaps helped by the constant incursions of Aunt Abby and Aunt Sallie T., usually in mourning, but even their crape forged by Worth. My Mother loved May and Gladys dearly; she enjoyed having them in the house, and appreciated their cheerful amusement at my Father's pro-Boer sentiments—this was something in accordance with her own high and elegant scale of values.

That particular visit of theirs covered the opening of the twentieth century—according to the German Emperor, and many more; others, including my Father, held that the new century would only open on the last stroke of twelve on December the 31st, 1900. Arguments about this were endless, but for us and for the Whites my sister Cora's word was law; she plumped for December the 31st, 1899, and organised our celebrations after my Father had stumped off to bed at ten, pronouncing firmly that there was to be no "nonsense" that night. We assembled at half-past eleven in Tiss's big bedroom on the top floor, because Cora's was above our parents' room; there we drank cocoa round a blazing fire, and watched the hands of the little clock on the mantelpiece creep nearer and nearer to the hour of twelve—I found time to envy the lovely golden pig-tails dangling down over May and Gladys's bright dressing-gowns. (Grace and I still wore our hair cropped like little boys, because my Father had a theory that this made it grow thick later in life—it worked for some of us but not for all.) A minute before the hour Tiss threw open the windows, saying to us little ones, with a thoroughly Day sense of the dramatic—

"Listen! This is the beginning of a new century; you will never live to see the end of it."

Her words sent a shivering sense of time and change and fate running cold down my spine. I have never in my life been so excited. I ran to a window and leaned out into the darkness, snuffing the cold scentless air of a winter's night, and waiting for this strange and wonderful thing, a new century, to begin. After a pause that seemed like eternity itself—and the beginning of a fresh century somehow brought eternity very close—on the stroke of midnight the bells began to peal from all the churches round about: up from Old Windsor and Datchet, across the Green from the village, near and clear from Beaumont Chapel just below the garden fence, more faintly from Egham down under the hill and Wraysbury away across the Thames—the air was full of the sound of bells. When it died away we could just hear, in the distance, a thin sound of cheering. They little knew, those good Surrey yokels, issuing from the pubs full of beery and unquestioning optimism, what sort of a century it was that they were greeting with cheers. Nor did we; we kissed one another, and exchanged laughing good wishes for a "happy century," and stole away to bed. I lay awake for a long time that night, hugging a vague sense of wealth—historical wealth—because I had been awake and heard those bells, and seen a new century begin.

Chapter 11

*I*T WAS during our ten years at Ridgemead, that ugly and well-loved house, that "going abroad," such a wonderful and exciting thing, began for Grace, Jack and myself. Our first trip was to Paris in 1900, to see the Exposition Universelle; my Father took us all. I remember almost nothing of the Exhibition, but Paris I loved. We had an apartment up near the Etoile, and used to eat our unwonted breakfasts of coffee and croissants and curled shells of sweet butter out on the balcony of the tall, grey, severe house, looking at lilacs and chestnut-trees in bloom against the astonishing background, to our country-bred eyes, of the grey and severe walls of other tall houses, with high windows and narrow wooden shutters. And I remember with an intensity which astonishes me now the broad avenues full of chestnuts in flower, and the clear *high* quality of the light; the restaurants overhanging the Seine or in the Bois de Boulogne, where at night lamps were reflected in water or shone between the dark stately shapes of trees; and the heavenly, heavenly taste of foreign food. I greedily demanded second helpings of all the dishes with the richer and more exotic sauces, which pleased my Father very much— though he consistently refused to eat "made dishes" at home he loved continental cooking abroad, and was delighted with my *gourmandise.* My Mother smiled tolerantly on us both.

After Paris came Switzerland. I developed "glands," and had to have an operation for them; Fräulein Bé declared that Switzerland

167

was the one place to cure glands—Maudie Cassel, an earlier pupil
of hers, had been cured of glands by living, it seemed, on top of
the Furka Pass for months; we gathered that Sir Ernest Cassel
had built a sort of mountain palace on those high Alpine pastures
for the purpose. My Mother sent to Hatchard's for a Baedeker
and began to read out to us descriptions of various resorts which
caught her fancy. I wanted to go to the Eggishorn, because I had
bought Tyndall's *The Glaciers of the Alps* in the Everyman Edition a year or so before, and had conceived an ardent desire to
see those blocks of ice, fallen off the Aletsch Glacier, floating
about in the Märjelen-See among meadows starred with gentians
—this sounded to me one of the most wonderful conjunctions in
nature, as indeed it is. But we were not as rich as Sir Ernest Cassel
—who in any case had only one child, not nine—nor as ambitious
as Fräulein Bé; to her and my disgust Brunnen on the Lake of
Lucerne was decided on, and to Brunnen we went.

I think there must always be some particular magic about a
first visit to the Alps, even for people not born, as I was, with
that inexplicable craving for heights and getting to the top of
heights. Trees, church-towers, the walls of old castles, hills—
no matter what the object I was never satisfied till I had reached
the top of it. But mountains surpassed everything else in this
respect. One of our rather dull brown geography books, mostly
filled with lists of exports and imports, nevertheless contained the
inspiring information that anything over a thousand feet high
counted as a mountain, and I was constantly pestering my Mother
about the heights in feet of the downs in Sussex and Dorset,
hoping that one of them would qualify for mountainhood—alas,
none did. Why do some children have these spontaneous desires
—unprompted, unencouraged? Anyhow I had them, and that first
summer in Switzerland was for me "all a wonder and a wild
desire," although because of that operation for glands my activities
were rather restricted.

Brunnen, in spite of Fräulein Bé's contempt, was a charming
introduction to the Alps. True there were no glaciers, and only

one very modest snow-capped peak, the Uri-Rothstock; but this bore on its crest true perpetual snow, which glittered with snow's special dazzle under the mid-day sun. The small resort stands at one angle of Lucerne's many-angled lake; looking up towards Flüelen, where William Tell shot the apple off his small son's head, looking down towards Gersau and Lucerne; it lies also at a confluence of valleys—the Muottathal running up between high grey mountain walls to the east and another, more open, passing northwards behind the Rigi to the Lake of Zug; where they meet, a flat riverine plain expands, in which stands the little mediaeval town of Schwyz, full of old timbered houses; the whole is dominated by the twin peaks of the Grosse and Kleine Mythen, blunt-headed spears of pink rock for all the world like two giant spear-heads from the Stone Age. The plain is full of light and open to all the sun, but Brunnen is always airy from the draughts drawing up or down the converging valleys and the two arms of the lake.

Our quarters here were peculiar and amusing. We stayed at the Hôtel Eden, owned by the Schoeck-Fassbind family; it was very full and my Mother, Grace, and I had to be accommodated in Herr Schoeck's studio, a huge room on the top floor with a sky-light, and stuffed birds and animals everywhere, and the artist's rather intimidatingly dramatic canvases on walls and easels. Beds and washstands had been summarily interposed among these startling objects, making them somehow even more startling; but we were perfectly comfortable, and the views up and down the lake from the huge windows more than compensated for going to sleep with a stuffed lammergeier with outstretched wings suspended from the ceiling above one's head. In one respect the Eden was ideal from my Mother's point of view. After the disaster at that fête in Paris, when several of her acquaintances were burned to death, she had developed a horror of fire, and always travelled with a strange contraption which could be strapped to the feet of a heavy bed or wardrobe; to it was attached a coil of knotted rope down which to make a get-away if trapped by the flames. But the Hôtel Eden was built right against the mountain, so that while from the front it appeared to be six or seven stories high, each floor had an exit at ground level at the back—and my poor Mother was able to pack away her fire-escape in its canvas case and forget about it.

The Schoecks were a delightful family, cultivated and musical, and my Mother in the easy fashion that was natural to her promptly made friends with them; very soon we were spending our Sunday evenings in their private rooms, listening to music and being regaled with coffee and cakes. There were at least three sons at home for the holidays from the University at Zürich, and a charming niece, Mathilde, who acted as *Bureau-Fräulein*; all these young people, their friends and even their parents played some instrument or other, and their pleasant heavily furnished sitting-room was the scene of small private concerts, week after week. Othmar Schoeck—as I remember him the youngest and the stockiest of the three brothers—played the piano with something of the same cool, scholarly quality as did Donald Tovey; it was no great surprise to me to learn, thirty years later, that he had become a well-known composer.

My own entertainment was one of my Mother's chief problems that first summer in Switzerland. I was not considered strong enough to join my sisters in the long mountain expeditions which they undertook four or five days a week, but I was fizzing with activity and energy, and had to be occupied somehow. My Mother solved it with one of her usual uninhibited and brilliant organisations. In no time at all she had established the fact that the hall porter in the Eden had a large flock of girls and boys, who spent their summers in a most agreeable and lucrative fashion, climbing the local hills to pick edelweiss and alpenrosen, the rose-red aromatically-scented dwarf rhododendron of the Alps, and then selling them to the trippers off the lake steamers from Lucerne. To these youngsters I was forthwith attached, not at first for their all-day flower-gathering expeditions, but to help with the bunching and selling. Even for this they made early starts, at 6 A.M. or thereabouts, so when I went to bed in the studio I used to tie a string round my ankle with a shoe-horn attached to the further end, which I left dangling out of the window; on this the porter's children tugged till I woke, dressed in a flash, and ran down to join them. The flowers which they had gathered they always cached for the night in the still pools of the Muotta, off the main stream racing grey-green in its broad bed of pale stones, set with clumps of wild anchusa which glowed like blue fire in the early sunlight against that white background; barefoot, the lot of us, we pattered out to the pools and sat down on the stones, still chilly with dew, to tie the cherry-pink and silver flowers into little bunches which we arranged on wooden trays and left in a patch of shade while we ran across to the porter's house in the town for a simple breakfast of coffee and rye bread—after an hour or so in the open air this tasted far more delicious than the hot rolls and quince jelly at the hotel. When the first steamer from Lucerne came in we were ready and waiting on the quay, our trays suspended by leathern straps from our necks, crying our wares—"Edelweiss! "Alpen-rosen!" It was mostly the girls who did the selling, though whether this was because the boys thought it beneath their dignity, or were less attractive to the tourists, I never found out. The tourists seemed to find us little girls quite sufficiently attractive; even before the ladies from New England in their rimless eyeglasses disembarked we could hear them exclaiming from the rail of the steamer how "cunning" we were, as we stood holding out our bunches. By now my hair had been allowed to grow, and because it was so curly and got so tangled I wore it in two Gretchen plaits from a centre parting; I used to listen, delighted, to the familiar American accents saying—"Look at that one with the long plaits! Isn't she just a *typical* little Swiss girl?"

Brunnen is one of the Four Forest Cantons, which give to the Lake of Lucerne its native name of the *Vierwaldstätter See*; in these cantons German is spoken, and as in Paris with French, so here I was delighted to find that my schoolroom German, already perfectly fluent, worked. My Father was quite right about the entertainment value of speaking modern languages, as I then began to realise; from the outset I could rattle away to my little companions, and they to me. Soon I also picked up from them the curious archaic form of German which is their native speech, Berner-Deutsch or Schwyzer-Deutsch; it was to prove very useful to me later in life. But during that first summer at Brunnen I learned something of far greater importance than Berner-Deutsch: that to get the most out of foreign travel one must enter, as far as possible, into the life of the country one is in, at all levels. Those Sunday evenings with the Schoecks and my impersonation of a little Swiss girl with the porter's children gave me an insight into Swiss life and character which I could never have had otherwise.

Brunnen is a wonderful place for flowers. The plain and the valley-floors have their own treasures: wild columbines, purple or sulphur-yellow, standing thick all through the meadows that wait to be cut for hay, with wild thalictrum and monkshood fringing the streams that water them; in the pinewoods through which a path climbs up to Axenstein grow the small intensely-scented cyclamen which the Swiss call *Alpenveilchen*, "Violets of the Alps"—and out on the dizzy narrow ledges of the limestone cliffs which overhang the Axenstrasse, the slender white St. Bruno's lilies, and a stocky orange one like a dwarf tiger-lily can be found by those with a good head for heights. All these I picked and brought down to my Mother, who identified them in Schröter's *Alpine Flora* and taught us their Latin names; and from their further walks my sisters brought home the mealy-stemmed yellow Alpine auriculas with which the country-boys fill their hat-bands on their Sunday outings, and the tall red gentians that smell like tea-roses—they, and I, carried back our finds in those absurd vasculums, long shallow tins painted green and slung from a green braid, which are to be bought in all Swiss towns. The flowers were, of course, a delight to my Mother, and most of all if she could see them growing herself. When we made expeditions here and there in the little open horse-carriages

—so much better from the botanical point of view than a rushing car—she was constantly prodding the driver in the back with the bamboo handle of her huge green-lined parasol and bidding him stop because she had caught sight of some fresh treasure by the roadside; I would be sent to pick it—"With the root-leaves, mind," she would adjure me, "and only one." We usually hired the same carriage, and the *Kutscher* got to know this habit; he would pull up reluctantly, making appropriate sounds to his horses, and ask gloomily of the world at large—"Noch eine Blume? Ach Gott!" If the flowers she saw were already familiar to her, my Mother contented herself with happy cries as we passed—"Oh, look, there is so-and-so!—look Cottie! Gracie, look!" On one occasion Grace, thus called upon to look at a bugloss, muttered stolidly—"I don't know Blue-gloss from Adam's apple." She was always a patron rather than a devotee, and could never be brought to share in my Mother's enthusiasms.

A number of the American aunts and cousins came out to join us at Brunnen that year—little Aunt Jane, so neat and precise and tidy; Aunt Abby; Aunt Sallie T. and some of the Glennys, "Aunt Slark's" grandchildren, including tall Cousin Emma and handsome Walton—it was there that Walton so impressed me by throwing his cigar into the lake before handing Grace and me into a boat. Most of them stayed in the Vierwald-Stätterhof, which was grander and more expensive than the Eden but lacked the delightful Schoecks, but we were together all the time—driving, strolling through the sunny little town to buy embroideries and peasant-made lace, making expeditions all over the lake, or simply sitting and chatting. I could not help observing how much more free and lively her relations' intercourse with my Mother was in Switzerland than at home, owing to the absence of "Jim," my poor Father—it was a question of the two climates again. Aunt Abby, regrettably, exhaled a climate rather resembling my Father's; she disapproved violently of my friendship with the porter's children and all that flower-selling, and remonstrated with my Mother about it, who fortunately for me paid no attention. Not so Aunt Sallie; it "tickled her to death" that I should be taken for a Swiss child, and she actually got up early one morning and marched down to sit on a seat on the quay to see it all happen for herself.

For my elder sisters, Therese and Cora, the trip to Paris in 1900 and the many subsequent Swiss sojourns were by no means the beginning of foreign travel. My Father's business required him to make journeys abroad constantly, and he often took one of them with him, for the fun of the thing—thus Cora went to Russia in 1893, Therese a year or so later, and more than once; in 1900 Therese and Helen had both accompanied him to Denmark, Norway, and Sweden. He still had business connections with Spain, and took my sister Cora there, but once only; her good looks and masses of glorious light-brown hair caused her to be so mobbed in the streets—especially by ladies asking if the hair was all her own, and un-dyed?—that he decided that Spain was no place for his daughters. He was always going to Canada and America too, but usually alone. But these business interests of my Father's are perhaps worthy of fuller mention, since they form a part of the whole story of railway development in Europe and Asia, and particularly of the impact of the rapidly expanding American steel production on that development during the last two decades of the nineteenth century, and the first few years of the twentieth. In fact he was himself one of the focal points of that impact.

Since his original purchase of that ton of copper in Manchester before he was twenty, his interest had always been in metals, as we know; and from 1870 onwards he had also been closely linked with the metal industry in the United States—it was after all on a business trip to New Orleans that in the house of the Slocombs, long-established iron-founders, he met my Mother. But by the time my personal recollections begin his affairs had shifted north-wards from Louisiana to Pennsylvania, where the Baldwin Loco-motive Works—as they were then called—were producing engines more powerful than anything hitherto known, in Europe at any rate, and the Pennsylvania Steel Company was forging rails of great strength. Meanwhile Europe was requiring more and more railways, and my Father set out to visit foreign Governments— most continental railways were State-owned—to persuade them in the first place to purchase Baldwin engines. Often, indeed usually, he was successful; but the big Baldwin locomotives— drawing much longer and heavier trains, at a higher speed, than anything previously employed—presently began to play havoc with the permanent way: whereupon the foreign Governments moaned to my Father. His answer in substance generally amounted to—"That's the worst of those cheap rails"—and he was usually successful in getting the French, or the Germans or Russians, to place an order for rails with the Pennsylvania Steel Company. It was a sort of mercantile cross-ruff.

The two American firms concerned were so pleased with these efforts that they presently appointed my Father to be their European agent for the sale of locomotives and spare parts in the one case, and of rails, ties, bolts, and whatever else concerns the completion of a rail-road in the other. Owing to the kindness of the Bethlehem Steel Company I have a photostat copy of my Father's draft of his contract for the European Agency of the Pennsylvania Steel Company. It contains one important clause. After the words—"We to be your sole selling agents for the British Isles, their Dependencies and Colonies, and Europe" the document goes on—"A good many sales are effected in London for delivery in other countries, as for instance Chile, Argentina, China, Japan, etc.: and such business, although done for countries outside of the list named above, to be transacted through us, and to be treated as London Agency business."

This agreement went through, and from the year 1896 till 1911 my Father held these two agencies. The words I have quoted give an idea of how wide a field his dealings covered, and I have been at considerable pains to check and verify from independent sources, like the chief engineering magazines, some of the results of his activities. What, after all, was a late-Victorian or post-

Victorian child told about its parent's business? Directly, hardly anything; but there are certain recollections which stand out sharply in my mind, and these correspond with the bald facts gleaned from contemporary publications.

There was, for instance, the Christmas Day when he went to London. Now Christmas for my Father was a sacred family festival: one spent it among one's nearest and dearest, with as many blood-relations as possible also gathered in the house—and no one else. But I recall a certain Christmas morning when—after we children had as usual paraded the passages at 6.30 A.M. in our dressing-gowns, singing "Christians, awake; salute the happy morn," at the pitch of our voices—a telegram came for my Father, and he ordered round the brougham and went off to the City, an unheard-of thing. There was general dismay—Christmas, and my Father not there! Church, the tree, the carols went on as usual; we were still doling out and unpacking presents in the high hall after tea when, ushered by a rush of cold air, my Father came in, chill from the winter's night, in his huge brown broadcloth over-coat lined with Russian sables. He threw his arms round my Mother, exclaiming—"Forgive me for leaving you and the children! But I've made twenty-five thousand pounds to-day."

The draft agreement already quoted mentions one per cent as my Father's commission on most sales, so I conclude that on that Christmas Day he must have put through a deal to the tune of two and a half million pounds—which though a fleabite to-day, round the turn of the century represented a very tidy sum. I also draw the conclusion that the transaction was almost certainly with the Russian Government, because in those days Russia still used the old Julian Calendar, so that their Christmas fell eleven days later than ours—it was the Bolshevik Government which adopted the Gregorian Calendar in 1918.

Russia figured largely in our eyes as children; my Father was always going there, and bringing us back delicious little presents, silver-gilt brooches or belt-buckles with eagles on them, and absurd ladle-like gold spoons inset with translucent coloured enamels. Then there was that overcoat of his, lined throughout with the soft, chocolate-dark backs of sables, which we loved to finger and smell—it had a strange furry smell which we liked. Even more spectacular was the knee-length fur mantle which my Mother used to wear in cold weather and out skating; it was composed entirely of sable-*tails*! A much older cousin told me once that this astonishing garment had been ordered for the Empress of Austria, the beautiful and tragic creature who was stabbed to death on a lake steamer in Switzerland, but that she didn't like it and sent it back, whereupon my Father bought it for his wife. I cannot conceive why it should have failed to please the Empress, for it was delicious: in narrow ribs with the points of the tails projecting in level rows, like tiny flounces of fur, all down its length, and slits for the arms to poke through; my Mother looked ravishing in it too, with a little round muff of sable-tails to match, and a bonnet trimmed with three or four more, tufting up among little velvet bows above her pretty dark hair and her gay brown eyes. And of all the "business associates" who came to stay in Surrey—some of whom, like the Converses from Philadelphia, whose family business Baldwins was, were perfectly charming—by far the most startling to us was the Russian Minister of the Interior. I have forgotten his name, Count Something, but he was a small grey man, very precise in manner and in his dress, which was also grey, and talking rapid harsh French; to our delighted astonishment he used to kiss my Mother's hand, bowing low over it, when he came down to breakfast, but even more striking were his goings-on at prayers, which took place immediately afterwards. When the twelve maids filed in, rustling in their starched prints, to kneel at a row of chairs below the windows, and we had pushed our own chairs back from the table to kneel in front of them the little Russian, rising too, pushed his chair *in*—and then, retreating into a corner, stood at attention, as remote as possible from the proceedings, till my Father had finished his reading from the Old Testament and his extempore petitions. All this I observed, fascinated, peeping through my

177

fingers; I thought his behaviour very strange, almost hostile. All our Catholic relations—the Ruspolis, Cousin Hattie Barbellini, whose husband was a Papal Chamberlain, and the beloved Brazzas always knelt quite cheerfully at prayers. In fact I got a fairly definite impression that "the Russians" were difficult people to deal with.

My impression was correct enough, even though my reasons for it may not have been very sound. For one thing Russia had something mysterious called "broad-gauge" railways, so that if they bought Baldwin locomotives—this much we overheard—these had to be specially constructed. In fact in 1895 and 1896 alone they bought an aggregate of 138 Baldwin engines of the four-cylinder type for various railways. When I first heard the expression "broad gauge" I asked my Father what it meant, and he explained that in Russia the width between the two lines of rails was about five feet, somewhat wider than that in use in other European countries. Childlike, of course I asked him why?—and I still remember his explanation: so that in the event of war and an invasion of Russia, European rolling-stock could not be used on Russian lines. Railways had not figured very much in the only two wars I knew anything about, the American Civil War and the Boer War, and I puzzled over this pronouncement for a long time. Later in my life I was to recognise fully the strategic importance of the Russian broad gauge.

I think it very improbable that my Father actually supplied any of the rails or engines for the Trans-Siberian Railway itself, an enterprise in which he took such a deep interest that he actually contemplated taking his wife and all his nine children along it as far as it went in 1901, when he conceived the new century to begin—unluckily for us, this romantic project was never realised. But perhaps not really so unluckily; the eight-day trip across the Trans-Siberian, which I was myself destined to make in 1941, passes chiefly through the dullest country in the world—thousands of miles, dead flat, of birch, pine, and plough, birch, pine, and plough—all in square blocks, with melting snow in the ditches, and no birds but the unlucky magpies. Siberia as seen from the train *is* finally the abomination of desolation, until one reaches the rolling downs and mountain ranges round Lake Baikal, set with poplar-trees with white stems and copper-bright leaves—and, later, the brown uplands of Manchuria, where little horses, the most courageous in the world, breed in flocks like sheep, tended by horsemen clad in filthy quilted silks and plastered with silver jewellery set with corals and rough turquoises; they came aboard our train and sat, smelling strongly, drinking tumblers of tea in the dining-car. There the wild geese come skeining down onto the sky-filled meres in such dense masses that I have seen a lake turn from blue to brown under my eyes as the huge flocks of the migrating birds circled, descended, and settled on the water.

The Trans-Siberian Railway was begun in 1891, and only completed in 1904. The Russian Government, in an early example of that spirit of insanely exaggerated nationalism which now besets most of the world, issued a rescript that only Russian-made material was to be used in its construction. However, about the time of its completion the Russo-Japanese War occurred, and as a result of the economic stresses which this occasioned the Russian Ministry found itself compelled (I quote from *The Engineer* of June the 16th, 1905) "to give large orders for locomotives . . . for the Siberian Railway and other Russian Railways." "These orders have been given out to Russian and foreign firms alike," *The Engineer* notes on November the 17th of the same year, adding that "a special Commission has been formed to obtain new rolling-stock." Apparently the Russians were always the same, at least up to the close of the last war: their home-made products did not last, nor could they properly maintain and service the first-class machinery which, in spite of this rescript, they imported from abroad. The rescript itself closely resembles Russian tactics to-day —a propaganda nonsense put out for home consumption, while the Government largely ignored it in their actual dealings. For an essential part of the final scheme of the Trans-Siberian was the building of its southern extension, the Chinese Eastern Railway, from Manchouli via Harbin and Mukden down to Dairen, to link up both the warm-water ports of the Yellow Sea and the products and markets of China—with its population of four hundred million—with the great trans-continental line; it had great strategic as well as commercial importance. The Russians built it under a form of agreement with China which in fact secured to them complete liberty of administration; oddly enough this agreement was not made directly with the Russian Government, but with the Russo-Chinese Bank—in spite of subsequent modifications this railway, with all its later links and branches, was still a source of friction and disputes between Russia and China when my husband and I were at the Legation in Peking in 1926 and 1927. Initially, however, it was purely a Russian enterprise, and its interest for me lies in the fact that between 1898 and 1900 no less than 148 Baldwin locomotives were purchased for it; they cost somewhere about £4,000 apiece, and my Father sold them. Moreover Kent's *Railway Enterprise in China* states explicitly that for the section from Harbin to Dairen—then called Port Arthur—"rolling-stock, rails, and all materials were imported from Philadelphia, and landed at Port Arthur and Newchwang." Philadelphia was of course the exit port both for the Baldwin Locomotive Works and the Pennsylvania Steel Company. For other Russian railways he sold a further 100-odd engines of a heavier type.

These purchases recall the terms, already quoted, of my Father's agreement with Pennsylvania Steel—that sales effected in London for delivery in places outside Europe, including China and Japan, should be transacted through him; the terms of the Baldwin Agency (of which I have unfortunately not been able to procure a copy) were, I know, substantially the same. These dealings of my Father's, the engines especially, appealed to our imaginations; well do I remember my excitement on some trip abroad—my Father took Grace and me to Paris again in 1904—at being shown an enormous engine, the biggest I had ever seen, with a peculiar short stumpy funnel and the name BALDWIN on the side, hissing and humming gently in front of the long train we were about to enter, and hearing my Father say complacently—"*I sold that.*"

My childish recollections of things which made an impact on our lives fit in again, very neatly, with the Russo-American quarrel over the sugar tariff, though at the time we knew nothing of the cause. In 1901 we realised that somehow or other things were not going so well—there were more of the rather futile attempts at economies; my Mother looked anxious and fretted over "the books," the tradesmen's weekly accounts, and tried to cut down her charities at the back door, where a stream of the sick and needy—and I fear also the worthless—paraded regularly for soup, clothes, medicines, and letters to hospitals; as for my Father, he growled over the vast cheques which he had to write for those same "books," and was even shorter in temper than usual. Moreover, instead of the whole family migrating to Dorset that summer Grace, Jack, and I were sent there by ourselves: to a farm, in charge of a rather half-witted under-nurse called Paine. It was not nearly so much fun as going with my Mother: we lived inland, there was little swimming and no going out in boats—what I remember best of that sojourn is that the farmer's bull ran loose in a field which we had to cross to get to the road; we were not particularly frightened of it, but when my Father came down to see us he insisted on its being shut up, and after we left we heard that it had killed a man. I also recall that Paine and we three children one day managed to consume three whole roast ducks at a sitting, because each of us wanted to have the treat of picking a carcase! Children have digestions like ostriches, but Paine was certainly mental to allow this.

The historical reason behind these domestic troubles was that in 1901 the American sugar producers, alleging that the Russian growers were receiving a government bounty, succeeded in getting a discriminatory duty imposed on Russian sugar; the Russian Government retaliated by imposing in their turn discriminatory duties, 20 to 30 per cent higher than their normal tariffs, on American iron and steel goods, including locomotives. No wonder my Father was upset. This state of affairs lasted till September, 1905, when the Russian duties were removed, fairly clearly in gratitude for President Theodore Roosevelt's assistance in bringing about peace between Russia and Japan, though this was never explicitly acknowledged: the official statement merely refers to "misunderstandings" in the interpretation of the most-favoured-nation clause when the duties had been imposed.

My Father's enthusiastic praises of "Teddy" Roosevelt about that time lend colour to this view. He was usually extremely well informed about everything relating to the iron and steel trade. On February the 11th, 1901, we find him writing from London to F. W. Wood, then the President of Pennsylvania Steel—

> There is a rumour just now of a big deal either consummated, or contemplated, in which Federal Steel, Carnegie's, the Wire Company, and some others, seem to be merging. It isn't clear here yet whether it is only Carnegie selling out his interest or whether the whole Carnegie concern is being taken over. The prime movers are said to be Morgan and Rockefeller. . . .
>
> In old days, I know that Morgans here had an interest in Joliet, afterwards in Illinois Steel; that was merged into Federal, I presume their interest always growing. Recently it was given out that Carnegies were going to put down a sixteen million pipe plant; I suppose threatened competition made Morgan try and buy.
>
> The advent of the Standard Oil interest into Copper has not, so far apparently, been very successful, and certainly hasn't been very advantageous to the trade, those who are outside the combination benefiting by it, seemingly, more than the insiders.
>
> It seems very questionable whether it is advantageous that great trades should be, more or less, controlled by financiers who do not understand the trades they seek to monopolise!

He goes on to remark that during recent months "we have constantly had pointed out to us that they [Carnegies] were out of competition because they were unable to sell a rail under .10 phosphorous," and concludes—

This big Combination, if it goes through, will no doubt be very powerful, and control a great deal; but wherever there has been a ring that I have known of, it has always been a good thing for the man outside it.

I reproduce this letter partly for the light it throws on "big business" half a century ago, but also because of a note on the first paragraph sent to me by a present member of Bethlehem Steel—which subsequently absorbed the Pennsylvania Steel Company. This gentleman writes:

That rumour was well founded. There had been a meeting at the University Club in New York on December 12, 1900, attended by J. P. Morgan and various financial and steel men. At that meeting C. M. Schwab [how often I heard my Father speak of him!] presented the possibility of a merger. The result was the formation of the United States Steel Corporation. . . . Mr. Sanders' prediction that Federal Steel, Carnegie, American Steel and Wire, and others would be included proved to be correct. Doubtless there were persons in the United States who had information of what was under way, but it is interesting to see that the news had also travelled overseas.

I find these old business letters of my Father's curiously moving. He was always so burningly keen on whatever he was doing, from stalking or driving four-in-hands to pruning shrubs; so eager to give his American associates any information that might be of use to them. The letter I have quoted is not an isolated one; I have copies of others too, in one of which, also from 1901, he writes almost wistfully: "It is very sickly that prices keep slipping away so here, and that orders keep passing us; there have been plenty of them if our prices had been right. Your trade is so much better than Europe's now that it's hard to get down low eno', no doubt. I find it so in locos"—an obvious reference to his concurrent Baldwin agency. Evidently more than fifty years ago dollar products already had a way of pricing themselves out of European markets.

By 1901, too, the first great flush of railway expansion in Europe was beginning to decline, and my poor Father's fortunes began to decline with it. There was no immediate *débâcle*; we continued to go to Switzerland—to Mürren, Zermatt, and Courmayeur; the Wickhams and the Sanders cousins continued to come and pay long visits, so did the American aunts; and the attempted economies did not prevent my Father from joining Mr. Ross at Kinlochewe every autumn for the stalking and fishing. Mr. Ross's fortunes were not declining in the least; as my Father's went down his went up; his interests had by now shifted from railways to coal, and he was richer than ever; but his heart had begun to trouble him, and he usually crossed the Atlantic in his own steam yacht—it was quieter than a liner, he said. In those later years I was old enough to register both him and his wife better: he was short, bearded, benevolent, and rather silent, except when he could be persuaded to launch into reminiscences of the old days when he was building the Canadian Pacific Line through the Rockies in the early eighteen-eighties. We listened eagerly to his stories of prowling bears, or "wash-outs" after a sudden storm, and the difficulties with his men during the bitter winters, when fifty or more degrees of frost made all work impossible but lumbering —felling trees for use as struts in tunnels and embankments; on one occasion when the temperature was "forty below" and the men refused to work he went round the camp at night and broke every single thermometer—after which he had no more trouble. All contemporary accounts of this undertaking agree, however, that "Ross's" were always the best camps: better food, better lodging, and all-round better treatment, in spite of his toughness.

As for Mrs. Ross—Annie, as her husband and my Father called her—I can see now what an interesting product of the age of expansion in iron and coal she was. The millionaire's wife, with her wonderful jewels and her French clothes, still kept the fresh warm-heartedness of the sonsie Scottish country lass that she had been when her James married her in Morayshire more than thirty years before, a warm-heartedness as fresh as her still-lovely complexion; and there was a caustic quality even about her affection that was very Scots. She openly pitied and scolded my Mother for having all those children—she had confined herself to one son, Jack, a tall young man with his mother's height and good looks—and seemed to think that quite enough. My Mother never argued, but she had a trick of quietly changing the subject which usually silenced good Annie Ross, for all that she had by now assumed—quite unconsciously, I feel sure—much of the manner as well as the appearance of a great lady; her husband's position in Canada had really forced her into this. But her affection and her naïveté kept breaking in—or breaking out; that was what made her so beguiling. She was really only interested in two things, people and clothes, and on both she made utterances of trenchant frankness.

"Not over my *lap*, dear—this is a Doucet dress!" she exclaimed one day when I carried the cream-jug to her at tea.

I was always rather a favourite of hers—excessively pretty and *dégagée* herself, she liked pretty people, even if they were only children, and I was a pretty, fearless child; I have often remembered since one prophetic utterance that she made when I was only about ten. I came running in, with filthy hands and a torn frock, to the room where she sat in all her elegance chatting to my Mother, pouring out a long tale about having climbed a tree and found a magpie's nest. My Mother was genuinely interested in the magpies; Mrs. Ross's comment, however, was—"My dear Marie, that child will *have* to become a writer, to relieve herself of her flow of language."

But a far more important element in the life of our family than the Rosses—fond as we were of them—or any other business associates was the succession of long summer visits which my four elder sisters, in particular, used to pay to our Italian cousins at Brazzà, in northern Italy—a place so unusual and entertaining that it demands a chapter to itself.

Chapter 12

*M*Y *MOTHER'S* was not the only wedding from that yellowish house in New Orleans which took a bride away to foreign parts. Some ten years later my cousin Cora Slocomb, Uncle Cud and Aunt Abby's only child, went from it to her marriage with Detalmo di Brazza. Two very exogenic marriages: one to the tall, fair, blue-eyed English businessman, the other to the dark, stocky, bearded Italian count from Friuli. Many novels—and even more numerous unfortunate unions—have caused foreign counts, especially Italian ones, who married wealthy girls from the States rather to stink in American nostrils; but there was nothing spurious about Cousin Detalmo. He was extremely rich himself, to begin with; as for his family, when the Emperor Charlemagne completed his conquest of Italy about A.D. 800, and made an earlier version of Domesday Book, inventorying his new possessions in detail, di Brazzas were already living at Brazzà, and place and family were duly listed. There was nothing that even New Orleans could object to about such a connection, except that Italy was so far away; and I think Aunt Abby was really extremely gratified by it. She had every reason to be, on saner grounds than those of wealth and social prestige, for Detalmo proved to be the most devoted of husbands to not the easiest of wives, and a uniformly dutiful and courteous son-in-law to, I should say, one of the most difficult mothers-in-law who ever existed.

186

This marriage, which brought her niece and girlhood's companion to Europe, close at hand, meant a great deal to my Mother. Cousin Cora, speaking in the accents of home—"our own tongue, in which we were born," as the Acts of the Apostles say of Pentecost—and familiar with all her home connections and surroundings was constantly popping across to England to see her Aunt Marie, once she was established in Friuli: she had the money, she had the energy—goodness, what energy she had!—and over she came. As small children we didn't like her so much as some of the other relations: busy, bustling, a little vociferous—mostly about what interested her at the moment—she was rather too like Aunt Abby for our taste at first, though we liked her pretty eyes and curly hair, and her extraordinarily gay sweet smile; in evening dress she was lovely, for she had as beautiful a neck and arms as I have ever seen: full, and milk-white. Moreover she was warmhearted, generous, and affectionate, quite without her Mother's rather harsh censoriousness, and in time we became very fond of her. "Nenaine" was her old nickname; what it derives from I don't know. We little ones called her *"Cousin* Nennie" rather carefully, since though she was our first cousin in fact, in age she was practically a contemporary of my Mother's.

Perhaps this is as good a place as any to dwell a little on Brazzà and my Cousin Cora's life and activities there—because if her visits to England meant much to my Mother, our visits to Brazzà meant almost more to my sisters, and later to me. (Being older, naturally they began to go to Italy in the summer much sooner than I did.) The old Castello di Brazzà which we knew so well no longer exists, it was burnt down during the Austrian inrush after Caporetto, in the first World War—a long white seventeenth-century building with a series of large rooms opening out of one another along the *piano nobile*, mostly with painted and gilded beams across their ceilings, and full of ancestral furniture, some of it beautiful, all of it imposing and dignified. Outside were the regulation North Italian surroundings: cypresses, stone tables under stone pines, marble seats in the shade, hot white paths in the sun, the ruin of the earlier Castello, with a high keep and crumbling walls, on a knoll behind the house—and at every turn breathtaking views of the Julian Alps, a sea of blue crests curving in a great semi-circle round the flat plain, set with white houses and white-stemmed poplars with plumy tops.

Here Cousin Cora entertained, skilfully and lavishly, every summer; the great house could hold scores of people, and scores it was made to hold, of the most diverse description. There was always a substantial number of relations from England and America as a basis, and of Brazzas too: the old Countess, Detalmo's mother, who lived to be a hundred and five and could remember Napoleon's armies entering Italy, was there every year. She had had seventeen children, and was constantly teased by her family because she had forgotten the existence of one son, Tommaso, who had died as a child—it was a tradition in the Brazza family, going back for centuries, that if a son was called Tommaso he would die young and be forgotten, and it was fascinating to hear the old Contessa deny, almost with oaths, that she had ever borne such a child. There came also, year after year, Count Pierre di Brazza, the explorer, who gave his name to Brazzaville in the French Congo. From earliest youth he had always had a passion to explore and colonise in Africa, as the English and Belgians had done; and since he could not do this for his own country—less prone then than later to African adventures—he offered his services to the French Government, became a naturalised Frenchman, and gratified his early desires to the full by opening up the French Congo—he married Thérèse de Chambrun. My sisters recall him as the most amusing of companions, and very kind to little English girls; he had a remarkable knack of catching up snakes by the tail and breaking their backs with a single flick of the wrist—this accomplishment he used often to display when the well-being of picnics, a great feature of life at Brazzà, was menaced by the presence of some serpent. In the family he was called Pipo; he used to electrify my sisters by cleaning up the gravy on his plate not with a piece of bread but with his fingers, which he then sucked indelicately—especially if the dish was cuttle-fish stewed in its own ink, which he loved.

There were lots of other Brazzas too—naturally, in a family originally seventeen strong. Of them I myself remember best Ascanio and Francesco—with the latter at one point I fell in love. Francesco was an enthusiast for electricity in all its forms, and worked with Signor Marconi to produce wireless telegraphy; I believe he was really something of a genius. He was thin and gaunt and wild, alternating between rapid and rather lewd chatter (which luckily we couldn't very well follow) and fits of moody silence—when he was lewd at table the family used to shish him vigorously, at the same time giggling delightedly; when he was moody they left him alone.

On this *couche* of relations, American, Italian, and English, Cousin Cora built up a most varied assortment of people in her summer house-parties. A standing dish was the Grand Duchess of Saxe-Weimar, accompanied by her lady-in-waiting, a chamberlain, and a chaplain—who came in very handy on those Sundays when the curate at Sta Margherita, whose business it was to come over and say Mass at the Castello, either overslept, or swallowed a drop of water when cleaning his teeth so that he could not say Mass at all. Cousin Cora liked intellectuals, and they liked her; the learned Dr. Hodgkin and Nellie, my sister Cora's friend, came constantly and seemed to mix in very happily with the Grand Duchess—whose presence turned the big rambling overflowing house into a sort of miniature court, with white gloves, and curtseys, and careful precedence about seating at meals. All this was extremely stimulating—it was very amusing for my sisters to have to make curtseys to a splendid old lady who was delighted with their fluent German.

But everything at Brazzà was amusing. Nonnino the butler, who really ran the whole place, and his troop of rather gauche youths, recruited for the summer from the country-side, waited at table in white cotton gloves, and the food which they handed in this unaccustomed dress was a delight, and full of unexpected things

—like those cuttle-fish which Count Pierre enjoyed so much, or tiny birds spitted on silver skewers with bay-leaves in between, lying on a bed of polenta. And on Fridays meals were further enlivened by the regular argument between Cousin Detalmo and his female relatives about whether he should or should not eat the meat provided for the Protestant guests. In the tenth or eleventh century the Pope of the day, as a reward for some military services rendered by a Brazza, had given the family a dispensation in perpetuity from abstinence on Fridays, and Detalmo—really very reasonably—could not see why he should not avail himself of this saecular permission when there were cutlets, or duck and green peas actually being passed round. But his sister-in-law Countess Vera, his daughter Idanna, his and Cora's only child, any other Brazza ladies who might be present, and even his wife—who had not become a Catholic, but thought eating meat on Fridays set a bad example—would round on him with the utmost vigour and at the pitch of their voices; their remonstrances resounded through the great room, while Cousin Detalmo stuffed his mouth with meat, roared with laughter through his iron-grey beard, and re-counted the Papal permission, the country footmen meanwhile trying to hide their delighted smirks behind those white cotton gloves.

We got to know the various Brazza relations quite well, and the country-side and its activities too: the vintage; gathering mulberry-leaves to feed the silkworms in early summer, and whipping the silk off the cocoons with a whisk of twigs later in the year; picking and stripping the maize, putting figs and prunes out to dry in the sun on muslin frames. We became familiar with the neighbours too—Asquinis and Pasolinis and so forth, meeting them year after year. Those long summers at Brazzà made Italy, for us, a sort of second homeland—not in the least the Italy of the expatriate English in Rome or Florence, but an *Italian* Italy, dyed-in-the-silk. (When long afterwards I tried to set some of it down —with my Cousin Idanna's permission—in *Enchanter's Night-shade*, I rather nervously sent the typescript to Daniele Varé, who came from the Veneto, in case I had got it all wrong. He returned it with these words: "It is an extraordinary thing that it should have been left for you, an Englishwoman, to write the first adequate novel about country-house life in the Friuli." I was satisfied with that.)

Cousin Cora did much more than merely entertain a great many people very well. I have said that she had abundant energy, and from the outset she turned her attention to improving the lot of the peasants on her husband's estates. These were large, both round Brazzà itself and away to the east, in the mountainous Slovene-speaking district, where there was another big property, Savor-gnan—the full family name was Brazza-Savorgnan. Social welfare was not much developed in Italy in the eighteen-eighties; poverty, ignorance, a most lamentable lack of hygiene, and rural immorality on a scale that amounted almost to promiscuity were what the young Countess di Brazza found when she came to her new home. The Friulan peasants are lusty vigorous people, hot-headed, obsti-nate, intelligent, and largely without the slyness and the nervous cruelty of the South Italians; they have a big dash, so it used to be said, of Ostrogoth blood—anyhow, grey or grey-blue eyes, stone-pale faces and tawny hair, Titian's "Venetian red," were common among them in my youth. They talked an amusing dialect, closely related to Ladin; Idanna had picked up a lot of it and used to teach it to me. (Dogs, I remember, were called *lis changs*.)

Onto these people Cousin Cora directed her reforming energies. She made them clean their houses. She cajoled or harried the priests, causing them to insist on the marriages of pregnant girls, and getting them to preach sermons on such uncongenial themes, to Italian ears, as the duty of chastity and sobriety. She hunted the doctors in Udine, the local town and provincial capital, out into the country districts to look after the people there; she herself harangued the women in her fluent and rather prettily American-ised Italian on maternity hygiene. But she was quite practical enough to see that what was wrong, with the women and girls any-how, was poverty and idleness, and these she set herself to remedy

191

by founding schools. Not for the three R's—except in England, where Miss Charlotte M. Yonge's heroines were teaching quarrymen's children to read and write, elementary education had hardly reared its head in Europe by then. No—the schools which my cousin founded had an economic aim; they were to teach the making of lace.

It may have been partly her Mother's collection in the house in New Orleans which gave Cora di Brazza this quite brilliant idea; she too had been brought up on Mrs. Palliser's *Great Book of Lace*, and really knew a lot about the subject; moreover lace-making as a remedy against poverty had been started in Italy only a few years before her marriage, and quite close by. The winter of 1872 was a cruel one; the lagoons round Venice froze, and the fisherfolk of Murano and Burano were reduced practically to starvation. In the past both these island towns had been centres for the lace-making industry, and a certain Signor Fambri of Venice determined to revive it to help the people. He discovered one old woman—her very name survives, Cencia Scarparola—who still kept the ancient skills, and set her to teach the fresh generation; the ladies of the patrician families of Venice helped him with money, lace to be copied, and their personal efforts; in particular a beautiful young widow, the Countess Andriana Marcello, devoted the rest of her life to this work. Queen Margherita of Italy, when still Princess of Savoy, became president of the Burano school; after her husband's accession to the throne she allowed the superb Crown laces to go to Burano to be copied, and later entrusted them to the school there for repairs—in fact she would send them nowhere else to be mended.

Since Brazzà is only some ninety miles north of Venice the American bride of course soon met all the Venetian ladies, among them the Countess Marcello, who became her close and dear friend; and once my cousin had taken stock of the needs of the peasants on her husband's estates it was only to be expected that she should turn to lace-making to relieve them. In 1891 she founded her first school near Brazzà, after a small show of peasant industries in the Castello, to which the whole country-side thronged—"with the object," she herself wrote "of developing the small household industries and thus forming a means of accessory occupation and emolument for the large peasant families during the long winters, when the ground in this part of the country is frozen or snowbound." The wording may be heavy, but the idea was admirably sound—"accessory occupation," keeping women and girls profitably employed in their own homes while they keep an eye on the babies and the stewpot is one of the best solvents of poverty there is. The young American Countess first set to and learned to make lace herself, and then taught six of the most intelligent local girls; at the show, with her native sense of salesmanship, she had these six girls sitting twiddling the bobbins beside their stuffed "pillows," with the result that, to quote her again—"the vast public remained enthralled, and could not be persuaded to move on; and the jury decided that this handicraft was best adapted to the requirements of the Province." Her first six girls became instructors of others and within two years she had opened three more schools; the original one, at Fagagna, had a hundred workers within the first twelve months.

Many people have made the mistake of starting or developing peasant industries without looking ahead for markets in which to dispose of them, and still more without first ascertaining what type of peasant product will command a sale in the world at large. Not so my cousin. Our common Grandfather was a very successful man of business, and she had inherited his shrewdness and capability. Soon she was hurrying off to Paris with samples of the work produced by her pupils—many of whom, as she said, were "orphans, or lame, or deformed, or very miserable; on the slender threads wound about their bobbins hangs their whole means of homes and existence." She talked to shop-keepers in Paris and London, and learned what were the most saleable patterns, and lengths, and breadths; thereafter she paid her girls by the piece, basing their earnings on the wholesale prices then obtaining in Paris, and her retail prices likewise on the current French ones. Because the work was so good, and sold in such a businesslike fashion, the demand for it spread, and shops in Milan and Venice were soon eagerly buying "Brazzà lace."

My Mother thrilled to all these efforts. If she had been capable of envy I think she would really have envied her niece Cora both for the extent of the need around her, and her relative freedom to work at relieving it. Cousin Nennie would come hastening across from Paris and down to us in the country to pour out hopes, plans, complications, and aspirations, in her rich soft voice, to her dear Marie—who gave her that unmatched warmth of sympathy that was her great gift. And when the really big opportunity came, and the younger woman grasped it with both hands, my Mother's pride and pleasure were unbounded. Though I was too young to remember it myself, "Cousin Nenaine's Lace Exhibition at the World's Fair" became one of those legends which decorated my childhood, taking place alongside of Captain Elisha's escape or Uncle Cud's ride. And to-day, studying with some care the facts about that performance of my cousin's, I have come to feel that it was well worthy of her ancestors.

It was barely a year before the World's Fair opened that Cora di Brazza learned that there was to be a Woman's Section in the Chicago Exhibition of 1893; but she realised at once what that could mean for the lace schools of Italy, if properly handled, and she proceeded to handle it herself. Through the Ministry of Commerce she booked space in the Italian portion of the Woman's Building for an exhibit, for which she made herself responsible. She approached Queen Margherita, who was already interested in the Burano School, and persuaded her to lend many of the priceless royal laces to be sent across the Atlantic and exhibited. I don't think Cousin Nenaine was yet a Lady-in-Waiting to the Queen, as she was afterwards for many years; but she got the royal laces, and where the Queen led, other great ladies were only too glad to follow suit, and lend their family laces too. On those lines alone the exhibit was a superb one; and after admiring the classical examples the visitor in Chicago could go on to look at show-cases full of modern work from not less than fourteen of the Italian provinces, with a young woman sitting by with a price-list to book orders.

To organise such an exhibit, insure it, and get it shipped across the Atlantic in under a year might seem quite a good job, but it was not nearly enough for my Cousin Cora. People would ask questions; they must be informed; and she proceeded to sit down and write a catalogue, in the form of a history of the making of lace—and a very good history it is, full of information very difficult to obtain outside the Proceedings of Learned Societies. Characteristically, she took the subject right back to the earliest making of textiles, including things then being discovered in the lake-dwellings at Robenhausen and elsewhere, the laces described by Homer and figured on Greek vases, and the fringed and netted ornaments from Egyptian tombs—photographs or sketches illustrated such objects as were too precious to be allowed to leave their various museums. In the course of these researches she identified for an archaeologist in Rome some mysterious little pieces of worked bone dating from the third century, which he had come on in his current excavations; they defeated him completely, but when she showed him some modern bobbins he instantly recognised what he had unearthed, and allowed her to take some of the ancient Roman lace-makers' tools to exhibit in America. Her exploring brother-in-law, Count Pierre, was laid under contribution to send back from Africa specimens of the beautiful *pukas* or slung bags worn by chiefs of the Ogowe and Abomba tribes, woven by men out of the fibre of pineapple leaves and adorned with elephants' whiskers—some of those *pukas*, strangely enough, contained stitches still in use in Venice, such as the lovely *Punto in Aria*.

Hastening here and there, over Italy, over much of Europe, cajoling curators, hurrying draughtsmen and photographers, she secured her examples and her illustrations; then she went back to Brazzà and dashed off her catalogue-cum-history at lightning speed. She asked and obtained permission to dedicate it to the

Queen, with a signed royal photograph to use as a frontispiece; finally she sailed for the States with her MS. and her illustrations, and by more harrying of publishers she contrived to get the book printed and bound in time for the opening of the Exhibition. It sold like hot cakes, and she devoted all the proceeds to defraying the expenses of taking the lace exhibit over to Chicago—adding a good deal out of her own pocket as well.

The Exhibition was a wild success, and gave a great fillip to lace-production in Italy; orders flowed in, and "accessory occupation and emolument" was assured for hundreds of women and girls in peasant homes for a long time to come. I have spoken of this as my Cousin Cora's "performance," and a notable performance it was—she *was* a performer, and it was her magnetism and intelligent instinct for showmanship, joined to a great deal of extremely hard work, that brought such benefits of honest employment and relief of poverty to so many humble souls. I have no patience at all with the timid introverts—shrinking alike from publicity and from the work involved—who decry such doings. It is the happy extroverts, who don't in the least mind behaving rather extravagantly and risking a little ridicule, who really get things done. My Mother—who had inherited much of Sarah Eliza's Quaker quietude, a core of stillness at the heart of her busy life—fully recognised this, and always stood up for her ardent, busy niece; and Cora di Brazza had as well the lifelong approbation and affection of one of the really great women of her time, Queen Margherita—the only Queen in history, so far as I know, who was also a first-class mountaineer. (From my childhood this always enlisted my admiration for her.)

These foreign connections, with their lively Continental characters and interests, and their even more lively conversation, greatly mitigated the rather grim stodginess of our low-church English upbringing. What my Father made of it all I simply don't know; I cannot look back maturely enough to get inside his mind about the Italian relations, Ruspolis and Barbellinis as well as the di Brazzas, in the least. He was very fond of his niece

Nenaine because she was pretty and lively and made up to him very cleverly—and though my Father's principles would never have allowed him any such goings-on as those of his father-in-law with Jenny Lind and the rest, he was quite reasonably and humanly at the mercy of pretty women who made up to him in the right way. Of course, except for Nenaine herself they were all Catholics, which was most unfortunate, especially for them— for their chances of eternal salvation were slight; and he read, and caused us to read, Spurgeon's Sermons aloud on Sunday afternoons more copiously than ever after one of these visitations.

I think my Mother must have been rather clever about all these relations of hers, because my Father was neither a patient nor a tolerant man, and did not suffer people he disapproved of at all gladly; moreover there were an enormous lot of them, and they kept on coming all the time. But he liked company, no one more; he loved to hear or to tell a good story, he loved to laugh, and the American aunts made him laugh a lot, especially Aunt Sallie T. and her husband. I see now that my Mother kept the balance very skilfully by perpetually having his people to stay, her sisters-and-brothers-in-law and their numerous offspring; the suggestion that the Wickhams should spend Christmas with us, or some of the Sam Sanderses be invited always came from her— and as they were all devoted to her, they always came. My Father, too, had travelled enough to be familiar with the manners of most European capitals, and in spite of his stubborn religious prejudices he was surprisingly broad-minded about other things—at a time when for a woman to smoke, in England, was outrageous he would never condemn it, because delightful women in Moscow and Rome always smoked, he said—and were prettier and cleverer than the local old Gorgons who so condemned the habit. He peremptorily forbade us, his daughters, to smoke, but that I think was a measure of economy; there were six of us, his specially imported Egyptian cigarettes were enormously expensive, and if you had six girls in a house all smoking like chimneys, where would it end?

He was very fond, in a rather patronising fashion, of Cora's husband Detalmo, who often escorted his wife on her dashes to England to get counsel and sympathy from her Aunt Marie—it was rather touching how the younger, wealthier, and far less encumbered woman, with her wide-flung activities and her exhilarating social orbit still clung to the person who had been her beloved adviser and support in her difficult childhood. My Mother—with six children, with seven, with eight, with nine— like her mother before her stayed quietly at home, bringing us up, gardening, and peaceably but very consciously serving God, as she had learned to do before she was twelve years old; but she had something to give to her brilliant niece, and that niece came regularly to get it. How well I recall those inrushes of Cousin Cora's on winter evenings, when the London train had got in: richly dressed, smelling delicious, eager, voluble, happy; her soft cheeks as she kissed us still cold from the long drive up from the station in the brougham, her voice warm and caressing while she tumbled out startlingly frank praises of us all—"Why, little Cottie's going to be a beauty too!" "Detalmo, where is my *large* bag?"—and when the faithful Detalmo brought it, out came the presents she could not wait to give even till she had taken off her furs. As for us children, we adored Cousin Detalmo. He had a ravishing defect of speech which made him pronounce all his R's and some of his L's as W's—we used to listen eagerly for examples of this, and were delighted by the confusion which we overheard resulting when he told the rather rustic booking-clerk at our country station that he wanted a "wound twip" to Water-loo. He was always losing things, and he had a most happy idiom for that too—whether it was a train or an umbrella, he had always lost it "by a combination."

Detalmo, who took most things very coolly, simply worshipped his wife—slavishly, adoringly. He made fun of her enthusiasms and teased her about the embarrassments into which they some-times led her—which she would re-count as cheerfully as Aunt Sallie T. herself—but his full-throated laughter was always affectionate. One way and another I am sure she led him the dickens of a life, but I believe he loved every moment of it. He had the sweetest nature of any man I ever encountered—I never heard him say, or saw him do, a harsh or even a sharp thing; laughter and gentle mockery were as far as he went. He took his religion as lightly as everything else—hence his persistence in eating meat on Fridays if it was going. The Brazzas, too, had always been Royalists, which in the last quarter of the nineteenth century meant that one was rather anti the Vatican; and I think it was this tradition quite as much as their common interest in lace-making which caused Cousin Cora to remain one of Queen Margherita's Ladies-in-Waiting for so long.

That brought us much interest too, at second-hand. To get over a heart-break my sister Therese was sent out to Italy for two whole years; there she shared in the annual winter migration from Friuli to Rome, where innumerable Brazzas hived together in a huge mouldering Palazzo not far from the fountain of Trevi, each unit in its own apartment, on various floors. Nenaine somehow arranged to attach my sister to her in some capacity or other, so that she attended all the Court functions; we were highly entertained to hear of the necessity for her having extra evening dresses, in mauve and in white, for official half-mourning, and of the special shoes made to match, but low-heeled and easy-fitting, to render the long hours of standing endurable. To us it all sounded even more picturesque and fascinating than Mardi Gras in New Orleans, because this was *real*, and the other was only make-believe—and children, those great specialists in make-believe, have a correspondingly keen sense of reality. Real Kings and real Queens, about whose forbears we had read in the history-books, and whose current activities we saw recorded in pen-and-ink sketches in the *Daily Graphic*, were something quite different from Rex and Momus and Comus, parading and make-believing, just like us only far more grandiosely, away on the shores of the Gulf of Mexico. And history itself came home to us, came right into that comfortable drawing-room in Surrey, when my Mother read aloud to us my sister's lively letters, in which the very utterances of these characters were sometimes quoted. The Arch-Duke had said so-and-so, and Princess Y. had made him laugh by answering that—and the old King had frowned, because it was a little saucy of her. Here, I felt, was history walking and talking; the present was all arrayed to turn into the past, and get into those books which I so much enjoyed, Miss Agnes Strickland's *Lives of the Queens of England* and *Lives of the Queens of Scotland*. As a small girl I envied my sister Therese exceedingly.

Chapter 13

*I*N 1904 we left Surrey and went to London. My Father was now a man of sixty, who had worked hard all his life, and in spite of his superb physique I think he was beginning to find those early morning starts and double train journeys something of a strain; but undoubtedly the main reason for the change was economy. No horses, no stablemen, no gardeners and bills for plants and bulbs—for while she had a garden my Mother simply could not stop buying things for it—no sheep: all this would save a lot of money; and with nine children all at the stage of requiring education or dress allowances or both, he needed to economise. I have never spoken of the sheep before, but they were so characteristic of my Father that I must mention them. His ideas about food, though arbitrary and frightfully troublesome to the housekeeper, were sound, and strongly held; he considered, prime beef and venison apart, that the only meat fit to eat was six-year-old Exmoor mutton—and since no English country butcher could supply this he used to purchase from Devonshire farms an annual supply of wether lambs, and run them on till they were in his view fit for the table. They were folded all about the place, and it was one man's work to shift the hurdles, clip the fat creatures in due season, and feed them with hay, turnips, and oil-cake—I must say the meat, dark in colour and beautifully flavoured, was delicious, the best mutton I ever tasted. These animals, in various stages of growth, had accompanied us to

Surrey from Porters—like the orphans, also in various stages of growth. What a menagerie!

The move to London ushered in the one rather unhappy period of my girlhood—it filled me with despair, and though my Mother said nothing about it, I knew that she hated it too. Once more she had to leave a garden which she had made beautiful just as it came to perfection: the borders full of delicious old-fashioned things now unobtainable like Raby Castle carnations, and that dusky-apricot rose, Anna Olivier, named by a rejected lover for a girl who had been a beauty in New Orleans before my Mother's day; had to leave the woods that she had filled with daffodils, and the open slopes by her covered with pheasant's-eye narcissus, blooming in May among her flowering shrubs, and all the other roses, planted with such loving skill wherever a rose could stand, climb, or droop—as her Carmine Pillars drooped in crimson cascades over the whiteness of huge old syringas. Oh, yes—she was in despair and so was I, exchanging all this for London with its grime and murk, and horizons pricked with chimney-pots, after our ever-changing views over the Thames Valley, and of Windsor Castle through the beeches that bounded the lawn.

We moved to another ugly but extremely comfortable house; ugly comfortable houses seemed to be almost a speciality of my Father's. This was that large lump of dark sooty red brick which still stands by itself in Elm Park Gardens, fronting on the Fulham Road; I believe it is now turned into flats, but we filled it to overflowing, diminished as our establishment was. Yah had been pensioned off and settled in a cottage; Fräulein Bé had retired to Germany, and a succession of rather inferior creatures acted as *dames de compagnie* to Grace and myself, escorting us about London and speaking German and heavy Teutonic French with us; the last of the orphans had been planted out in "good places" and Mrs. Ledger likewise pensioned off. It was a general winding-up and drawing-in—which Providence in a way completed when my youngest brother Bobbie died of meningitis two or three years later. He had always been ailing, and could never have come to good, but my Mother had loved him with the despairing intensity reserved for the lame duck; all the same in her deepest heart I think his death was a relief, at least from the gnawing anxiety of what would happen to him if she died first.

My Mother understood perfectly what leaving Ridgemead, the only home I had really known, meant to me, and did some very percipient things about it. For one thing she let me help about the move. She took me up to London with her to go over the empty house, allocate the rooms, and measure the walls for our furniture; crawling about the dusty floors with an inch-tape and a note-book, feeling for the first time the *chemical* unpleasantness of London's dirt on my skin, I nevertheless had the comfort of being useful—a comfort she had learned to value herself so long ago. She gave me a pretty bedroom with a big bow-window looking west, from which I could watch London's sunsets down the rather drab vista of the Fulham Road; there was a plane-tree just outside, so that I could hear the rustle of leaves at night —harsher and more metallic than the rustle of country leaves, which carried no mineral burden of soot, but much better than no leaves at all. For my lessons she allotted me a charming little room at the back of the house leading out of the drawing-room; it was nearly all windows, with a wide low window-seat, and overlooked the lawns and shrubberies extending down the whole length of the Gardens to the line of plane-trees at the farther end—on autumn evenings, with bonfires burning and a blue dusk filling the enclosed space, I could almost believe myself in the country.

For the actual move as many of us as possible were of course got out of the way; Bobbie and his governess were parked with Yah in her cottage, and Cora was detailed to take Grace, Jack, and myself away to the seaside for the Easter holidays. On Cora's initiative we went to Worthing, because it was close to the Sussex Downs and Cora, now a don at Oxford at her old college, had become as much interested in ancient man as she had formerly been in butterflies, under the influence of her friend Barbara

Freire-Marreco, who had already done some interesting work on the Pueblo Indians of Mexico. Here I had my first introduction to a subject which has twined, a bright thread, through all the rest of my life, emerging like the flecks in a piece of tweed as and when I have had time and opportunity to work at it—archaeology. In the chilly spring sunshine we tramped all day over the downs, tracing out prehistoric cattle-tracks and looking for dewponds, or else spent hours up at Cissbury Ring, searching for flint implements. Cora taught us how to recognise a worked flint: the "bulb of percussion" swelling away at right angles from a tiny surface and, if it was a well-worked tool, the secondary chipping round the edges of the flake. While our elders measured and paced and examined, Grace, Jack, and I, down out of the wind in the huge surrounding ditch, combed through the chalky earth thrown out in front of rabbit-burrows on the slopes of the vallum, looking for scrapers and flakes, and always in hopes of coming on an arrowhead; Cora passed our finds in review over lunch. It was a very good bit of preliminary instruction in field-work.

Besides hunting for the works of prehistoric man, we set about imitating them. Cora told us that "secondary flaking"—the work, small and fine as embroidery, round the edges of knives and arrowheads—had probably been made by gentle pressure with a bone tool; that was enough for us. The beach at Worthing was covered with large sea-smoothed flints, and on any days when we were not up on the downs we sat, our backs against a groyne, chipping away at these. How beautiful and surprising the elastic quality of flint is! We soon found that by striking one stone sharply against another it was easy to produce lovely delicate flakes, each with its curving bulb of percussion, for all the world like the ones we found at Cissbury or picked up crossing the ploughed fields on the way there, except that ours were of a smoky grey, lacking the white patina conferred by lying for centuries in a chalky soil. The secondary flaking was much more difficult, but with practice—children have such endless time at their disposal—and by working our shoe-horns and tooth-brushes down into mere butts, we managed to reproduce the works of primitive man fairly closely as we sat on the shingle, looking up now and then to watch the plumes of smoke from passing steamers.

I made another discovery during that spring at Worthing. The rather dingy seedy hotel where we stayed contained a surprising quantity of books, and one day I pulled out from the shelves two or three faded volumes entitled *Poems and Ballads*, by Algernon Charles Swinburne. I looked into them; I was at once enchanted; and soon I was carrying this most unsuitable mental food for a girl barely in her teens down to the beach, there to read "The Garden of Proserpine" with my back against the groyne, instead of wholesomely ruining my toothbrush on flint flakes.

> *Here, where the world is quiet,*
> *Here, where all trouble seems*
> *Dead winds' and spent waves' riot*
> *In doubtful dreams of dreams;*
> *I watch the green field growing*
> *For reaping folk and sowing.*
> *For harvest-time and mowing,*
> *A sleepy world of streams.*

I seldom read Swinburne now, but when I recall those lines I see so clearly the long flat sweep of the coast towards Shoreham, misty and etched with a black hatching of groynes, and feel the chilly sea air, and hear the "spent waves" sucking at the shingle not far from my feet. In fact those volumes which I devoured were first editions, and I have often half-regretted since that I didn't simply walk off with them: the landlord was an illiterate oaf who had taken over the house, books and all; he would have been none the wiser or the worse, and I should have had something I valued. I hadn't very much money to buy books with, we had to rely on putting them down on our lists of Christmas or birthday "wishes"; and though I had fooled my Father over *The Bible in Spain*, I realised that even he knew enough not to go buying me Swinburne. This not in the least from what I had read: the more startling things in *Poems and Ballads* such as "Our Lady of Pain" slipped off my innocence and ignorance like water off a duck's back—the written word really does not corrupt in the same way as the visual image, on the films or in "strips." But I had somehow picked up the idea that Swinburne was "improper," and in fact was rather surprised to find that there seemed to be nothing much wrong with him.

Looking back, I sometimes wonder why I found those first years in London so distasteful; I was homesick for the country, of course, but that did not altogether account for it. I think one reason was a certain unease in the house. In London my Father's prejudices came into much more direct conflict with his family's ideas of living than they had done in the country. His ban on the theatre was still absolute, and here were half a dozen grown-up young people living in a town full of theatres. Of course the elder ones all went; it was impossible to expect them not to, and to save trouble they said next morning at breakfast that they had been to a concert. I was more intransigent. I made no attempt to go myself—not out of virtue, I simply had no idea of what I was missing, and anyhow I was so accustomed to being "too young" to do what the others did that I let it alone. But on one occasion this question of theatre-going brought me into my first furious collision with my Father. My godmother Coralie Boord, who was endlessly good to me, had telephoned to ask me out to dinner; I was given a latch-key and put on my best dress; she came to fetch me and together we clattered off in a hansom, up the Fulham Road and the Brompton Road and along Knightsbridge to dine at the Berkeley—after which to my great astonishment she took me to a play. It was something completely childish and innocuous like *Where the Rainbow Ends*, and I thought it rather silly, I remember; but it was fun to be in that unknown and wicked place, a theatre, and I looked about me with the greatest interest. Next morning at breakfast my Father asked what we had done with ourselves?

Breakfast in London was now at eight-fifteen instead of seven-forty-five, but my elder sisters were gradually edging themselves into the position of either coming down very late, or having it in bed, so that morning, as often happened, my parents and I were alone.

"Godmother Tiny took me to see *Where the Rainbow Ends*," I said flatly.

"Was that at a theatre?"

"Yes. I didn't know beforehand." I felt I had the right to say that.

To my surprise my Father merely grunted, and said no more. But a couple of days later, when again the three of us were breakfasting alone, the post was brought in and we all read our letters. There was one for me from my Godmother which simply said, "I think you ought to see this"—enclosed was a long remonstrance to her from my Father in which one of his favourite phrases, "You know what my views are" occurred more than once. I read it; it made me furious; I flamed out at him. How dared he scold dear Godmother Tiny?—she was only being kind. He reiterated that she knew his views about the theatre. Yes, we all knew them—and they were *mad*, I stammered. "What about the others? They go, and you know perfectly well that they go; *they* lie to you and call it concerts; I go by accident, and when I tell you the truth, you simply make trouble for me. You force them to lie, and accept their lies to salve your own conscience—but isn't lying worse than going to any play?" I had never felt myself on a better wicket—I was prepared to be eloquent.

My Father was greatly taken aback by this outburst from his youngest girl, his pet and darling; he hesitated over his reply. I was then only fifteen, and my excursion into ethics must have come as a great shock. But I was thoroughly roused, and went on—

"From to-day, I shall not go to the theatre till I am twenty-one.

207

After that I shall go, as often as I please, and if you don't like it, I will no longer live under your roof." (There had been something in the letter about those who lived under his roof.)

This was very bombastic and tiresome of me; but I stuck to that pronouncement for six whole years, thereby missing Sarah Bernhardt's last visit to London, and the elder Guitry's too. I find it hard now to reconcile myself to that loss, but it was mainly my own fault. At the time my Father just rang the bell for prayers, and when they were over rose rather heavily, and went off to the office without saying any more. When he had gone I turned to my Mother, who had sat completely silent, distress in her face, during this scene. "Wasn't I right?" I demanded. "You know it's all true."

My Mother sighed. "It's almost never right to make an upset," she said, and went off to do her housekeeping.

The question of religion became more acute in London, too. At Englefield Green the choice lay between St. Jude's Church and the Park Chapel, unless the more energetic walked the four miles across the Park to hear the glorious singing at Matins in St. George's Chapel at Windsor, and then the four miles back; we often did this in summer, and always at Easter—in my case for the sheer and simple rapture of hearing the trebles' voices ringing up into the perpendicular vaulting as the choir walked in singing as an introit "Jesus Christ is risen to-day." My Father raised no objection to this, nor to the Park Chapel; since the old Archdeacon was a neighbour and friend, and certainly not "high," he hardly could. But in London St. Paul's Onslow Square, where Prebendary Webb-Peploe was still preaching the pure milk of the fundamentalist word, was only a few minutes' walk away, and he saw no excuse for our not all trooping thither with him on a Sunday morning. This also, however, he found it impossible to enforce. At Oxford both my elder sisters had become moderately high-church, and Helen followed suit; Cora was by now a rather brilliant scientist, and though she never found any serious difficulty in reconciling science and religion—and indeed later wrote a most remarkable synthesis of the two—neither she nor the others could stomach the ill-informed bigotries of St. Paul's, except as an occasional act of grace, a kindness and courtesy to my Father. St. Peter's Cranley Gardens, with regular early Eucharist, was within half a minute of our door, and altogether London was even fuller of churches than it was of theatres: magnificent services at St. Paul's Cathedral, Westminster Abbey, and Southwark Cathedral, and all over the place preachers of high quality to whom it was an intellectual pleasure to listen: Skrine in Ennismore Gardens, H. R. Gamble at "St. Sloane"—Holy Trinity Sloane Street—and Shuckburgh Swayne in Cranley Gardens next door. So it came about that we arranged a sort of roster among ourselves, taking it in turns to be detailed for Sunday duty at Onslow Square, while the others betook themselves to more congenial places of worship. My Mother, God bless her, who disliked the services and sermons there as much as any of us, went uncomplainingly every single Sunday, just as she had escorted her mother-in-law to the "Meetings" of the Plymouth Brethren years before, and came home with peace on her face and in her heart. As for my brother Harry, he looked up some well-known preacher in the list of Church Services in *The Times*, and then went off to stroll with his friends in Hyde Park, returning to lunch with André Mangeot to play Bach to us afterwards, and a lively and convincing account of the sermon he hadn't heard.

But over my confirmation matters came to a head. Both my eldest sisters had come to have something of the same motherly and protective feeling for me as Aunt Abby had had for my Mother; and as Aunt Abby had taken little Marie down to New Orleans to learn French and get first-class schooling, so Therese took my preparation for confirmation in hand. She could not reconcile herself to my getting only such religious instruction as the good Prebendary, for whose confirmation classes my Father entered me, would furnish—and I am sure she was right; the only task I remember being set in the cold bare dusty room at St. Paul's where the classes were held was to write down how often the word "faith" occurred in the Epistle to the Hebrews. Therese had been impressed by the sermons of H. P. Cronshaw, then Vicar of St. Stephen's, Paddington, and decided to send me to him for instruction. How she managed this I don't know; it cannot have been easy, but she arranged it somehow, and presently I was going to the classes at Onslow Square on Tuesday evenings, and on Thursday afternoons jolting in a white horse-bus up through Notting Hill Gate and the purlieus of Bayswater to sit in Mr. Cronshaw's study and be instructed in the Christian Faith.

H. P. Cronshaw was a peculiar character. He had a deeply-lined, ravaged, ugly face, and in speaking an ugly voice, but in the pulpit the most beautiful and telling delivery I ever listened to, not excepting Cosmo Gordon Lang, later Archbishop of Canterbury. Cronje, as we came to call him, was a great Christian, convinced and convincing, but he had none of the sunny Franciscan sweetness of F. E. Hutchinson; he was a North-countryman, with a typically dour sardonic streak and a caustic tongue—he used this liberally on me. Ultimately we became tremendous friends: he married us, christened our eldest child, and in those later years took a thoroughly "sarky"—to use his own idiom—delight in telling my husband what a pest I had been to him during my preparation for confirmation. I was too shy to speak, I wept on the slightest provocation, altogether I was murderously tiresome. Now this was not in my normal character; as a child I had been bold and fearless, delighting such a penetrating and shrewd observer as Mrs. Ross by these very traits; and I think Mr. Cronshaw's experience with me throws a certain light on the Anglican practice in those days of preparing boys and girls for confirmation at adolescence. At that point in the development of young human creatures there is usually a tremendous flowering of the mind, accompanying the inevitable emotional upheaval; if ever there was a moment when "renouncing the world" seems exceptionally difficult and un-called-for it is precisely then, when the realms of literature and art, the kingdoms of the earth and the glory of them are opening before the eyes of youth—and if to all this is added the strain of taking a decisive step about religion it is small wonder that certain individuals should be rather thrown off their emotional or nervous balance. Certainly I was: I was extremely wretched the whole time that I was being prepared, and most miserable of all on the night of the confirmation itself—it was an evening one, at Willesden, and I can see now the gas-light on the wind-shaken almond-blossom outside the church above the black wet pavement as we went in, and can recall my despairing wonder whether it would ever again be right for me to let my heart be lifted up, as it always had been, by things like almond-blossom.

Anyhow it would all have been much worse, I am sure, at St. Paul's Onslow Square.

What interests me now is the way in which my Mother connived at all these goings-on, and the dual preparation. Clearly she felt it to be of real importance in my case, for she often came with me herself in the white bus that took us up to St. Stephen's Paddington; how she squared it all with my Father I don't know, but it was she who broke it to the poor old Prebendary, with the mixture of authority and sweetness that she could command on occasion, that I was *not* going to be confirmed with the rest of his troop—I heard it all going on as I sat in my little schoolroom, through the folding doors.

My Mother and I drew very close to each other during those years in London. We were as it were isolated in our desperate home-sickness for the country; the rest of the family thought London very much a change for the better. After a couple of years Grace came out, and then I was rather alone; Jack was at Wellington, Cora and Helen both at Oxford, Therese "slumming," as it was called, at the Lady Margaret Hall Settlement in South London, doing after-care for the Lady Almoner—then a very new-fangled appointment—at St. Thomas's Hospital; Harry, whom I adored, was at his Father's office all day and dined out practically every night—another thing my poor Father disliked extremely. Grace and Jenny were the only two permanently at home besides myself, and they also were out a great deal; they were both beautiful dancers, and at that stage cared more for dancing than for anything else, and there were among our circle of acquaintance plenty of friendly married women to chaperone them to dances night after night. This had its repercussions on our social life. Young men might be brilliant or worthy, they might speak with the tongues of men and of angels, but if they danced badly it profited them nothing, as far as my two sisters were concerned. So it was the young men who danced who were most often invited to the house; I still came down to dinner, which had now been postponed to seven-fifteen, and I found the company in London less interesting than that in Surrey, where dancing had not been a necessary qualification. My Mother was not at ease in this milieu either; it was something quite outside her experience that girls should dance with men whose parents were not lifelong friends of their parents, such a thing was not done in New Orleans. (True, she had danced and ridden with my Father, and though I am sure she never admitted the thought, it seemed to have led to this.) But the sons of her old friends in Hertfordshire did not dance really well, and though they came to the house occasionally, as partners my two sisters spurned them.

This also drew us together, my Mother and I. By some accident of heredity—far more important than eye-colour or proneness to rheumatism—my sort of people were her sort of people, and we could enjoy them together. Later on, when Helen, Jack, and I had started climbing seriously, and had our own circle of mountaineering friends she was exceedingly fond of most of them, like E. H. F. Bradby, George Mallory, Geoffrey Winthrop Young, and all the rest.

But before this happened I was rather at a loose end. I missed Fräulein Bé and the good hard work in her schoolroom: doing Latin proses, learning Ovid by heart, wrestling with Euripides, and skimming the cream off French and German literature under her enthusiastic direction. Poor Miss Metsch, the *dame de compagnie*, was not much of a substitute; I had to organise my own education more or less, and find my own occupations. For the

212

first I insisted on learning Italian, which I did with a withered little old master who came three times a week; he was a scholar and an enthusiast, made me learn the *Vita Nuova* by heart, and taught me to declaim Filicaia's bitter sonnet:—

"Italia, Italia, o tu, cui feo la sorte"—with an old-world rolling dramatic accentuation which has startled my Italian acquaintances ever since. "Who," they ask, "taught you to say it like that? It is amazing." Alas, I have forgotten his name.

My occupations were a little bizarre. In the holidays, when Jack was at home, we all skated at Princes, which I enjoyed immensely; there I met boys and girls of my own age, Enid and Ivar Campbell, and the young Gibbses and Trotters; it was a healthy normal outlet. But in the terms I did my own things. I had suddenly realised the existence of pictures, and dragged Miss Metsch not only to the National Gallery but to practically every picture-show in London as well. I also, still escorted by the unhappy Miss Metsch, frequented second-hand book-shops: not the well-known ones in the Charing Cross Road, but drab little places with racks of books outside, in Chelsea or at South Kensington Station or near Notting Hill Gate. Here I stood in the cold, hunting for books on mountaineering. In the first place I did this to fill my own shelves, but I had read a good deal of climbing literature since I first bought Tyndall's *The Glaciers of the Alps* years before, and was beginning to know what the plums were, and also what they were worth—since I wrote for their catalogues of Alpine books to Francis Edwards and Mr. Hutt or Dutt, the great specialist, who had a dark shop somewhere off Lincoln's Inn Fields. And gradually I began to add quite substantially to my pocket-money by buying, say, a second edition of Wills's *Wanderings in the High Alps* for two shillings, and selling it to Francis Edwards for seven-and-six. This was a most agreeable way of spending my time, however unrelished by Miss Metsch, and it taught me something which I was more than ready to believe anyhow—that there is usually money in specialised knowledge, if applied with sufficient diligence.

It had always been taken for granted that I, like my three older sisters, should go to Oxford; my Father had been greatly disappointed that Jenny and Grace refused to complete their education in this way, and wasted their time in frivolity. In fact both had a perfectly sound excuse: Jenny was delicate, and had anyhow compromised by spending two or three years at the Slade School; Grace, after an attack of scarlet fever in Surrey, caught teaching in the village Sunday school, had come out to Switzerland and swum in ice-cold glacier-water; this brought on Bright's Disease, and she was left a semi-invalid, obliged to live on fish, chicken, and Contrexéville water, which made a University career quite impracticable. I, however, was to go, and to do great things, as Cora had done; my poor Father had a pathetic belief in my powers. Two coaches were presently engaged, one to teach me mathematics and algebra, which I loathed, the other for classics. But it all went wrong, for a rather curious reason. My dear sister Cora, once a student herself and now a don, thought—really most reasonably—that the precious little youngest sister, brought up entirely in the schoolroom at home, would be at a terrible disadvantage if she tried to take her first examination without any previous experience; she suggested that I should go up and sit for Responsions at Oxford a year too soon, simply to learn my way round and get accustomed to an examination. My coaches concurred; I needed another year's work at least, but this plan should help when the time came. So I went.

Cora took me on this delightful outing. I had never seen Oxford, of which I had heard so much; the city was dreaming in its summer beauty, and I was in a dream of pleasure too—being shown round colleges, going on the river, taking tea at Queens with H. P. Cronshaw's brother George and in North Oxford with the beloved "little Hutch" and his wife. The morning and afternoon sessions in the Examination Schools were merely incidental interruptions to this round of delights: I ran in, wrote my papers light-heartedly and very fast, observing with pity the obvious agonies of some of the wretches who had *got* to pass this time, and then ran out again to wait for Cora—it was so hot that I often sat on the wide stone steps, looking across at the façade of Queens and the topmost pinnacles of All Souls, their stone crocketings white as flowers against the summer sky. The result of this casual treatment was what might, I suppose, have been foreseen—I passed easily, and that was my undoing. I was only seventeen, and the college authorities did not care to take girls under eighteen; I was bidden to wait for a year, and then come up. To fill in time I started reading Italian History with Greta Robertson, and at my Mother's instance put up my hair and began to go about—with very little enthusiasm at first. But when the year was up I decided to put off going to Oxford for another twelve months. My little brother had only recently died, my Mother was not too well, and I realised that she liked having me with her and carting me round in the afternoon to call on her elderly friends, with the pretty old French cardcase in embossed silver from which she pulled out cards if the friends were out. But when that second year had passed the situation at home was still the same, and once more I decided to postpone going to college for another twelve months—and by that time, as we shall see presently, it was too late. In the upshot I never went to Oxford at all, missed altogether the mental discipline and the serious scholarship which a University alone can give; intellectually I remained half-baked.

"If you'd ever been properly educated, with your wits, you'd have been a hell of a writer," my son once said to me—and I really think he may have been right.

My Mother's homesickness for the country did not diminish, nor did mine. Whenever we could we went down to Richmond Park or Kew or Hampton Court, to nourish our eyes with the sight of green things growing, and flowers in bloom even though in gardens not our own; if there was not time to go so far afield we took rugs and cushions, boarded a bus outside the door—buses in those agreeable days stopped where you wanted them to, not at fixed points for their own convenience—and got off at Brompton Cemetery. There, between the railway and that central space bounded by hideous cloisters where she now lies, my Mother had found a quiet spot where trees overhung a few neglected tombstones; we spread our rugs on the grass and passed a quiet hour or so in a green shade, almost oblivious to the roar of traffic down the Fulham Road.

But we both really lived for the summers in Switzerland. We seldom went for less than three months; we settled down—at Brunnen and later at Mürren—and were joined gradually by the American relations, in force: little Aunt Jane, Aunt Sallie T. and her widowed daughter Louisa Townsend with her boy, Idanna di Brazza and her father Detalmo—greyer than ever, but still prone to eat meat on Fridays; Cousin E. C. Day, Uncle Bob's son, and often some Glennys as well. Again the Southern accents flowed musically, again "the Day girls" enjoyed their anecdotes and their jokes, again Aunt Sallie amused herself, and us, by her mischief-making. There was usually one English contribution to this family gathering, and only one—Charles Masefield, whose eldest brother Reginald had married my cousin Doll Sanders, one of Aunt Isabel's many daughters; he took to attaching himself to us for his summer holiday. One year, soon after his wife's death, dear old Archdeacon Baly was persuaded to come too, and his venerable presence and great white beard presided at meals at the head of the long table where twenty or more of us all sat together. This was a manifest relief to the normal hotel curiosity of the other inhabitants of the Kurhaus: here at last was the patriarch, the husband—or perhaps even the father?—of one of those numerous elderly ladies round whom so many young people swarmed; presumably they were all related, but *how*? Aunt Sallie T. and Louisa of course simply made this confusion worse confounded—the so striking elder Mrs. Townsend constantly referred to the handsome and vivacious younger Mrs. Townsend as "my daughter."

"Chère Madame—a thousand excuses—but you wish to say

216

your daughter-in-law?" the courteous but desperately inquisitive foreigner would enquire.

"*Both*," Aunt Sallie would reply, delighted—"my daughter *and* my daughter-in-law!" This was nearly as good as the black pearl; age could not wither, custom could not stale her pleasure in teasing.

The fact was that during those Swiss summers we enjoyed much more of a family life than we had done since leaving Surrey; more of us were together, for longer on end, than was ever the case in London, and whereas in London all went their own ways, more or less, here we led a united life. Some might climb and some play tennis, but we all met at meals, all strolled along together to the station to greet or say goodbye to someone, all ate strawberry tarts at the *confiserie*, or picnicked up in the Blumental. And the presence of the aunts and cousins, year after year, gave a sense of background, of permanence, which our constant changes of residence had denied us at home. This lack of unity and a stable background became especially marked in London, where our heterogeneous acquaintance—Cora and her scientists, Therese and her almoners and social workers, Grace and Jenny with their cosmopolitan dance-partners, Helen's and my mountaineers—gave a restless, episodic, uncertain quality to our surroundings. But there was no uncertainty about our Aunts. We had known them always; they carried their own strong unity with them; wherever they were, they were at home—and among them my Mother was another person, gay and happy; she bloomed with zest and interest and fun. As for me, I found it all extraordinarily restful and delightful, and—something the young need so much, which I missed at home—those months of a real family life were full of reassurance.

Chapter 14

*T*HE years in London, little as my Mother and I enjoyed them, ran on quietly enough; when that life suddenly came to an end the shock was considerable even to young and resilient people, as I and my brothers and sisters were—to her it must have been frightful. As I have said her splendid health had at last begun to fail a little; to lessen her burdens my sister Jenny took over the accounts, never a strong suit of my Mother's, and the house-keeping, which she did extremely competently; we still had delicious food—oh, those chocolate meringues, filled with chocolate-flavoured cream, which were Jenny's own invention— and entertained liberally; but the household bills (for food alone) were brought down to the paltry sum of four thousand pounds a year, which seemed astonishingly moderate compared with our previous expenditure. In 1911 my Father took for us a small lodge on the island of Mull in Argyll, with shooting, fishing, and stalking on a modest scale; contrary to his usual practice he himself did not go up to Ross-shire, but remained in London; my Mother stayed with him. I suppose this one fact might have aroused our suspicions, but it didn't. Therese was now considered old enough —she was nearly forty—to act as chaperone, and all sorts of people came to stay: Doll and Reg Masefield, Reg's brother Charles, and no end of Grace's and Jenny's dancing young men. We shot, fished, stalked; sailed a chunky awkward island boat about Loch Scridain, swam in cold rough water before breakfast, set lobster-pots and revelled in what we hauled up in them, picked raspberries in the garden, and shelled peas on the wooden seats in front of the fuchsia-clad whitewashed house. We read Havelock Ellis's *The World of Dreams* aloud after supper—of trout or the lobsters—and jotted down our dreams during the night to read out at breakfast, sometimes confirming, sometimes disproving the great man's theories; we learned, and acted, Synge's *The Well of the Saints*. A dominie rode over eighteen miles on a pony twice a week to give me lessons in Gaelic. It was a lovely life, full of the sense of permanence and timelessness which is so essentially a part of the Highlands; we had the feeling that there was no reason why such a form of existence should ever come to an end. And then my Mother's letter came—brought by the postman who bicycled five miles over a rough track, took a cup of tea, and after an hour in which we hastily answered our letters, bicycled back again.

I remember that morning so clearly. 1911 was a summer remarkable for heat and drought, even in the rain-soaked West Highlands, and we were still living out of doors, in summer frocks, though it was already early September; we were sitting shelling the last of the peas on the seat by the narrow strip of lawn when Sandy Post came puffing up the path between the fuchsia-bushes, blown from his ride, and handed us the mail. The last of our summer guests had gone; we were alone. The letter from my Mother was addressed to Therese; when she had read it herself she summoned our attention, and read it out to us.

It was a pitiful story, and I realise now what it must have meant to my Mother to write it. The plain fact was that we were ruined. On the day of Bobbie's funeral, four years before, my Father had had what everyone took to be a chill; he stayed in bed for a whole day, something he had never done since he left his cradle. We all remembered that most vividly—our Father in bed by day was something unheard-of. But in fact it had not been a chill at all, it was a slight stroke, and thereafter his mind began to give way, though so slightly at first as to be imperceptible; however, it was enough to affect his business powers. In 1907, when Bobbie died, my parent had had two hundred and fifty thousand pounds safely salted away in sound investments; in the four intervening years he managed, with his poor deranged intellects, to disperse practically all of it by injudicious manipulations—carried out, as we learned afterward from his devoted manager, Mr. Watson, by opening a Bible on his desk in the office, and picking texts at random with a pin. Why Mr. Watson did not reveal these curious methods to my Mother earlier I cannot conceive, but by the time he did so practically everything had gone; there was just enough left to keep up the rather heavy premiums on my Father's life insurance policy, and to maintain us somewhere abroad very cheaply indeed—but that was all. The policy, my poor Mother explained, had to be kept up at all costs; it was for something like sixty thousand pounds and represented our sole future source of income.

She went bravely into details. The London house had already been let furnished as from December; later it would have to be sold. Jack could not go to Cambridge as Harry had done, he must start earning his living at once; I must give up all idea of Oxford, Helen of training her voice professionally. My Mother wrote in deep distress for *us*, fearing that we should find poverty very hard; of her own situation, dashed from luxury to penury just at the onset of old age, with an ailing husband on her hands, there was not a single word.

After Therese had finished reading this letter we discussed the future while we finished shelling the peas. We were all fairly determined on one thing: we were *not* going to live in a state of miserable economising in some cheap foreign hotel, we were going to earn our livings somehow. Grace was still a semi-invalid, but she was a wonderful needle-woman, and would sew; Helen thought she might after all make something out of her voice. Therese, characteristically, said there and then what she was going to do— go to America and teach English literature and history in some expensive school; and within a couple of months she was doing it. My own reaction, looking back, I find interesting. I had never stopped writing in secret, and I thought that I could perhaps make some money by it; after we had eaten those peas—ever afterwards so intimately connected in my mind with this startling change in our lives—at lunch I took a copy-book and pencil and went a little way up the hill behind the house to a place I knew well, and had come to love: a small glen running down towards the sea, in those days of early autumn full of vivid colour—the crimson of rowan-berries, the enamelled brilliance of blackberry-leaves in every shade from primrose to carmine. There, sitting on soft dry heather and leaning against a rock stippled with black and grey lichen, I wrote my first short story, *Pepita's Miracle;* some twenty-three years later it was published in America without the alteration of a single word, and brought me in a hundred pounds.

But at the time, when we returned to London and set about tackling our new mode of existence, writing seemed too speculative as a means of livelihood. True, Charles Masefield sent some of my poems and sketches to Brother John, presently to be the Poet Laureate; he replied in flattering terms but said—"Let her write a novel; that will show what her talent is really worth." Admirable advice from the literary point of view, but meanwhile I had got to *eat*; through the good offices of another Lady Almoner, Edith Mudd of St. George's Hospital, a climbing friend, I secured a job as assistant secretary in the Chelsea branch of the Charity Organisation Society, the justly famous old C.O.S. My hours were from nine-fifteen to six o'clock, and I was paid twenty-three shillings a week. Helen, with her University degree, got a much better job as secretary to the Juvenile Advisory Committee of one of those new-fangled creations of Will Beveridge's, the Labour Exchanges; we took a six-room flat in the Fulham Road for twenty-five shillings a week, and an ex-nursery-maid came to look after us—Grace was to live with us, sew, and keep house. Cora was of course completely self-supporting as a don, Harry went away to Australia, Jenny became private secretary to Adelaide Anderson, then Chief Woman Inspector of Factories, and an old family friend; through Mr. Ross a job was found for Jack in Canada, to which he sailed in December—my Father always had a profound belief in Canada as the country of the future. A few days after his departure my parents set off for Cannes; within less than three months the *diaspora* of our family was complete. "Never slept in Elm Park Gardens again" my Mother noted sadly against the date of her departure for Cannes.

My life in London at this stage is my story, not my Mother's, and has no place here—I will simply say that it was all tremendous fun; I never enjoyed myself better in my life. We were frightfully poor, although my Mother had coerced my Father into making us each a tiny allowance, less than half what we should have cost him for our keep on the Continent. Often I was actually *hungry*, a rather surprising experience for people brought up as we had been, but a useful one; because I ate so much at breakfast, besides my kipper or sausage, my sister Grace, a rigid and practical housekeeper, put two rounds of the loaf and as much butter as she thought proper on the table, and that was all I got, whatever I said. The ex-nursemaid cut me sandwiches for my lunch, which I ate in the Chelsea Polytechnic dining-room among the students, paying a penny for a cup of coffee, and if I was feeling rich, fourpence for a helping of pudding. None of this mattered in the least: I was well, I was absorbed in my work and the social problems it raised; I saw, and made, countless friends; I was as happy as a lark. At the C.O.S. I encountered Ethel Graham of Skipness, who was studying sociology, and she invited me to spend the Easter of 1913 at her home in Argyll. There I met my husband; by June we were engaged; and in October of that year we got married and settled down in London.

But from 1911 onwards my Mother's life was a hard one. My Father developed a bad heart and asthma; his health as well as economy demanded that he should spend his winters abroad. That first one they spent in Cannes; the following August our house was sold, and they came home to supervise the disposal and storing of the furniture and family possessions, always such a pitiful business—things which look perfectly happy and decorative in inhabited rooms take on such a derelict air in a repository. In October they went abroad again, this time to the Italian Lakes; it was there some months later that my Mother got my letter announcing my engagement. She had always hoped that I should marry, and had unobtrusively fostered the courtships of my various swains while we were still together; some of them even confided in her. (Another of the things I only realised later was with what dismay she must have gone abroad, leaving me and my two sisters to live in London earning our livings in a rough world, and entirely without her watchful supervision, or indeed any supervision at all.) But here I now was, engaged to an eminently suitable young man, even if he was only a younger son and far from rich; I think she was pleased, though I suspect that she secretly regretted some of the wealthier and equally suitable admirers whom I had refused. She and my Father came home for my wedding, performed by dear Cronje at St. Mark's, North Audley Street on Crispin Crispian's Day, 1913, and a few days later they returned to Cannes.

My Father, never an easy man at the best of times, was of course more difficult than ever now that he was ailing and *désœuvré*; he grumbled at waiters and complained to hotel managers, who in their turn complained of him. "Ah, the English! They desire always to warm the garden!" one proprietor exclaimed bitterly when my Father would persist in opening the windows of the hotel salon while the so cruelly expensive *chauffage centrale* was turned on. But my Mother managed to get a certain degree of pleasure even from these difficult sojourns: the things from which she had always drawn sustenance and delight, sea and sky, mountains and flowers, delighted and sustained her still; she wrote lyrically about the flowers grown for perfume-making on the Riviera, and the sunsets along the western shore.

What is quite astonishing to-day, in view of the conditions which prevailed in World War II, is the degree of mobility which my parents enjoyed in World War I. They came home for the birth of my first child in the summer of 1914—that of course was simple enough, as war had not yet broken out; but in October the same year, submarines or no, they set sail for Canada. With Europe at war my Father was more than ever convinced that Canada was the most stable country in the world, and he decided to transfer his few remaining assets, including that Life Insurance, there, to be placed in trust for his family. In fact this plan did not in the end work out for us as well as he had hoped: the trust company in which he placed his funds charged high fees, was completely inaccessible, and we had no possible means of checking their proceedings—however, fortunately for him he was not to know that.

They spent the whole winter over there, and my Mother amused herself in characteristic fashion by tracing out and tracking down all the living descendants of a first cousin of my grandfather's, Charles Dewey Day, whose father, Ithamar Day, brother of Captain James, had emigrated from New England to Canada—to Hull, as Ottawa was still called at the close of the eighteenth century—because he was unwilling to live under any flag but the British. His son Charles was one of the few members of the Day family to enter public life: he became a Member of Parliament and Solicitor-General, and was at one time a member of Her Majesty's Executive Council for Canada; for several years he was Chancellor of McGill University. In 1842, when only thirty-six, he became a Judge of the Court of Queen's Bench in Montreal, and at some point he presided over the Commission of five lawyers which framed a new Legal Code for the Province of Quebec, combining the old French Code with many of the features of English Law. (It was presumably as a result of his labours that when I was taken to hear a case being tried in the High Court at Montreal in 1942, I listened to pleading and evidence alike being heard both in English and in French, which amused me very much.)

This Judge Day originally owned the portrait of my Grandfather's Grandfather, Captain William Day, painted by Thomas Hudson, Court painter to George II, after a particularly successful piece of privateering on behalf of the English Crown, when Captain William brought five French ships as prizes into Plymouth; as Charles Day's only son died in infancy he gave the portrait to my Grandfather, from whom it passed in due course to my cousin E. C. Day. My Mother carefully notes that the Museum in Montreal "would welcome" a photograph of this, and makes a memo that when she returns to London she must look out the copy that had been given to my youngest brother, now dead, and send it to Montreal. She went to immense pains to have as many of the family portraits as possible photographed, and gave us each framed copies, but as these were old and faded by the time I started to write this book I set about procuring fresh ones. This involved an immense amount of correspondence with America, and I was amused and touched when among my Mother's papers I came on endless letters exchanged between her and my Aunt Jane more than fifty years ago, when she was engaged on the same enterprise. All her problems cropped up over again for me—the inexperienced photographer who produces bad results, the frenzied enquiries as to who had the portrait of "The Grandmother with the Gun." My Mother guessed where it probably was—with one of her cousins, Thomas Davis Day's daughter—but she never secured a copy since owing to the "grand family split" she could not, or at least did not approach her. I was more fortunate, and the photograph of Abigail Hinman's portrait which I reproduce here I owe to that same "Cousin Sarah's" great kindness; she went to infinite trouble to have it specially taken for me.

My Mother wrote down a full account of this Canadian connection, and the sequence of her efforts to ascertain and verify all the facts she could; it makes pleasant reading to-day, for it shows her happy and interested in the task and in all the incidentals connected with it. She learned amongst other things that Charles Day, the Judge, had been passionately interested in bees, and in the Canadian wild-flowers; this reminds her of her own father's love of both, and she notes—"My Father used to charge us never to gather too many wild-flowers, but to leave plenty to seed"; and she records his dictum "that it should be made obligatory by law that every person should plant one tree a year, and that for each cut down, two should be planted." A very right-thinking man, my Grandfather. She also recalls in this connection that a certain Richard Day, probably a nephew of that Robert who emigrated to America in 1634, sought permission from Charles the Second to re-plant Windsor Forest by sowing it with acorns, at his own expense!—she even mentions that she has traced his correspondence with Lord Conway on the subject among the State Papers in the Record Office. Happy woman—thus busying and contenting herself with research in a strange city, while one of her sons was at the front, and the other on his way there.

It will be seen that genealogy was one of her passions, and she pursued it with the same pertinacity and accuracy that she devoted to wild-flowers and sea-weeds. Her own family's records in America, going back for eight generations, were too well known to require much attention, but she was anxious to pursue her researches into their English forbears and connections—Dolbeares and Hinmans as well as the tree-planting Days—and while still in Montreal she lists several places where the parish records remain to be searched: Norwich, Windsor, and Eton amongst others. I had done quite a lot of this searching of records with her and for her when I was a girl—in Devonshire, and at the Record Office and Somerset House as well; all those Lutheran governesses forced us to write German script, so that even the semi-gothic handwriting of early wills and registers, which completely foxed most country parsons, presented no great difficulties. My Mother did some really remarkable work on her husband's forbears, the Brookings and Sanderses, to which this book owes much.

After this genealogical interlude in Canada, again braving the submarines my parents re-crossed the Atlantic in May, 1915, and spent the summer in England; in September, with most of northern France a battle-field, they calmly set out again for Cannes, and remained there in perfect tranquillity for nearly a year, only returning to England—still quite calmly—in August, 1916. To-day, with the sufferings and restrictions and complications of 1940–1945 in mind, it seems almost incredible that two frail old people should have been able to wander to and fro across Europe like that in the middle of a war in which France was involved—however, they did it, and did it without any particular difficulty except for the curiosity aroused in Customs officials by my Mother's flask. She always liked to drink water at all hours, and a great deal of it; to this end she carried when travelling a huge wicker-covered flask containing nearly a quart, slung round her person on a strap—this was always sniffed at suspiciously by douaniers at all frontiers, and their incredulous disgust when the contents proved to be indeed nothing but water had afforded us many good laughs on journeys to Switzerland and Italy in happier days. However, 1916 saw my parents' last journey on the Continent; after their return in August they spent a few weeks in London to see us, and then went off to another of those depressing hotels, this time at Seaton in Devonshire, where my Father died before the year was out.

But those years of the first World War, journeys apart, brought to my Mother an anxiety which I was later to share, and a tragedy which I was spared. By the summer of 1914 my brother Harry had returned from Australia, and he joined the Life Guards as a private twenty-four hours after the war broke out; he went out to France with the first draft, before the end of September. He amused us with accounts of some of his fellow-recruits at Windsor, less accustomed to riding than he, who when first issued with a saddle, of course with the girths buckled, wandered dismally round from the front end to the back of the horse allotted to them, wondering where they could slide the contraption on. Harry enjoyed his war enormously; he soon became a corporal, then a corporal of horse, and after some months was given a commission;

he was in Flanders to the very end of the war, and never got a scratch.

My brother Jack, as we know, had been sent to Canada after the family *débâcle*; he was placed in the Trade Commissioner's office, but he didn't like it, and without a word to anyone set about getting himself another job. The one he particularly wanted was advertised in the press with the express stipulation that "all applications must be in the applicant's own hand-writing." Jack, bless him, wrote an execrable hand; he sent in his application typewritten throughout, including the signature, and got the job—in the teeth of over a hundred other candidates. This calm, shrewd assessment was typical of him. On August, 1914, he too joined up, as a private in the Royal Montreal Regiment, the 14th battalion of the First Canadian Division, and sailed for Europe in October. Alas, my Mother just missed him; indeed the boat on which she and my Father were travelling passed the convoy bringing the Canadian troops to Europe somewhere in the Atlantic. This was a cruel disappointment—she had so counted on seeing her beloved youngest-but-one in Canada. She never saw him again; by the time she and my Father returned to England in May, 1915, he was dead.

We, however—and how I wished it could have been my Mother instead of me—saw a good deal of him while the Division was in England, during the three months before they went to France in February, 1915. Jack was now rather a splendid person: the stout stolid little boy who in the face of three years of persecution had refused to renounce his family's pro-Boer sentiments had turned into an immensely tall young man—calm, poised, laconic; modestly self-confident, humorously affectionate, and with a dry deliberate wit which made him very good company. George Mallory and Geoffrey Young were both extremely attached to this brother of mine, of whom they saw much in London and in the Alps before he went to Canada.

When Jack arrived in France with his regiment my brother Harry was of course already there; on a winter's night, coming down out of the line, he heard that "the Canadians" were moving up, and eventually the Life Guards actually passed the Dominion troops; Harry dismounted and ran up and down their ranks in the dark calling his brother by name, but in vain—it was an off-chance, and it failed; like my Mother he never saw Jack again.

The first German gas attack on April the 22nd, 1915—in the course of which my younger brother fell—was a desperate business. This new horror took the allied troops completely by surprise; the attack was directed against the French right near its junction with the British left, then held by the Canadians, and the Algerians and some of the French Territorial troops on the Canadians' left fled, though the Tirailleurs and the Zouaves remained in position, gas or no. But the Germans pressed on fast through the gap left by the retreating French troops till they actually menaced the Canadian Brigade Head-Quarters. The 14th battalion, in which my brother served, was ordered up to cover the H.Q.; the Canadian divisional artillery was directed to assist those of the French who still held their ground. The 13th Canadian battalion fought till their last man had fallen, and by early next day some ten battalions were strung out attempting to cover the gap between where the Canadian left had been when the attack began, and the canal; among them was the 14th. The terse phrase in the Official History—"The ten battalions did not form a continuous line . . ." covered hours of very confused fighting of which it gives little hint, except perhaps to professional soldiers; my brother's company, for example, spent much of the day reaching out to right and left to try to establish contact with the rest of the battalion, or any other Allied troops, while the remainder ran up and down such trenches as they had, or dug at furious speed, "loosing-off as often as we could so as to look as if there were more of us" as one of his friends put it. In such circumstances it was little wonder that many of the battalion, my brother included, were subsequently posted as "missing, believed killed."

Some time in May a Memorial Service was held in St. Paul's Cathedral for the Canadians who had fallen; this too, my Mother just missed, and I wish she had not, for it was extraordinarily moving—the most moving occasion of the sort that I ever remember. The shock of the use of gas, the gallantry of the raw unseasoned overseas troops in holding the gap and preventing a German break-through, their terribly heavy losses all stirred the public imagination; the cathedral was packed to the doors, and the whole great space heavy with emotion. Winnington-Ingram, then Bishop of London, preached the sermon, but it was off-key right from the text: "They asked of Thee life and Thou gavest them long life, even for ever and ever." That was not what was in the minds of that great throng of people—they were thinking of what all those young men whom they loved had gone through before they died: the fears, the desperation, the confusion, the cruel gas—and the hymn met their need:

> *There no more the powers of Hell*
> *Can prevail to mar their peace;*
> *Christ the Lord shall guard them well,*
> *He who died for their release.*

That was it—the powers of Hell had been unleashed against them, but now it was over, and they were at peace. I cannot describe the effect of hearing those words, sung as they were sung that night.

Since Jack, like so many others, had only been listed as "missing," till the end of the war and beyond my Mother continued to hope against hope that he might turn up as a prisoner, or in some hospital. We had no such hope; Grace in particular had contacted all his friends, and learned that he had been seen to fall just before a short retirement took place; no one saw him alive again.

Chapter 15

AFTER my Father's death in 1916 my Mother had a few years of relative peace and tranquillity. That life-insurance policy duly fell in—though it was over a year before we got a single cent from Canada—and she found herself in easier circumstances, and bought a small house on the borders of Chelsea and Fulham; Besa, who had retired from selling Fullers' sweets, and Miss Copus, the old sewing-maid who had helped me to make the Boer flag, with a rather senior orphan came to look after her, so that she had the daily companionship of two faithful souls who had been her friends for thirty years or more—such a priceless boon in old age. The house was close to Brompton Cemetery, and without even crossing a road she could stroll up to that quiet spot under the trees where she and I used to sit, or take flowers to my Father's and my little brother's grave; it was roomy and comfortable, in its Victorian way, with a big pleasant garden behind containing a huge old pear-tree and a plot of grass where she had her tea in summer; there were borders for bulbs and flowers, and Besa's stout form might be seen weeding or watering under my Mother's directions—she would straighten up, with her fat comfortable chuckle, when any of us walked in, and drop her trowel or can to clasp us to her ample bosom with some crack about having a new job—her purple-veined cheeks were just as fresh and pleasant to kiss as on that day when I ran away to Windsor and took refuge with her. Here my Mother's friends, old and young, came to see her—it was surprising how many figures in uniform ran up those shallow steps and knocked at the front door; and there were rooms always ready for Grace and Harry when they came on leave.

For Grace went to war too; in fact she had a rather remarkable para-military career. After nine years of invalidism on a rigid diet—there was nothing bogus about this, for the Bright's Disease had in fact left her with not quite one whole working kidney—she determined to do something for her country, like everyone else. She began sensibly and cautiously, going down three days a week to the East End to work for the Soldiers' and Sailors' Families' Association; presently she increased this to five days. Finding that she could apparently manage so much she took a job as a clerk in the Admiralty for some months—and the next thing we heard was that she had joined the W.A.A.C.s as a sub-lieutenant. The medical examination would seem to have been rather superficial, the enrolling authorities apparently relying on a signed statement from each applicant that she had never suffered from any organic disease—Grace put her name to this document without a qualm, and very soon was sent out with a draft of girls to Rouen.

This sister of mine had almost the firmest character of anyone, man or woman, I have ever known; and in the W.A.A.C.s these qualities, not always too comfortable in family life, were of the greatest value—she found herself completely, and rose in rank rapidly: presently she was what corresponded to a Major, then to a Colonel. She maintained rigid discipline—no tunics unbuttoned at the neck, no button-holes or brooches, no make-up; all the same the women under her adored her, and what is more they used to come to see my Mother when they were on leave and tell her so. During the winter of 1917–1918 Grace was at St.-Omer, living in Nissen huts on bully beef; there were air-raids twenty nights out of thirty, and no shelters were provided for the women at that hurriedly improvised H.Q. Several of her W.A.A.C.s described to my Mother how when the alarm went Grace would get up, pull on a pair of gum-boots and a trench-coat over her pyjamas, and without her helmet walk bareheaded from hut to hut to calm and steady her girls. This method was as shrewd as it was brave—"Some'ow you 'ad to be'ave yerself, seein' 'er goin' round with 'er pretty 'air under all them bombs," as one cockney woman said. A by-product of Grace's work in the Army was an unfailing supply of chars and "helps" for the small house on the Fulham Road; wounded, invalided out, or finally demobilised, there was always someone eager to come and work for "the old lady." When after the Armistice my sister had been moved to York, where she was Commandant for the whole of northern England, on one occasion she telegraphed to say that she was coming home for the week-end, and my Mother instructed the ex-W.A.A.C. char to make up her bed, put hot bottles in it, and "dust"; going up presently with a vase of flowers she found the woman in a welter of "turning-out"—scrubbing paint, polishing floor and furniture. She remonstrated.

"Oh, Jones"—reluctantly, my Mother had adopted the Army habit of surnames, in England hitherto confined to parlourmaids —"Oh, Jones, there was no need to do all this turning-out." The woman rounded on her.

"When Miss Grice comes 'ome she's going to 'ave 'er room *clean*. I'd go to 'ell for that girl."

I cherish a picture clipped from one of the daily papers of my Mother and my sister Grace leaving Buckingham Palace after His Majesty King George V had given her the O.B.E.—my Mother, wearing a pointed widow's bonnet, is smiling up happily into her daughter's rather severe face, under the hideous W.A.A.C. hat. Undoubtedly that was a very happy day for "the old lady," and I daresay she thought, as I did at the time, of Abigail Hinman: my sister's false declaration about her health was very much in the spirit of the goings-on of the Grandmother with the Gun at the siege of New London.

Grace's health in fact constituted much the most remarkable aspect of her activities in the war, and I add this post-script about it. Late in 1917 I happened to meet Dr. Herbert Morley-Fletcher, who had looked after her ever since we came to London thirteen years before—he was therefore perfectly familiar with the extent of her physical disabilities. He asked after her; I told him the sort of life she was leading at St.-Omer, and how she had said, on her last leave, that she found that a diet of bully-beef suited her very well! He screwed his dark intelligent gaze on me.

"What she is doing is *medically impossible*," he said. "It is the most complete victory of spirit over matter that I have ever known, or ever heard of."

Grace spent all her leaves in that pleasant small house, with the wide spaces of sky behind and in front, across Chelsea Station towards the river; so did Harry. Once more my Mother's roof was the family centre to which we all gravitated—Helen from her big job in the Ministry of Munitions, where she organised the work and welfare of nineteen thousand girls and women; Cora, now married, from her home in Coventry; I was close by in Lexham Gardens, and ran in as often as I could; so did Jenny. While the war lasted there was constant anxiety on Grace's and Harry's account, and more than twenty years later, when my own son was all through the retreat to Dunkirk I could enter as never before into that anxiety; but on the whole how blessed it was, after the dreary years of exile, wandering from hotel to hotel, merely to be *still*, and among her own possessions.

The one absentee was Therese—and anxiety about her far outlasted the war years. Early in 1914 she had come back from the States and taken a job in Russia, a country which had always had a great appeal for her since she first went there with my Father twenty years before. In theory she was to teach English and deportment to the little grand-daughter of old Princess Tenisheff, in the Orel province, or "government" as it was called—there had been a divorce, and the child lived with her grandmother; in practice, since there was already the "*Française*" to teach French and the "*Hollandaise*" to teach German, her duties seemed to consist mainly in seeing that the child got an English amount of air and exercise, in keeping the old Princess company, and helping her with her entertaining in the huge rambling country-house among the birch-trees. Therese had a pronounced gift for languages and picked up Russian in no time; she loved the place and the people, and her letters gave a vivid account of country life in Russia during the last three years of the old régime. The Tenisheff estates were vast; a private railway ran from the main line junction at Orel out to the house, on which both passengers and merchandise were carried in the Prince's private trains; apart from tea, sugar, and caviare the place was practically self-supporting—even in fish, which were caught in the lake, two or three miles long, lying on one side of the house. But the Tenisheffs were on the best of terms with their peasants: every child born on the estate, for instance, was brought up to the house for the elaborate baptismal rites of the Orthodox Church to be carried out in the presence at least of the old Princess, who supplied a christening-cake, a present, and in need a robe—my sister used to watch the gaily-dressed little processions come trailing across the narrow wooden foot-bridge, nearly a mile long, which spanned the lake, and trailing away again afterwards, laughing and singing as they went.

When war between Austria and Serbia became imminent there took place the famous "Russian mobilisation," which looms so large in the histories of the time; my sister saw on the spot how it was actually carried out. Prince Tenisheff was "President of the Council of the Nobles for the Orel Government" and in this capacity had to sign all the mobilisation notices himself; they were written out in longhand by his clerk, and when duly signed Therese and her little pupil drove to all the villages for miles around in a small *troika* drawn by three ponies, and with a hammer and tacks affixed them to the village tree, the proper place for such things—after her early experiences with my Father's four-in-hands Therese was a first-class whip, and loved driving the *troika*. Men on horseback dealt with the rest of the province; the whole business occupied some days. To me there is something at once exquisitely mediaeval and most Russianly inept about any part of this national task being entrusted to the foreign governess and the child in their pony-cart. However, these primitive methods apparently worked all right: on the due day—or rather night, for the private trains and wagons were to leave for the junction about midnight —more small parties, an endless stream of small parties, crossed the long wooden bridge over the lake, their bobbing lanterns reflected in the dark water, and gathered at the private station; there, among homely bundles of baggage and provisions, so unlike a brisk Western mobilisation, there were long scenes of farewell, men and women kissing and sobbing, till at last the coaches chugged and clanked away to Orel, and the reduced parties trailed back across the bridge, their lanterns still bobbing, and the sound of weeping echoing back from the silent lake.

Fairly late in 1916 the Tenisheffs, disturbed by the way the war was going, decided to move down to one of their properties in the Crimea in order to be near an escape-route by sea in case of need; they disbanded all three foreign governesses, and the Dutchwoman and the Frenchwoman somehow struggled home— after the revolution the Tenisheffs themselves were never heard of again. But my sister's thirst for Russia was still unslaked, and she promptly took another post, this time in St. Petersburg. It was a considerable contrast to the Tenisheffs, with their feudal simplicities and eighteenth-century elegance; the husband of her new employer was an Armenian sweet-manufacturer from Erzerum, enormously wealthy, whose rather fragile wife wore in her ears cabochon emeralds or rubies as big as hazel-nuts. However, the two children were charming, and they lived in a big airy apartment, high up, on the Kamennostrovski Prospekt; for the summer of 1917 they moved out to a delightful villa on the Gulf of Finland. It all seemed *couleur de rose*. And then in the autumn of that year came the October Revolution—first the Menshevik, later the Bolshevik; my sister was an eye-witness of both.

From then onwards all postal communication ceased; our letters were returned to us, none arrived. Late in 1917 some fiend in human shape called at the Foreign Office and dropped an unstamped letter from Therese addressed to my husband; this person might, we felt, have come in and said who he was, and how he had got out, and in what sort of shape he had left her—but he didn't; he handed the letter to the hall porter, and walked away. It was to my Mother, and said briefly that she, Therese, had always been intensely interested in revolutions—she had in fact taken the French Revolution as her special period when reading history at Oxford—and that now, with an actual one in progress under her eyes she proposed to stay and see it through. After that letter we heard nothing for nearly four years, till on a day in the spring of 1921 we read her name in *The Times* among a list of British subjects who were being repatriated from Russia through the frontier station of Terioki, on the borders of Finland.

Those four years of silence and anxiety were hard for my Mother, but she took them with her usual resigned tranquillity; as in Jack's case, she refused to believe the worst, and this time she was right. A room was always kept ready in the small house for Therese when she should return, and gradually it became filled with copies of *The Times*. Before the mails to Russia shut down, my Mother had posted *The Times* regularly to my sister; when she could no longer do so she started keeping them for her, in case there should be something she wanted to look up. This was perhaps reasonable for a matter of a few months, not longer; but the ritual once started took on a sort of perpetual motion of its own—to stop it would have been tacitly to admit the possibility that my sister might *not* come back. So every month Besa did up some thirty *Timeses* in a bundle with string, and made the orphan or the char climb the step-ladder to pile them on top of the big double Maple wardrobe with the mirror doors; when they reached the ceiling two piles were made in corners, and finally a fresh accumulation was begun in the box-room. How they were disposed of in the end I have no idea.

A few days after that paragraph appeared in the papers my sister reached London. She was gaunt and haggard; her hair quite grey, her pretty blue eyes enormous in her thin face; she brought

237

little with her but a flat loaf of sour greyish-black bread full of sawdust, to show us what people ate during revolutions. Three and a half years under the Bolsheviks had left her, at first, with some very odd habits. She was normally the most self-controlled of people, regulating her life with an iron discipline that had even a touch of asceticism about it; but for the first month or so after her return, as Besa found to her astonished dismay, if the leg of mutton was left in the dining-room instead of being removed at once to the larder, Therese was liable to finish it, or as near as no matter; and it was more than a year before she could be persuaded to leave her door unlocked when she left the bedroom, even in the afternoons when the char had gone and there was no one in the house whom she had not known since she was a child. My Mother, of course, was perfectly patient with these peculiarities while they lasted, and as we listened to Therese's accounts of life in Petrograd during the first years of the Bolshevik régime it was easy enough to understand their origins. A shortage of fats so acute that when for a colossal sum the sweet-manufacturer managed to buy a bottle of cod-liver oil for the two children they would lick the spoon interminably—or lie, and declare that they had not had it that morning; such a shortage of meat that my sister, like everyone else with any sense, carried a sharp carving-knife in her belt, so that if one happened to see a horse fallen dead of starvation in the street one could cut off some pieces to take home, stuffed in one's high felt boots to escape observation—otherwise it would have been stolen on the way. The endless visits, by night and by day, of newly appointed Commissars, who came to raid the flat for eatables or valuables; the battle with lice, with only cold water in which to wash one's own and the children's clothes; Therese used to beat the clothes on the kitchen table with a rolling-pin to kill the lice that way, and then shake out the corpses, sweep them up, and keep them in a tin till the next time there was enough fuel to have a fire and do some cooking—usually about twice a week. The Armenians' servants all left or were taken away, and presently the fragile wife was got into a hospital; Therese had to do everything, and cope with the children as well. The flat was on the seventh floor, and of course the lift stopped working almost at once; she told us how after a year of near-starvation she was so weak that it became almost a routine, on reaching the top of the last three flights of stairs, to roll over and *lie* on the landing, so that if she fainted she would at least not fall downstairs again.

The competition to get into hospitals, where there was a little more to eat, was so acute that men and boys used to hawk matchboxes containing lice infected with typhus on the streets; typhus patients had to be admitted without question. "*Guaranteed* typhus lice," they would hiss urgently, holding out their hideous wares in your face. But it was all pretty hideous. I have never forgotten her account of the first two or three days of delirious freedom, when the whole populace ran amok in the streets, killing and torturing policemen and dancing round them with laughter and silly glee while they died in agony. Most indicative of all of the Russian character was the business of the trams. St. Petersburg had an extensive and excellent tram-way system, run by foreign or foreign-trained engineers and employees, German or Belgian, I forget which. During those first two or three days of giddy liberty the native inhabitants took over the trams and drove them themselves; ignoring schedules and routes they charged about the city, sending the heavy and expensive machines along the tram-lines at headlong speed with an incessant clanging of bells and loud cries of joy—there were so many head-on collisions that the streets became blocked with wrecked trams, and it was weeks before the system was got into working order again. There was, of course, forced "national work" for everyone for so many weeks in the year, whatever their normal employment; Therese twice spent a couple of months in the summer working as a navvy on building railway embankments, pushing wheelbarrows of earth up steep slopes. She was a big strong woman, and too courageous to mind things like blistered hands or a strained back, but her health never completely recovered from the protracted over-work and under-nourishment of those years. She did indeed learn all about revolutions.

My Mother was of course overjoyed to have Therese safely back, and living with her; they got on very well together, and during her three years in the States my sister had seen so many of the relations, and visited so many of the family homes that they had endless matter for conversation, apart from the Russian saga. Therese was the only daughter permanently resident in my Mother's house: after being demobilised Grace married Bertram Bircham, Legal Adviser to the Ministry of Labour, and lived in a lovely house at Worplesdon which she ran with the same ruthless efficiency that she had displayed in the W.A.A.C.s; Helen built herself a delightful little abode at Wentworth in Surrey, only a few miles from Windsor Great Park; Jenny had a flat in London; my brother Harry came and went. Still my Mother was the family centre, as her mother had been before her. One by one the American aunts died off—as my Mother was the youngest sister this was only to be expected, though Aunt Jane survived her by a year or two; but as the aunts died grand-children came along, to give her intense pleasure. She had been with me in London when my first child was born, a few days after the outbreak of war in 1914—when she gave me those reminiscences of the American Civil War; she stayed with us at Godalming in the house which George and Ruth Mallory lent us when George, who had been a master at Charterhouse, abandoned school-mastering for soldiering; there my son was born in 1918. Finally she used to come down to Bridge End, the beloved fifteenth-century house at Ockham where we went in 1919, and lived to see my youngest child born and growing there. She crooned lovingly over all three of them; I used to listen, with a curious sense of time repeating itself, to her singing to my children the same darkie songs that she had sung to me when I was a child. Sometimes she went down to visit her devoted and admiring sister-in-law my Aunt Isabel at Haslemere; but for the most part she sat quietly in her own house, where her children, her nephews and nieces, and her friends young and old came to visit her. Her interest in them and in all their activities was as keen as ever; only when she sat alone a settled sadness would come into her face. But then Besa would bring in a cup of tea and stay for a little cheerful chat, and tell her who had rung up to announce themselves for supper. Tranquil sunset years: three blue photographs of Stonington still hung beside her dressing-table, and more and more often she recurred in talk to the scenes of her youth—" 'a babbled o' green fields," the last happy resource of the old or the dying.

Her death was of a piece with her life. Her heart began to trouble her, and the complaint was diagnosed as a *sequela* of yellow fever, which she had had as a girl in New Orleans; Hodgkin's Disease, and at her age incurable. Quietly she made her preparations to leave the world which in spite of difficulties and sorrows she had enjoyed so much. She went slowly and methodically through all her papers, a little at a time, as her small stock of strength permitted, destroying everything that was not of permanent interest, like her genealogical studies; recognising how difficult her handwriting was she got in a typist and dictated the most important results of these, and had copies made for us all—this when breathing and speech were already becoming difficult; she made Besa write down her final dispositions about her furniture, and left a special note that I was on no account to wear mourning for her, as she knew that my husband disliked it. Few deaths can ever have given less trouble of a practical sort. The doctor who attended her was a youngish man whom we hardly knew, a pupil of Herbert Morley-Fletcher's, who sent him to us; he became devoted to his patient, and was greatly struck by her serene patience and constant consideration for others, even during suffering that became increasingly severe. He told us flatly that the use of certain drugs might prolong her life by a few weeks or even months, but that he was not going to give them. "I will do everything in my power to ease her; I will do nothing to make her live an extra week, or even an extra day," he said. To inspire such a degree of devotion in a stranger when on one's deathbed must be unusual; she did, however—and on a sunny day in May, when the big pear-tree outside her window was white with blossom, she slipped peacefully away.

In 1941, for the first time, I visited the United States. When the Germans marched into Hungary, where my husband was British Minister, in April of that year we had to leave the Legation in Budapest hurriedly, and since Italy was an enemy and Yugoslavia in process of being over-run by the Panzer Divisions, the only route home open to us was across Russia and Siberia, down through Manchuria via Harbin to Dairen, and on across the Pacific to America—round the world, in fact. From Harbin, or rather from the frontier station at Manchouli right down to Dairen, the old Port Arthur, we were travelling over the Chinese Eastern Railway, for which my Father had sold both rails and rolling-stock nearly fifty years before. It was a long and in parts a very tedious journey; we had been eight weeks on the road when we reached San Francisco, just half-way home, whereas from Budapest to London direct normally takes about thirty-six hours.

From California I went first to New Orleans to spend some weeks with our cousins. The place was still full of Glennys, and I had other friends there as well. I was glad to see the city where my Mother had grown up and come out, and I was of course bewitched, as every stranger must be, by its quite peculiar charm: the wonderful iron-work everywhere, flowering trees overflowing onto the sidewalks from gardens dense and scented with exotic shrubs and flowers; the French-speaking darkie servants in people's houses, and the *warm*, civilised quality of the life, even in homes where poverty had begun to strike. I loved the place, I loved the people—I was driven out into the country to lunch at old plantation houses, where it was easy to envisage that scene of the door that opened of itself. But—and I have often wondered why—except out on the plantations and in one or two of the oldest gardens, like those on Coliseum Street, somehow I could not recapture the city of my Mother's youth. Whether this was because she herself was never much good at cities, or because the new

America had invaded New Orleans too much, rather swamping its earlier character, I cannot say. Certainly this invasion had taken place. Factories had sprung up on the outskirts; and within the city itself, as I went about lecturing for the Red Cross and meeting people of all sorts, I was vaguely aware of what seemed to be two concentric social circles—an outer one, rich, rather new, and slightly at a loss in its surroundings, and an inner one, usually by no means rich and certainly not in the least new or modern, which gave an impression of being somehow compressed and driven in on itself by that more active, not to say more vociferous outer ring. There was far greater ease at the centre, in spite of age or straitened circumstances—a sort of traditional quiet and simplicity which I found very appealing. I would have liked to linger there for months, sitting in the great heat on screened verandahs above gardens blazing with colour, and watching the play of feature on fine chiselled faces while I listened to stories from the past—my Mother's past, and that of her kinsfolk—related in the deep voices that had been familiar to me from the far-distant days of my earliest childhood.

But I had to go North to join my husband and my daughter in Washington, and to make plans. After a few super-heated days there and some hectic ones in New York, at last I found myself sitting in a train going up to Boston to stay with friends in Massachusetts; though I did not realise it at the time, travelling now over a rail-road in whose construction my grandfather, James Ingersoll Day, had taken a part. And as I sat looking out of the window that afternoon—I was alone—I was overtaken by a very strange experience. It was a fine summer's day; where the line hugged the coast, wooded headlands, low, close-grown and green, ran out into the sea, with reed-fringed rocky inlets between them; worn grey boulders stood up out of the sward in the pastures, and inland rose taller woods, all bathed in the strong summer sunshine. This New England landscape, simple, homely, rather austere, is quite unlike anything in the Old World; I was seeing it for the first time, and yet something within me cried out strongly—"I have been here before." By the time I reached Boston, now rather shaken by the extraordinary vividness and intensity of this impression, I had already realised why it had come to me—my Mother's wistful, often-repeated descriptions of the landscape she loved had given me a mental picture of it so clear and strong that when the living reality was unfolded before my eyes it seemed completely familiar. She had been dead then for close on twenty years, but her own country-side, the country-side of the happiest part of her childhood, brought me very close to her.

And the year that followed was to bring me closer still. All through the spring of 1940 my son, like her sons before him, had been on active service in northern France as an infantry officer, and the days before we learned that he had got out at Dunkirk had been wretched with anxiety; now, in 1941, he switched to the R.A.F. and became a bomber pilot, and the anxiety began all over again. Moreover London, where my family settled down again at the end of September, 1941, was being blitzed; both my daughters were air-raid wardens. During the year and a day that I spent in America I realised at last, fully, what had lain behind my Mother's calm manner and sweet welcoming smile as she waited—sitting, sitting, sitting, in her little London house—for news: of Harry, of Grace, of Therese. Now, more than twenty years later, I sat in a beautiful old house on Garden Street in Cambridge, Massachusetts, writing about the Spanish Civil War, or rattled about the Eastern States lecturing for my bread and butter; but though I was more active, perhaps, I waited as she had waited. The wheel had come full circle: then, finally, I entered into her experience. I had kind—oh, the very kindest of friends, who understood somehow that the things of nature could do for me what they could not; they took me out into the country to stay with them, and drove me all over Massachusetts and New Hampshire and Connecticut. There I saw autumn, winter, spring, as my Mother had seen them—and because *places* meant so much to both of us, the New England country-side gave her to me all over again.